D0975345

# KIRSCH'S GUIDE TO THE BOOK CONTRACT

# Kirsch's
# Guide
# *to the*
# Book
# Contract.

*for* Authors, Publishers, Editors and Agents

*by* Jonathan Kirsch

ACROBAT BOOKS
Los Angeles

Acrobat Books
PO Box 870
Venice, CA 90292

The title and trade dress of *Kirsch's Guide to the Book Contract* are trademarks of the author.

**Important Caution to Reader**: The model contract and the discussion of its terms and conditions in *Kirsch's Guide* are offered for general reference only. No book can replace an attorney's advice based on the latest developments in publishing law. Only an attorney who is expert in the field of publishing law and familiar with the circumstances of a particular transaction can render effective advice and assistance. Readers of *Kirsch's Guide* are urged to consult a qualified attorney to address their specific questions and concerns.

Cover design: p*h*.D.
Page design: William Morosi

Kirsch, Jonathan, 1949–
    Kirsch's guide to the book contract : for authors, publishers, editors, and agents / Jonathan Kirsch.
        p.    cm.
    Includes bibliographical references and index.
    ISBN 0-918226-35-X
    1. Authors and publishers—United States—Popular works.
I. Title.
KF3084.Z9K57    1998
343.7309'98—dc21                                                    98–35077
                                                                        CIP

Manufactured in the United States of America
10 9 8 7 6 5 4 3 2 1

For Dennis Mitchell
*My law partner and cherished friend — an attorney of
superb skill and perfect integrity, a trusted confidant,
and a real mensch without whose encouragement,
support, good advice, and good cheer, none of my books
would have been written.*

And, as always, for Ann, Adam and Jennifer Kirsch
*"...inscribe us in the book of life..."*

# CONTENTS

# HOW TO USE *KIRSCH'S GUIDE*

Back in 1976, when I was both a law student and an aspiring young writer with a first novel in hand, I was thrilled when my agent secured an offer from a publisher and sent me a contract to sign. The contract was a stately if slightly musty document, printed on legal stationery and affixed to a sheet of blue paper known among lawyers as a "blue back." Yet it might have well been chiseled in stone, and for more than one reason.

First, as an aspiring writer with a first novel in hand, I lacked the clout—and, for that matter, the courage—to demand any changes in the niggardly deal that the publisher was offering for my work. Second, and even more significantly for our purposes, the book publishing industry was a courtly and tradition-bound industry, and the typical book publishing contract was a collection of legal "boilerplate," that is, standardized and highly technical legal provisions that had not changed much in the previous century or so.

"Sign here," was the implicit message of the blue-backed document, and so I signed, much more mindful of the meager advance that would follow in a few weeks than the nuances or the nuts-and-bolts of the document in front of me.

Today, however, book publishing is in the midst of an authentic revolution, both technological and economic, and the book contract is changing so fast that one simply cannot speak meaningfully of a "standard" book deal.

Ownership of the major publishing houses in the United States is being consolidated into a few multinational conglomerates. At the same time, the advent of fast, cheap, and accessible technologies for designing, typesetting, and printing books has prompted the growth of literally thousands of independent publishers—ranging from self-published authors with a single book in print to entrepreneurial publishing houses from various quaint and colorful communities around the country that successfully compete with even the biggest New York publishers. Thanks to both the withering of the Communist bloc and the flowering of commercial and copyright treaties among the nations of the world, entirely new markets have opened up for American publishers. The explosive growth of computer-based technologies and the Internet hold out the prospect of even more tumultuous changes in the publishing industry. The best evidence of this brave new world of publishing is the increasing number of telephone calls that I receive from small-town, single-title publishers around America that seek legal advice in response to offers received by E-mail from Poland or China or Brazil.

As a result of the sea change in publishing, the negotiation and drafting of a book contract is now a lively exercise for deal-makers and the attorneys who assist them, one that demands both insight and foresight. Thus, the focus of *Kirsch's Guide to the Book Contract* is to assist authors, publishers, editors and agents in fixing their sights on a moving target, and the pages that follow are designed to enable a non-lawyer to read, understand, and negotiate a book contract in all of its new subtlety and complexity.

## The Contract as the Bible of a Book Deal

Ideally, a book publishing contract is a resource that defines all aspects of the creative, legal, and financial relationship between an author and a publisher. That is why a typical book contract is so long, so dense, and so well-armored with boilerplate, all of which is intended to anticipate and answer all of the questions that may arise in the future dealings between author and publisher. If care is taken in negotiating the terms of a book contract and reducing the terms to a formal written agreement, then both the author and publisher will know in advance what to expect of each other, and a happy and successful publishing venture is more likely to follow. In that sense, the book contract is the Bible—or, perhaps even more aptly, the Constitution—of any deal between an author and a publisher.

To assist the reader in making sense of the book publishing contract, *Kirsch's Guide* begins with a model contract in its entirety, organized by topical headings that correspond to the titles of the various chapters that follow. Then the model contract is fully deconstructed and carefully annotated, clause by clause.

**Cross-References.** Cross-references to related subjects within the pages of *Kirsch's Guide* are indicated with an arrow: ➤. References to its companion volume, *Kirsch's Handbook of Publishing Law*, are indicated by: "See".

Each clause in the model contract is explained in detail in the text of *Kirsch's Guide*—what the clause means, how it affects the rights of the parties, and how it might be modified to accommodate special circumstances or demands. Although the specific wording of a book contract will vary from publisher to publisher, and from deal to deal, the clauses in *Kirsch's Guide* are comparable to those found in most book contracts now in use in the publishing industry, and the discussion of each clause in *Kirsch's Guide* should permit the author or publisher to decipher the comparable clauses in a specific contract under negotiation.

*Kirsch's Guide* can be used as a template by an author, agent, publisher, or editor in reviewing, negotiating or drafting a book publishing contract to make sure that all of the basic points have been covered in the contract. The model contract and the clause-by-clause explanatory text can be used to interpret, evaluate, and apply the workings of a typical clause to each point under negotiation in a book deal. Above all, *Kirsch's Guide* is intended to assist an author, agent, publisher, or editor in understanding the meaning and effect of the various technical clauses in a contract, adopting a reasonable position in negotiation, and revising a standard form to reflect the deal that is actually struck between the author and publisher.

Not every clause will be subject to intense negotiation, of course. The most important points in any book contract, which I call "deal points," are likely to be the subject of active bargaining. The routine clauses found in the boilerplate are likely to be lightly negotiated, if at all. Yet, as we shall see, *every* clause in a book contract is potentially important and perhaps even crucial.

### How *Kirsch's Guide* Is Organized

No two book contracts in common use are exactly alike. Both the sequence and the substance of various topics—transfer of rights in the author's work, advances and royalties, preparation and editing of the manuscript, time and manner of publication, and so on—vary from contract to contract. Some publishers, for example, choose to start off the book contract on a cheery note with the advance and royalties, if only for the positive psychological effect on the author. At least one major publisher, though, confronts the author at the outset of its contract with "warranties and indemnities"—those dreary and even fearful legal assurances that most authors find so off-putting—and does not get around to the delicious subject of the advance until deep into the boilerplate.

For the sake of clarity and coherence, the model contract in *Kirsch's Guide* generally tracks the life cycle of a book deal. Priority is given to the most urgent interests of authors and publishers: what rights are the authors conveying to the publisher, and how much is the publisher paying the author for such rights? Thus, Chapter One is devoted to *Introductory Clauses*, Chapter Two addresses *Transfer of Rights*, and Chapter Three discusses *Author Compensation*. The subsequent chapters follow a typical book deal: *The Manuscript; Publication; Copyright; Accounting; Warranties, Representations, and Indemnities; Options, Noncompetition, and Other Rights and Restrictions;* and *Cessation of Publication*. The final chapter discusses *General Provisions*, and is followed by a Glossary of publishing terminology. Finally, the Index to *Kirsch's Guide* permits the reader to find his or his way to specific topics in the main text of the book.

> **Tips and Tactics for Authors and Publishers.** Along with a general discussion of each clause of a typical book contract, you will find a series of boxes with tips and tactics for negotiating the deal as well as alerts and cautions about seemingly innocuous clauses that could affect you in unexpected ways. Matters of special concern to authors are marked with this icon: ✍; items of concern to publishers are marked with this icon: 📖.

## Deal Points in a Book Contract

The most important variables in any book publishing contract are the so-called "deal points"—that is, the basic

**Deal Points.** To assist you in finding your way to the all-important "deal points" in *Kirsch's Guide,* each clause that relates to a deal point is marked with this icon: **$**.

terms of the deal between an author and publisher that define what rights the publisher is acquiring from the author and how much the publisher will be obliged to pay the author for the use of such rights. More effort and attention are expended on the negotiation of deal points than any other element in a book contract; indeed, the deal points are often the *only* negotiated points in a book contract, and the rest of the boilerplate is sometimes left unnegotiated or sometimes even unread!

Deal points usually include the following basic elements, each of which is discussed in detail in *Kirsch's Guide.*

☐ **Advance**: How much money is the publisher willing to pay to the author as an advance against royalties and other forms of author compensation? How will the advance be paid—as a single lump sum or as a series of installment payments? What is required to trigger the payment of the advance—delivery of the manuscript, acceptance of the manuscript, publication of the book, or some combination of these and other triggering events?

☐ **Rights**: What rights in the author's work is the publisher acquiring? Some publishers seek to acquire *all* rights in a manuscript, including not only the right to publish the author's work in book form but also audio, electronic, foreign language, motion picture and television, and other so-called "secondary" or "subsidiary" rights.

☐ **Territory.** Where will the publisher be entitled to exploit the rights acquired from the author—in the United States and Canada only, in a specified foreign country or foreign language, or throughout the world?

☐ **Term.** How long will the publisher be entitled to exploit the rights in the author's work? Some contracts remain in effect for a specified number of years, after which the rights revert to the author, but it is more common for the publisher to seek rights "for the duration of copyright" or even "in perpetuity."

☐ **"Multi-Book Deals" and Options.** Is the publisher seeking rights in a single work of the author or more than one work? Some book contracts are "multi-book deals" in which the publisher acquires rights to a specified number of works by the author. More common are option clauses that permit the publisher to acquire the author's next work on specified terms at its discretion.

### "Boilerplate" in a Book Contract

A contract that confined itself solely to the deal points would be short and sweet. But a great many other legal, financial, and business issues are usually included in any standard contract, and these points tend to be covered in the standard clauses that are informally called boilerplate. Precisely because it is regarded as "standard"—and because it is often dense, highly technical, and thus hard to understand—the boilerplate is sometimes overlooked in negotiations between the author and publisher.

The circumstances in which a boilerplate clause actually comes into effect may be so remote that it does not seem very important at the time the contract is being negotiated. The "out-of-print" clause, for example, addresses what happens when the publisher is no longer actively printing and selling copies of the book—a circumstance that every author *hopes* will never come to pass! And yet the wording of the out-of-print clause may be crucial to determining if and when the rights to the book revert to the author. A poorly worded out-of-print clause can result in the book slipping into a kind of publishing limbo.

That is why much of *Kirsch's Guide* is devoted to a patient consideration of the "fine print" in a standard book contract—what it means, how it works, why it should be carefully drafted, and when it should be aggressively negotiated.

---

**A "Model" Contract:** The sample clauses in *Kirsch's Guide* are drawn from the model contract, but, in many cases, several variants of each clause are given in the main text. For that reason, the model contract illustrates only one of many possible approaches to the various deal points and boilerplate clauses in a book contract.

---

**Clarity and Confusion in Contracts**

The challenges that always face the deal-makers and the attorneys are whether to use specific terms and provisions or general ones; whether to cover each and every contingency in a publishing deal or rely on the "custom and practice" of the publishing industry; and whether it is more advantageous to pin down the details or allow some "wiggle room" within a contract. The answers to these questions may determine whether a conflict will arise in the future between author and publisher, and, if it arises, whether it can be resolved without the aggravation and expense of a lawsuit.

Some words and phrases that appear in a book contract are what lawyers call "terms of art;" that is, terminology that has an accepted meaning in a legal context or in the "custom and practice" of a particular industry. "Advance," for example, is a simple word that is understood to carry a great many subtle and complex meanings in the real world of publishing, i.e., an advance is generally understood to be "returnable" and "recoupable" but "nonrefundable," all of which are crucial terms in themselves. (➤*Advances, Page 104*) Thus, it is probably not necessary to include an exhaustive definition of "advance" in every book contract, although some contracts are clearer than others on the question of when and if an author must give back the advance.

But, more often, a decision must be made on whether to spend the time and effort to flesh out the terms of a specific deal or to rely on a general understanding. As a general principle, a publisher tends to prefer a broad and general contract clause since the very breadth seems to work to its advantage: a contract that grants "electronic rights" to the publisher can be interpreted to mean *all* electronic rights, but a clause that lists specific electronic rights is more likely to mean *only* the specified rights are granted.

Even so, a general clause may raise more questions than it answers. For example, it is not yet clear what constitutes an "electronic right" in today's fast-changing publishing industry. Does the right to download a book from an electronic database, print it out on paper, bind it, and sell it to a bookbuyer—"publishing on demand," as it is called—constitute an electronic right, or a print publication right, or both? (➤*Electronic Rights, Page 76*)

Sometimes the choice between clarity and confusion is regarded as a strategic decision—an author or publisher in any given book deal may *prefer* ambiguity in a given clause, since the lack of specificity allows the parties to take whatever position they deem advantageous if the clause is called into question later on. A contract that grants a publisher "electronic rights" in the author's work and says nothing more on the subject, for example, allows the publisher to argue for an expansive definition that includes subsidiary rights not actually mentioned at all. Perhaps the best example of intentional haziness is the notion of "allied and ancillary rights," a phrase that is often attached to motion picture and television rights and is intended to capture a set of related subsidiary rights without going to the trouble of defining them. (➤*Allied and Ancillary Rights, Page 89*)

More often, however, clarity, precision, and completeness are in the best interests of both parties. If an author or a publisher expresses a concern about some issue that is not satisfactorily addressed in a book contract, my impulse as an attorney is to add some language to make it clearer—even if I believe that the issue is unlikely to arise or that the contract already covers it. That is why, for example, authors tend to favor—and I tend to use—certain clauses that are not strictly necessary: "*All rights not expressly granted to Publisher are wholly reserved by Author*" is probably a superfluous clause in most contracts, but it makes my author-clients and me much more comfortable to see it in black and white! (➤*Reservation of Rights, Pages 56, 228*)

The essential point of a book contract is to establish the rights and duties of an author and publisher so that each one knows what the parties are entitled to expect of one another. Long experience in the publishing industry allows the drafters of contracts to anticipate what frictions and conflicts may arise in the future, and the book contracts now in general use provide the mechanisms to work them out. Ideally, a well-considered and well-drafted contract will answer the most important questions before they are asked.

## Plain English or "Legalese"?

At an early point in my law practice, I set myself the goal of drafting contracts in plain English rather than the highly technical language favored by attorneys. Contracts in the common language of everyday life, I thought, would be accessible, practical, and "user-friendly." But I soon discovered that I was wrong. "Legalese"—highly technical words and phrases used by attorneys—allows a contract to be shorter in length and more accurate in meaning than does plain English.

What non-lawyers call "legalese" is often known by lawyers as "terms of art"—that is, words and phrases with specific and well-understood meanings and effects: a kind of legal shorthand that has developed over time. "Consideration," for example, is a single word that summarizes a whole body of contract law, and any effort to avoid its use in favor of plain English requires a great deal of explanation and explication. Indeed, my early efforts at drafting in plain English produced exactly the opposite of what I had intended: the plain English contracts were longer and wordier. And I was always concerned, and rightfully so, that my own innovative language would somehow blur the legal concepts that were so sharply defined in the technical vocabulary of contracts in general and publishing contracts in particular. Today, I am no less committed to clarity and functionality in the drafting of contracts, but I am thoroughly convinced that the language of lawyers is the right one to use in a legal document.

## The Role of the Agent

An agent may play a great many roles in the life and work of an author—advisor, cheerleader, confidante, mentor, editor, and more. But an agent is, above all, a salesperson. He tries to find as many potential buyers as possible for the author's work, and seeks to extract the best price available from the interested buyers. The qualities that one seeks in an agent include an up-to-date and far-reaching Rolodex, a ready knowledge of trends and developments in the book industry, the ability to negotiate a good deal, and lots of experience in doing so!

An agent may play a great many roles in the life and work of an author—advisor, cheerleader, confidante, mentor, editor, and more. But an agent is, above all, a salesperson. He tries to find as many potential buyers as possible for the author's work, and seeks to extract the best price available from the interested buyers. The qualities that one seeks in an agent include an up-to-date and far-reaching Rolodex, a ready knowledge of trends and developments in the book industry, the ability to negotiate a good deal, and lots of experience in doing so!

The best agents have closed lots of book deals with various acquiring editors at a great many publishing houses. They know what a particular editor at a given house likes and dislikes in a book project; what books he has acquired; how much he paid for them; how well they did in the market; and how large an advance an editor can offer without checking with a boss or a committee.

Agents will generally focus on the deal points, at least at the outset of negotiation, and it is not unusual for offers and counteroffers to be exchanged in a kind of urgent shorthand that focuses only on the dollar amount of the advance, the maximum royalty rate, the rights to be acquired by the publisher, and the territory where the rights may be exploited. But a skilled and experienced agent will not overlook the boilerplate of the book contract, and the value of a book deal can be significantly affected by subtle changes in the words and phrases that appear in an otherwise tedious chunk of fine print.

An experienced agent may have negotiated so many deals with a particular publishing house that certain deal points are conceded in advance by the publisher. For example, one agent of my acquaintance always asks for and usually gets a "bestseller bonus" that obliges the publisher to pay an additional advance for each week that the author's book appears on the *New York Times* bestseller list. By now, the editors with whom he works regard the bestseller clause as a standard clause in the contracts that he negotiates on behalf of his clients—and so the bestseller clause has become what is known as "agent's boilerplate." Indeed, one of the advantages in working with a seasoned and successful agent is that new clients enjoy the benefit of the agent's boilerplate that already appears in the contract forms that a publisher uses when dealing with the agent.

An experienced agent will be far more adept, insightful and effective in dealing with the legal technicalities of a book contract than an attorney who lacks long and specific experience in the book publishing industry.

### The Role of the Attorney

Most agents are *not* attorneys, however, and so the author may wish to consult an attorney who is experienced in book contracts and publishing to review and comment upon the contract itself, to suggest amendments and modifications, and to work on the wording of especially problematic contracts. Some agents work with attorneys who represent the literary agency, not the author, in addressing such legal issues, and some authors prefer to retain and consult attorneys of their own. But the fact is that few book contracts are reviewed by *any* lawyer unless the dollar amounts are especially large or the legal issues are unusually problematic.

The author should bear in mind that the review of a book contract by a lawyer who represents the *agency* rather than the *author* poses some risks of its own. A lawyer owes a duty of the highest order to his or her clients. If the client is the agency rather than the author, and there is a conflict between the agency's best interests and the author's interests, the agency's interest will come first. The most common example of a potential conflict of interest is the so-called "agency clause," which establishes the agent's right to collect advances, royalties, and other payments from the publisher (➤*Agency, Page 203*). The agent always prefers an ironclad agency clause that irrevocably ties the agent to the book project, and the author often prefers a clause that allows the agent to be dismissed at a later date. For this reason, the author would be best served by an attorney whom she hires on her own initiative and pays out of her own resources.

Another potential conflict of interest between an author and an agent relates to one of the great unspoken truths of the publishing industry. Since agents will deal over and over again with the same publishers on behalf of different clients, it is natural and inevitable for the agent to cultivate the acquiring editors, ingratiate himself with them, and avoid ugly confrontations or excessive demands on behalf of any given author. After all, the agent wants to close the deal, earn the commission, and move on to the next deal, while the author may insist on tough bargaining over a particular deal point. If there are any potentially unpleasant points to negotiate between author and publisher, it may be in the best interests of both the author and the agent to turn the issues over to the author's attorney. Indeed, an attorney is often used as the bearer of ill tidings and the "bad cop" in a business transaction, which is exactly why lawyers are so reviled—and yet secretly admired, or so I suspect.

An attorney, however, cannot take the place of an agent unless the lawyer is positioned to "shop" a book with the same expertise and experience that an agent brings to a book project. I routinely explain to my author-clients that I will present a project to one or more specified publishers at their request, but I will not canvass the publishing marketplace in search of the best deal. I always emphasize that it is only by shopping a book to a great many publishers that one can determine the market value of any given book project. The agent is usually the best person to shop the book, and the lawyer is best used to evaluate, negotiate, and fine-tune the book contract and related legal documents.

Attorneys with genuine experience in publishing are not plentiful, especially outside of New York City, although publishing lawyers (including the author of *Kirsch's Guide!*) can be found in Los Angeles, San Francisco, Chicago, and other places where publishing is a sizable industry. Consulting a divorce lawyer or a personal injury lawyer to review a publishing contract, however, is no more appropriate than, say, consulting a proctologist for a psychiatric problem.

## "Clout"

Whether or not a publisher is willing to make concessions to an author depends largely on the perceived value of the author's work and how much the publisher wants to publish it. Of course, an author with a string of bestsellers, enjoys more "clout" in the negotiating process than a first-time author. And even a fortunate first-time novelist may find himself with some clout if his work has attracted the attention of several publishers that are willing to bid against each other. More often, however, the author is likely to find that publishers are willing to make only modest concessions and improvements in the course of even the toughest negotiation.

Authors are often under the impression that a literary agent who has made lucrative deals for other authors will be able to work the same magic with every client. A "hot" literary agent—one whose six-figure deals are written up in *Publishers Weekly* or even in the daily newspaper—will always find a mailbox full of unsolicited manuscripts from yearning authors. And it's true enough that a first-time novelist who is lucky enough to be taken on by an agent with an impressive client roster is going to get more attention from the publishers than one who is unrepresented or whose agent is less celebrated. When it comes to a marginal book project, the fact that the author is represented by an agent with clout may make the difference between a thin deal and no deal at all.

The hard truth, however, is that the author and the book he actually writes, rather than the agent or the lawyer who represents him, are what really matters in any publishing deal. And the only way to determine the market value of a book project is to find out how much a publisher is actually willing to pay for it. If a manuscript draws an offer from a single publisher, then the publisher's best offer *is* the market value of the book!

## The Importance of a Signed Contract

No matter how rich or how poor the deal turns out to be, a book contract is essential to a successful legal and financial relationship between an author and a publisher. As a general proposition, the United States Copyright Act provides that *no* exclusive rights in a work of authorship are conveyed by an author or acquired by a publisher in the absence of a "signed writing"—that is, some form of written agreement that bears the signature of the author. Once signed, the contract will govern the rights and duties of both the author and publisher throughout the term of their agreement, which may last a lifetime and, often enough, a good many years after the author is dead and gone! So the care and attention invested in the negotiation and drafting of a contract will be paid back throughout the long life of a book deal.

Still, authors and publishers alike tend to take a casual and sometimes haphazard approach to their contracts. I am hardly the only author who was so intent on seeing his first novel in print and cashing his first advance check that he did not bother read the contract before signing it. Recently, I was shocked to receive an advance copy of a new book by one of my clients, beautifully printed and handsomely bound, even though I was still actively negotiating the contract with the publisher's attorney. The publishing house had put the book into print without a signed contract! And sometimes I am presented with a deal that is defined not by a formal contract but by a collection of letters, memos, and other scraps of paper on which the author and publisher have scratched out some kind of book deal. Whether out of enthusiasm or desperation, pure optimism or pure cynicism, both authors and publishers are sometimes so intent on the book that they pay scant attention to the book contract.

The problem with such informality, of course, is that the author and the publisher put themselves profoundly at risk. The author who delivers a manuscript to a publisher without a signed contract in place may find that the publisher has a very different idea of what rights have been acquired and what payments are owed. The publisher that goes to press without a signed contract may find that the rights to publish and sell the book are clouded or nonexistent. Without a clear and comprehensive agreement in writing, signed by both parties, neither author nor publisher can rely on their respective rights and duties with clarity and certainty.

### The Use and Abuse of Model Contracts

Nowadays, as I have already noted, the book contract is a moving target, and every clause in a book contract may be the subject of vigorous negotiation and creative drafting. Although the model contract in *Kirsch's Guide* is intended to embody the most commonly used clauses, the fact is that any given contract in actual use may differ from the model contract in various ways, great and small. That is why, for example, I recommend against the use of an "off-the-rack" contract, no matter what the source. The best contract is one that has been thoughtfully evaluated and modified to apply to the deal struck by an author and publisher for a specific book project.

Nevertheless, there are a great many contract forms in circulation. Some have been cobbled together over time by many hands and passed around among publishers, each one tweaking the contract slightly before passing it along—with the result that a contract may look like a cut-and-paste job precisely because it *is* one. Other contract forms are available in published sources such as *Kirsch's Guide* and other books on publishing law, whether written for lawyers or laypersons. A few model contracts have been drafted by specialists of one kind or another with the lofty motive of achieving *the* ideal contract, the most impressive example of which is the model contract offered by the Authors Guild, an association of professional writers with a staff that possesses admirable skill and deep experience in contract matters.

The problem with all model contracts, of course, is that they are models, not fine-tuned working legal documents. The cut-and-paste contracts are the worst of all: some clauses will be obsolete; some clauses will be inconsistent or even contradictory with other clauses within the same contract; and some clauses may be nothing more than gibberish. Even the best of the form contracts—and I do not exclude the one in *Kirsch's Guide*—will benefit from the attention of an informed and experienced publishing law attorney. And the model contracts like the one from the Authors Guild do not always mesh with the practices of the publishing industry in the real world.

### Marking Up a Book Contract

At some point in most book deals, one party—almost always the publisher—will present the other party with a proposed contract, and that's when the tough bargaining begins. The devil is always in the details, and the most important clauses are sometimes hammered out phrase by phrase, even word by word. When, at last, the contract has been negotiated to the satisfaction of both the author and publisher, care must be taken to revise the document itself to reflect the deal that has been made by the parties. Marking up the changes on a standard contract form is the last crucial detail.

By long tradition in the publishing industry, book contracts are often marked up by hand. Deletions are indicated by a line drawn through the deleted words and phrases; additions are written or typed in the margin at the top, side, or bottom of the page; and asterisks, arrows, or lines are used to indicate where the new material is to be inserted. All of these handwritten or typewritten changes ought to be initialed by both the author and publisher, and then the contract itself is signed. The advantage of a hand-marked contract is that all variations from the standard terms and provisions are immediately obvious to anyone who picks up the contract at a later date, whether a year or a lifetime later.

More recently, contracts in the book industry are revised on the word-processing equipment of the publisher. If so, it is very important to "redline" all of the changes—that is, all of the additions and deletions should be plainly marked in some form of typographical highlighting to permit ready identification of where changes have been made in the standard form. For example, newly added material is often set in **bold type** to show that it is not a part of the base document, and deleted material is ~~struck out~~ to indicate that it is no longer applicable.

Another approach to marking up a contract form is to use one or more additional documents, which may be called a rider, an amendment, an addendum, or an exhibit that set forth *all* of the changes in the standard contract, clause by clause. Riders, amendments, and the like can be used for a great many other purposes—to expand upon the description of the book that the author is writing, to list the artwork and other collateral materials that the author is obliged to deliver to the publisher, to provide for insurance coverage or other special terms, and so on. Such additional documents must be separately signed by both parties, and the contract itself ought to include a sentence that acknowledges the existence of the additional document and "incorporates it by reference" in the contract, i.e., "*This Agreement is modified by and subject to the terms of the Rider attached hereto and incorporated by reference in this Agreement.*"

Each of these approaches to changing or expanding upon the standard terms of a book contract is acceptable because each one allows the author or publisher to see at a glance exactly how the boilerplate of the contract has been changed in the negotiations. What is *not* acceptable is the lamentable practice of making the negotiated changes in the contract by entering them into the base document and then printing out a fresh copy of the contract. Without some form of highlighting, as described above, it will be necessary to read each and every word of the contract to determine if and how it varies from the publisher's standard contract.

### Using the Model Contract in *Kirsch's Guide*

*Kirsch's Guide* consists of a clause-by-clause analysis of a typical publishing contract. For many of the clauses, I have given more than one version in order to illustrate various approaches to the same deal point. For example, one sample clause in the main text illustrates how an author might grant *all* rights in her book to a publisher; another sample clause demonstrates how the grant-of-rights clause can be limited to a specific set of rights. (➤*Chapter 2: Transfer of Rights*) Some of these alternative approaches to the same clause are reflected in the model contract, too, but more often the model contract adopts only a single approach. So it is important to read and consider the various alternative approaches discussed in the main text before using the model contract. Above all, neither the model contract itself nor the general discussion in *Kirsch's Guide* is intended to replace the expert advice and assistance of an experienced publishing lawyer.

### State Law and Federal Law

Copyright is the specific form of "intellectual property" that is the focus of a typical publishing contract. Copyright law is federal law, and it applies with equal force and uniformity throughout the United States. In fact, the copyright law of the United States is recognized and enforced throughout the world by all countries that have entered into international copyright treaties with the United States. Thus, the basic principles of federal copyright law in *Kirsch's Guide* are generally applicable to readers throughout the United States.

Contracts, by contrast, are generally governed by state law. Although the law of contracts is very old and well-settled—and the publishing contracts in general use across the United States tend to look very much the same—a few specific points of law may vary from state to state. Often, a contract will specify that it is governed by the laws of a specified state, usually the state where the publisher's business is located. Thus, for example, the contracts used by major U.S. publishers invoke the law of the state of New York, and virtually all publishing contracts rely on the law of the state where the publisher's office is located.

For that reason, the cautious author or publisher will make sure that a contract is reviewed by an attorney who is familiar with the law of the particular state under which the contract will be interpreted and enforced.

*Kirsch's Handbook of Publishing Law.*

*Kirsch's Guide to the Book Contract* is a companion volume to *Kirsch's Handbook of Publishing Law,* a comprehensive survey of the legal issues that arise in the publishing industry. The two books can be used independently or in conjunction with each other. *Kirsch's Guide* focuses exclusively on book contracts and can be used without reference to *Kirsch's Handbook* in negotiating a book deal and drafting a book publishing agreement. The reader who needs further information and advice on other areas of publishing law—including, for example, copyright and trademark, dealings with agents and packagers, rights and responsibilities of co-authors and collaborators, defamation, invasion of privacy, idea protection, and so on—will find detailed coverage of these topics in *Kirsch's Handbook of Publishing Law.*

## A Note on Gender

The hypothetical author to whom I refer from time to time is imagined to be a woman in some chapters, a man in others. The publisher is identified as a gender-neutral "it" on the assumption that the publishing house is a legal entity such as a corporation rather than an individual, although publishers can be human creatures. And the publishers I've been privileged to work with over the years, both as an author and as an attorney, have possessed not only fine minds but big hearts, too.

# A MODEL BOOK PUBLISHING CONTRACT

Here is the model book publishing contract that is fully deconstructed and explained in detail in the pages of *Kirsch's Guide to the Book Contract*. Although there is really no such thing as a "standard" book contract, the model contract includes all of the clauses that are typically found in contracts commonly used in the book publishing industry. For some clauses, several alternative approaches to the same clause are given. Other clauses are given in one of several possible forms, and alternative approaches can be found in the main text; for example, the model contract grants all rights in the author's work to the publisher, but it is possible to mark up the model contract to allocate rights between the author and publisher. The clauses are organized under topical headings that correspond to the chapter titles used in *Kirsch's Guide*.

---

**An Important Caution to Authors and Publishers!** No single form contract is applicable to every publishing transaction, and any model contract—including the one in *Kirsch's Guide*—must be carefully reviewed, evaluated, and modified to correctly state the deal that has been struck by the author and publisher. The advice and assistance of an agent or an experienced publishing lawyer may be necessary to adapt a form contract to reflect a particular transaction.

---

## A Note on Numbering

Long ago, I learned that numbering paragraphs and subparagraphs in sequential Arabic numerals as illustrated in the model contract—1, 1.1, 1.1.1, and so on—is, far and away, the clearest way to organize a legal document. By using sequential paragraph numbering, the order and placement of any subparagraph is instantly recognizable by its own number. Every other numbering or lettering system—Roman numerals, for example, or a combination of letters and numbers—makes it necessary to flip back and forth in the contract to determine exactly where a particular subsection is placed. Thus, for example, "Paragraph 1.2.3" tells us immediately that we are considering the third subparagraph under the second subsection of Paragraph 1. The same subsection in a less utilitarian numbering system would be, for example, "I(b)(iii)"—and, crucially, the only number that would actually appear on the subsection itself is "(iii)," which forces us to leaf back through the contract to identify the section and subsection.

## INTRODUCTORY CLAUSES

This Publishing Agreement ("Agreement") is entered into as of [ *Insert date here* ] ("Effective Date") by and between [ *Insert name, address and legal capacity of Publisher* ] ("Publisher"), and [ *Insert name, address, Social Security number, date of birth, and citizenship of Author* ] ("Author") concerning a work presently titled *[Insert title here]* ("Work") and described as *[Insert description of subject matter, length, etc.]*

## GRANT OF RIGHTS

1.  **Grant of Rights.** Author, on behalf of himself and his heirs, executors, administrators, successors, and assigns, exclusively grants, assigns, and otherwise transfers to Publisher and its licensees, successors, and assigns, all right, title, and interest in and to the Work, throughout the world, in perpetuity, and in any and all media and forms of expressions now known or hereafter devised, including but not limited to all copyrights therein for the full term of such copyrights (and any and all extensions and renewals thereof), including but not limited to all of the following primary and secondary rights therein.

    1.1    *Primary Rights*

        1.1.1 "Hardcover Rights," including the exclusive right to print, publish, distribute, sell, and generally exploit the Work, in the form of hardcover editions of the Work, distributed primarily through book trade channels such as bookstores and libraries.

        1.1.2 "Trade Paperback Rights," including the exclusive right to print, publish, distribute, sell, and generally exploit the Work, in the form of "trade paperback" or "quality paperback" editions of the Work distributed primarily through book trade channels such as bookstores and libraries.

1.1.3 "Mass-Market Paperback Rights," including the exclusive right to print, publish, distribute, sell, and generally exploit the Work, in the form of softcover editions of the Work, whether as original editions or reprints, distributed primarily through the book trade, independent magazine wholesalers, direct accounts, and other customary channels of distribution.

1.1.4 "Translation Rights," including the exclusive right to translate the Work, in whole or in part, into foreign languages, and to use, adapt, or otherwise exploit any and all of the rights in and to such translation(s) anywhere in the world.

1.1.5 "Periodical Publication Rights," including the exclusive right to use and generally exploit all or any portion of the Work, in the form of excerpts, condensations, abridgments, or selections of the Work, in newspapers, magazines, and other periodicals, both in print and other media of publication, whether directly or through syndicates, either before ("First Serial Rights") or after ("Second Serial Rights") first publication of the Work in book form.

1.1.6 "Book Club Rights, including the exclusive right to sell copies of the Work to book clubs, or to authorize book clubs to print and sell copies of the Work.

1.1.7 "Photocopying and Facsimile Rights," including the exclusive right to grant or withhold permission for the duplication and transmission of all or part of the Work by photocopying, facsimile, or other like means.

1.1.8 "Microfilm Rights," including the exclusive right to use, adapt, or otherwise exploit the Work, or any portion thereof, in the form of microfilm, microfiche, slides, transparencies, filmstrips, and like processes attaining similar results.

1.1.9 "General Print Publication Rights," including the exclusive right to use and generally exploit all or any portion of the Work, in

.the form of condensed or abridged editions; bulk sales and other special sales, including but not limited to premium, promotional, corporate, and institutional sales; excerpts or selections of the Work in anthologies, compilations, digests, textbooks, and other similar works; Braille, large type, and other editions for the handicapped; book fairs; school editions and cheap editions; and unbound sheets.

1.1.10 "Direct-Response Marketing Rights," including the exclusive right to sell copies of the Work in any edition or medium authorized under this Agreement, through any form of direct-response marketing, including but not limited to any form of television, electronic media, direct mail, and catalogs.

1.1.11 "Audio Rights," including the exclusive right to adapt, use, or otherwise generally exploit the Work or any portion thereof in any form of sound recording and reproduction, including but not limited to audiocassettes, compact discs, or similar audio products of any kind or configuration whatsoever, whether now in existence or hereafter devised. "Audio Rights," as the term is used in this Agreement, includes the following specific applications and uses of sound recordings of the Work in any form of audio reproduction, including but not limited to audiocassettes, compact discs, or similar audio products of any kind or configuration whatsoever, whether now in existence or hereafter devised.

1.1.11.1 *Unabridged Sound Recordings*. The exclusive right to prepare and generally exploit unabridged non-dramatic sound recordings of the verbatim contents of the Work in its entirety without the addition of any other material whatsoever.

1.1.11.2 *Abridged Sound Recordings*. The exclusive right to prepare and generally exploit abridged non-dramatic sound recordings of the contents of the Work, or any portion thereof, without the use of any other or additional material whatsoever except incidental musical interludes and spoken introductory and/or explanatory segments.

1.1.11.3 *Dramatized Sound Recordings*. The exclusive right to adapt and use the Work, or any portion thereof, in preparing and generally exploiting dramatized sound recordings of the Work, including scenes, dialogue, and additional material, whether based upon the Work or otherwise.

1.1.12 "Electronic Rights," including the exclusive right to use, adapt, or otherwise exploit the Work, or any portion thereof, alone or in conjunction with other matter, in computer-based and similar electronic media and technologies for data entry, storage, retrieval, transmission, display, and output of any and all kinds, and/or like media and technologies attaining similar results, whether now known or hereafter devised. Without limiting the generality of the foregoing, "Electronic Rights" includes but is not limited to electronic, digital, and computer-based media and technologies of all kinds, and the storage, retrieval, transmission, display, output, and reproduction of data through such any such media and technologies, including, by way of example only, interactive media and multimedia in which the Work may be adapted and used in conjunction with other matter, whether such data is stored on hard drives or other fixed storage media, disks and diskettes, and other portable storage media, and/or remote on-line databases. "Electronic Rights," as the term is used in this Agreement, include the following specific applications and uses of the Work in computer-based and similar electronic media and technologies for data entry, storage, retrieval, transmission, display, and output of any and all kinds, and/or like media and technologies attaining similar results, whether now known or hereafter devised.

1.1.12.1 *Electronic Books.* The exclusive right to use and generally exploit all or any portion of the contents of the Work, but without the addition of any other material whatsoever, in electronic versions of the Work that are reproduced in the form of portable storage media and offered for sale or license to the consumer.

1.1.12.2 *Publishing-on-Demand.* The exclusive right to store, reproduce, transmit, and generally use and exploit all or any portion of the Work, but without the addition of any other material whatsoever, in the form of "Publishing-on-Demand" products and services. By way of illustration only, and without limiting the generality of the foregoing, "Publishing-on-Demand" refers to the manufacture and sale of copies of the Work by means of storage, transmission, and output of the Work in which the end product is a single printed copy of the Work for sale to a consumer.

1.1.12.3 *Databases, Networks, and On-line Services.* The exclusive right to store, reproduce, transmit, and generally use and exploit all or any part of the Work, but without the addition of any matter whatsoever, in a remote electronic database, network, or other on-line computer service, or similar system attaining like results, for use by consumers who are licensed to access the database, network, or service, and display and/or download the Work for their own personal use only.

1.1.12.4 *Interactive and Multimedia.* The exclusive right to adapt and generally use and exploit all or any part of the Work, whether alone or in conjunction with other material, in an interactive or multimedia product or service in any of the media or technologies described above.

1.2    **Secondary Rights**

1.2.1  "Dramatic Rights," including the exclusive right to use, adapt, or otherwise exploit the Work or any element thereof (including but not limited to characters, plot, title, scenes, settings, attire, and physical characteristics) in one or more live theatrical or stage presentations.

1.2.2  "Reading Rights," including the exclusive right to authorize the public reading of all or any portion of the verbatim text of the Work before a live audience, but without dramatization of any kind or the making of any audio, audiovisual, or other recording of the reading.

1.2.3  "Motion Picture and Television Rights," including the exclusive right to use, adapt, or otherwise exploit the Work, or any element thereof (including but not limited to characters, plot, title, scenes, settings, attire, and physical characteristics) in the form of one or more motion pictures and/or television programs of any kind, including but not limited to the right to disseminate such motion pictures and/or television programs by means of distribution and exhibition in theaters or otherwise, broadcasting, cable, satellite, telephone or other land lines, pay-per-view, closed-circuit, videocassettes, laser discs, digital video discs, and/or any other form of video transmission, exhibition, reproduction and sale, including but not limited to both analog and digital technologies and all other similar audiovisual media, whether now in existence or hereinafter devised.

1.2.4 "Radio Rights," including the exclusive right to use, adapt, or otherwise exploit the Work or any element thereof (including but not limited to characters, plot, title, scenes, settings, attire, and physical characteristics) for any form of radio programming, including but not limited to dissemination by broadcasting, cable, satellite, telephone or other land lines, pay-per-view, digital, closed-circuit or other forms of radio transmission, whether now in existence or hereinafter devised.

1.2.5 "Commercial Rights," including the exclusive right to manufacture, sell, and otherwise distribute products, by-products, services, facilities, merchandise, and other commodities of every nature or description, whether now in existence or hereafter devised, including but not limited to photographs, illustrations, drawings, posters, and other artwork, toys, games, wearing apparel, foods, beverages, cosmetics, toiletries and similar items, which may refer to or embody the Work, or any derivative works based on the Work, including but not limited to characters, plot, title, scenes, settings, attire, and physical characteristics.

1.2.6 "Future Media and Technologies," including the right to disseminate, use, adapt, or otherwise exploit the Work, or to authorize others to do so, by any means or medium of communication now in existence or hereafter devised.

2. **Territory.** The rights granted to Publisher in this Agreement may be exploited throughout the world.

3. **Term.** The rights granted to Publisher in this Agreement may be exploited in perpetuity.

## AUTHOR COMPENSATION

4. **Advance Against Royalties.** Publisher shall pay to Author, as an advance against royalties and any other amounts owing by Publisher to Author under this Agreement, the sum of [*Insert amount here*] to be paid as follows: One-third upon signing of this Agreement, one-third upon delivery and acceptance of the complete Manuscript, and one-third upon publication of the Work in the first Publisher's edition.

*A Clause for Escalating Royalties
Based on Retail Price*

**5.   Royalties on Publisher's Editions.** For each Edition of the Work published by the Publisher under this Agreement, Publisher shall credit Author's account with the following royalties on Net Copies Sold:

5.1 ____% of the Invoice Price on the first 5,000 Net Copies Sold of any Edition;

5.2 ____% of the Invoice Price on the next 5,000 Net Copies Sold of any Edition; and

5.3. ____% of the Invoice Price on sales in excess of 10,000 Net Copies Sold of any Edition.

5.4 "Edition," as used in this Agreement, refers to the Work as published in any particular content, length, and format. If the Work is materially revised or redesigned in any manner, or changed in length or content, then the Work as revised shall be considered a new "Edition" for purposes of this Section.

5.5 "Invoice Price," as the term is used in this Agreement, means the price shown on Publisher's invoices to wholesalers and retailers from which the Publisher's discounts are calculated.

*A Clause for a Fixed Royalty Based
on Publisher's Net Income*

**5.   Royalties on Publisher's Editions.** For each copy of the work published by Publisher under this agreement, Publisher shall credit Author's account with a royalty equal to ____% of Net Revenues from the sale of any and all Net Copies Sold. 5.1 "Net Revenues," as used in this Agreement, refers to money actually received by Publisher from the sale of copies of the Work, net of returns, after deduction of shipping, customs, insurance, fees and commissions, currency exchange discounts, and costs of collection.

5.2 "Net Copies Sold," as used in this Agreement, means the sale less returns of any and all copies sold by Publisher through conventional channels of distribution in the book trade, and does not include promotional and review copies, Author's copies (whether free or purchased by Author), or copies for which a royalty rate is otherwise set forth in this agreement.

The difference between the Invoice Price and the suggested retail price or cover price as such price may be printed on the dust jacket or cover of the Work shall not exceed 5% without Author's consent.

5.6 "Net Copies Sold," as used in this Agreement, means the sale less returns of any and all copies sold by Publisher through conventional channels of distribution in the book trade, and does not include promotional and review copies, Author's copies (whether free or purchased by Author), or copies for which a royalty rate is otherwise set forth in this Agreement.

6. **Reduced Royalties on Publisher's Editions.** For any and all sales of the Work in any Publisher's edition at discounts greater than the Publisher's announced wholesale discounts in the book trade; nonreturnable sales; direct sales; export sales; and bulk, premium and other special sales; Author's royalty shall be [*Insert reduced royalty rate, e.g.,* "one-half the full royalty specified for sales in ordinary channels of distribution in the book trade"].

7. **Author's Share of Revenue From Licensing of Rights.** Publisher shall credit Author's account with a royalty equal to Author's share, as specified below, of all Net Revenues actually received by Publisher for the exploitation or disposition of any and all rights in the Work by third parties under license from the Publisher.

| | Author's Share | Publisher's Share |
|---|---|---|
| Hardcover Rights | _____% | _____% |
| Trade Paperback Rights | _____% | _____% |
| Mass-Market Paperback Rights | _____% | _____% |
| Translation and Foreign Rights | _____% | _____% |
| Periodical Publication Rights | _____% | _____% |
| Book Club Rights | _____% | _____% |
| Photocopying and Facsimile Rights | _____% | _____% |
| Microfilm Rights | _____% | _____% |
| General Print Publication Rights | _____% | _____% |
| Direct-Response Marketing Rights | _____% | _____% |
| Audio Rights | _____% | _____% |
| Electronic Rights | _____% | _____% |
| Dramatic Rights | _____% | _____% |
| Reading Rights | _____% | _____% |
| Motion Picture and Television Rights | _____% | _____% |
| Radio Rights | _____% | _____% |
| Commercial Rights | _____% | _____% |
| Future Technologies | _____% | _____% |

# THE MANUSCRIPT

8.        **Delivery of Manuscript**. Author agrees to deliver the manuscript of the Work in the English language in its entirety ("the Manuscript") to the Publisher not later than [*Insert date of manuscript delivery*] ("the Initial Delivery Date") in the form of (a) a computer-readable file stored on one or more disks

in such format(s) and word-processing program(s) as Publisher may specify, and (b) two (2) computer-generated printouts of the Work, double-spaced on 8½-by-11-inch white paper, which Manuscript shall be approximately [*Insert word or page count*] in length and shall otherwise be acceptable to Publisher in form and content.

9.      **Artwork, Permissions, Index, and Other Materials.** Author shall deliver to Publisher, at Author's sole expense, not later than the Initial Delivery Date or such other date(s) as may be designated by Publisher, each of the following:

9.1      Original art, illustrations, maps, charts, photographs, or other artwork (collectively "Artwork"), in a form suitable for reproduction.

9.2.      An index, bibliography, table of contents, foreword, introduction, preface, or similar matter ("Frontmatter" and "Backmatter")

9.3      Written authorizations and permissions for the use of any copyrighted or other proprietary materials (including but not limited to Artwork, Backmatter, and/or Frontmatter) owned by any third party which appear in the Work and written releases or consents by any person or entity described, quoted, or depicted in the Work (collectively "Permissions").

9.4      If Author fails or refuses to deliver the Artwork, Backmatter, Frontmatter, Permissions, or other material required to be delivered by Author under this Agreement, Publisher shall have the right, but not the obligation, to acquire or prepare such any and all such matter, or to engage a skilled person to do so, and Author shall reimburse Publisher for all costs and expenses incurred by Publisher in doing so.

9.5      Author acknowledges and confirms that Publisher shall have no liability of any kind for the loss or destruction of the Manuscript, Artwork, Frontmatter, Backmatter, or any other documents or materials provided by Author to Publisher, and agrees to make and maintain copies of all such documents and materials for use in the event of such loss or destruction.

*A Clause Providing for Publisher's Unqualified Right to Reject the Manuscript*

**10. Publisher's Rights on Delivery.** If Publisher, in its sole discretion, deems the Manuscript, Artwork, Frontmatter and/or Backmatter, Permissions and/or any other materials delivered by Author under this Agreement to be unacceptable in form or substance, then Publisher shall have the right to terminate this Agreement without further obligation to the Author.

*A Clause Providing for Author's Right to Revise the Manuscript Prior to Rejection*

**10. Publisher's Rights on Delivery.** If Publisher, in its sole discretion, deems the Manuscript, Artwork, Frontmatter and/or Backmatter, Permissions and/or any other materials delivered by Author under this Agreement to be unacceptable in form or substance, then Publisher shall so advise Author by written notice, and Author shall have the opportunity to cure any defects and generally revise, correct, and/or supplement the Manuscript, Artwork, Frontmatter and/or Backmatter, Permissions and/or other materials to the satisfaction of Publisher, and deliver fully revised, corrected and/or supplemented Manuscript, Artwork, Frontmatter and/or Backmatter, Permissions and/or other materials no later than thirty (30) days after receipt of Publisher's notice ("the Final Delivery Date"). If such revised, corrected and/or supplemented materials are not delivered in a timely manner, or if they are deemed unsatisfactory in form or substance by Publisher, then Publisher shall have the unqualified right to terminate this Agreement without further obligation to Author.

11. **Termination for Nondelivery or Unsatisfactory Delivery.** If Author fails to deliver the Manuscript, Artwork, Frontmatter and/or Backmatter, Permissions, and/or other materials required under this Agreement, and/or any revisions and corrections thereof as requested by Publisher, on the dates designated by Publisher, or if Author fails to do so in a form and substance satisfactory to Publisher, then Publisher shall have the right to terminate this Agreement by so informing Author by letter sent by traceable mail to the address of Author set forth above. Upon termination by Publisher, Author shall, without prejudice to any other right or remedy of Publisher, immediately repay Publisher any sums previously paid to Author, and upon such repayment, all rights granted to Publisher under this Agreement shall revert to Author.

12. **Publisher's Right to Terminate Due to Changed Conditions.** Publisher shall not be obligated to publish the Work, if, in its sole and absolute judgment, whether before or after acceptance of the Work, Publisher determines that supervening events or circumstances since the date of this Agreement have materially and adversely changed the economic expectations of the Publisher regarding the Work at the time of making this Agreement. Upon making such a determination, Publisher may terminate this Agreement without further obligation by notice in writing to Author, and Author may retain [*Insert percentage of advance and other payments to be retained by Author*] of all payments previously made to Author under this Agreement.

## PUBLICATION

13. **Editing and Publication Format.** Publisher shall have the right to edit and revise the Work for any and all uses contemplated under this Agreement, provided that the meaning of the Work is not materially altered, and shall have the right to make any changes in the Work as advised by Publisher's counsel. Publisher shall have the right to manufacture, distribute, advertise, promote, and publish the Work in a style and manner which Publisher deems appropriate, including typesetting, paper, printing, binding, cover and/or jacket design, imprint, title, and price. Notwithstanding any editorial changes or revisions by Publisher, Author's warranties and indemnities under this Agreement shall remain in full force and effect.

14. **Review by Publisher's Counsel.** Notwithstanding any other provision of this Agreement, Publisher shall have the right, but not the obligation, to submit the Work for review by counsel of its choice to determine if the Work contains material which is or may be unlawful, violates the rights of third parties, or violates the promises, warranties, and representations of Author set forth in this Agreement.

14.1 Publisher shall not be obligated to publish the Work if, in the sole opinion of Publisher or its counsel, there appears to be a risk of legal action or liability on account of any aspect of the Work.

14.2 If, in the sole opinion of Publisher or its counsel, the Work is determined to require additions, deletions, modifications, substantiation of facts, or other changes to avoid the risk of legal action or liability, then Author shall make all such changes at the direction of Publisher or its counsel.

14.3 If Author declines to make such changes, or if Publisher deems the changes made by Author to be insufficient, or if Publisher or its counsel shall deem that such changes will not eliminate the risk of legal action or liability, then Publisher shall have the right to terminate this Agreement without further obligation, and Author shall be obligated to repay all amounts advanced by Publisher. Upon such repayment by Author, all rights granted to Publisher shall revert to Author.

14.4 Nothing contained in this Agreement shall be deemed to impose on Publisher any obligation to review or verify the contents of the Work, or to affect in any way the promises, warranties, and representations of Author and/or the duty of indemnification of Author, all of which shall continue to apply to the Work, whether or not the Work is changed at the request of Publisher or Publisher's counsel.

15. **Proofs.** Publisher shall furnish Author with a proof of the Work. Author agrees to read, correct, and return all page proofs within seven (7) calendar days after receipt thereof. If any changes in the proof sheets or the printing plates (other than corrections of printer's errors) are made at Author's request or with Author's consent, then the cost of such changes in excess of 5% of the cost of typesetting (exclusive of the cost of setting corrections) shall be paid by Author. If Author fails to return the corrected

page proofs within the time set forth above, Publisher may publish the Work without Author's approval of the page proofs.

16.    **Time of Publication.** Publisher agrees that the Work, if published, shall be published within twenty-four (24) months of the Final Delivery Date, except as the date of publication may be extended by forces beyond Publisher's control. The date of publication as designated by Publisher, but not later than the date of first delivery of bound volumes, shall be the "Publication Date" for all purposes under this Agreement.

17.    **Author's Copies.** Publisher shall provide Author with ten (10) copies, free of charge, of each edition of the Work published by Publisher. Author shall be permitted to purchase additional copies of the Work, at the normal dealer discount, to be paid upon receipt of Publisher's invoice, for Author's personal use and not for resale.

18.    **Advertising and Promotion.** Publisher shall have the right to determine the time, place, method, and manner of advertising, promotion, and other exploitation of the Work, except as Author and Publisher may set forth in a writing signed by both parties.

19.    **Use of Author's Name and Likeness.** Publisher shall have the right to use, and to license others to use, Author's name, image, likeness, and biographical material for advertising, promotion, and other exploitation of the Work and the other rights granted under this Agreement.

20.    **Revisions.** Author agrees to revise the Work as Publisher may deem appropriate during the effective term of this Agreement. The provisions of this Agreement shall apply to each revision of the Work by Author, which shall be considered a separate work, except that the manuscript of each such revision shall be delivered to Publisher within a reasonable time after Publisher's request for such revision.

20.1  If Author fails to provide the manuscript of a revision of the Work which is acceptable to Publisher, or should the Author be deceased, then Publisher shall have the right, but not the obligation, to make such revisions, or engage a skilled person to make such revisions, and Author shall reimburse Publisher for all its actual costs of making such revisions.

20.2   If Publisher engages one or more persons to make such revisions, then Publisher, in its sole discretion, may afford appropriate credit (including authorship or co-authorship credit) to such person(s).

# COPYRIGHT

21.   **Copyright Notice and Registration.** Publisher shall, in all versions of the Work published by Publisher under this Agreement, place a notice of copyright in the name of Author in a form and place that Publisher reasonably believes to comply with the requirements of the United States copyright law, and shall apply for registration of such copyright(s) in the name of Author in the United States Copyright Office. Publisher shall have the right, but not the obligation, to apply for registration of copyright(s) in the Work as published by Publisher elsewhere in the world. Nothing contained in this section shall be construed as limiting, modifying, or otherwise affecting any of the rights granted to Publisher under this Agreement.

22.   **Additional Documents.** Author shall execute and deliver to Publisher any and all documents which Publisher deems necessary or appropriate to evidence or effectuate the rights granted in this Agreement, including but not limited to the Instrument of Recordation attached hereto as an Exhibit to this Agreement.

23.   **Copyright Infringement.** If, at any time during the term of this Agreement, a claim shall arise for infringement or unfair competition as to any of the rights that are the subject of this Agreement, the parties may proceed jointly or separately to prosecute an action based on such claims. If the parties proceed jointly, the expenses (including attorneys' fees) and recovery, if any, shall be shared equally by the parties. If the parties do not proceed jointly, either or both parties shall have the right to proceed separately, and if so, such party shall bear the costs of litigation and shall own and retain any and all recovery resulting from such litigation. If the party proceeding separately does not hold the record title of the copyright at issue, the other party hereby consents that the action be brought in his, her, or its name. Notwithstanding the foregoing, Publisher has no obligation to initiate litigation on such claims, and shall not be liable for any failure to do so.

# ACCOUNTING

24.     **Accounting**. Publisher shall render to Author a statement of Net Units sold and Net Revenues from sale of Publisher's editions and other exploitation and disposition of rights to the Work, and other credits and debits relating to the Work and the rights granted in this Agreement, and pay Author any amount(s) then owing, for each six-month accounting period, not later than thirty (30) days following the close of each such period.

24.1 As used herein, "Net Units" shall refer to copies of the Work in any Publisher's edition actually sold and delivered, net of returns, damaged or spoiled copies, and promotional and Author's copies.

24.2 Publisher shall have the right to debit the account of Author for any overpayment of royalties, and any and all costs, charges, or expenses which Author is required to pay or reimburse Publisher under this Agreement, and any amounts owing Publisher under any other agreement between Publisher and Author.

25.     **Reserve Against Returns**. Publisher shall have the right to allow for a reasonable reserve against returns. If royalties have been paid on copies that are thereafter returned, then Publisher shall have the right to deduct the amount of such royalties on such returned copies from any future payments under this or any other Agreement

26.     **Audit Rights**. Author shall have the right, upon reasonable notice and during usual business hours but not more than once each year, to engage a certified public accountant to examine the books and records of Publisher relating to the Work at the place where such records are regularly maintained. Any such examination shall be at the sole cost of the Author, and may not be made by any person acting on a contingent fee basis. Statements rendered under this Agreement shall be final and binding upon Author unless Author sets forth the specific objections in writing and the basis for such objections within six (6) months after the date the statement was rendered.

27.     **Agency**. Author hereby authorizes and appoints [ *Name and address of Author's literary agent or agency*] ("Agent") to act as Author's agent in connection with this Agreement, including but not limited to the disposition of

any and all rights in the Work, any sequels to the Work, and any options to future work of the Author under this Agreement. Accordingly, Agent is hereby fully empowered by Author to act on behalf of Author, to collect and receive all sums of money payable to Author, and to receive any and all statements, notices, or other communications to Author in connection with this Agreement. Receipt by Agent of any such payments, statements, notices, and other matter shall be a valid discharge of Publisher's obligations to Author for such matters under this Agreement. This clause creates an agency coupled with an interest as between Author and Agent.

## WARRANTIES, REPRESENTATIONS, AND INDEMNITIES

28.    **Author's Representations and Warranties**. Author represents and warrants to Publisher that: (i) the Work is not in the public domain; (ii) Author is the sole proprietor of the Work and has full power and authority, free of any rights of any nature whatsoever by any other person, to enter into this Agreement and to grant the rights which are granted to Publisher in this Agreement; (iii) the Work has not heretofore been published, in whole or in part, in any form; (iv) the Work does not, and if published will not, infringe upon any copyright, trademark, or any other intellectual property rights or other proprietary rights of any third party; (v) the Work contains no matter whatsoever that is obscene, libelous, violative of any third party's right of privacy or publicity, or otherwise in contravention of law or the right of any third party; (vi) all statements of fact in the Work are true and are based on diligent research; (vii) all advice and instruction in the Work is safe and sound, and is not negligent or defective in any manner; (viii) the Work, if biographical or "as told to" Author, is authentic and accurate; and (ix) Author will not hereafter enter into any agreement or understanding with any person or entity which might conflict with the rights granted to Publisher under this Agreement.

29.    **Author's Indemnity of Publisher**. Author shall indemnify, defend, and hold harmless Publisher, its subsidiaries and affiliates, and their respective shareholders, officers, directors, employees, partners, associates, affiliates, joint venturers, agents, and representatives, from any and all claims, debts, demands, suits, actions, proceedings, and/or prosecutions ("Claims") based on

allegations which, if true, would constitute a breach of any of the foregoing warranties and representations or any other obligation of Author under this Agreement, and any and all liabilities, losses, expenses (including attorneys' fees and costs) and damages in consequence thereof.

29.1 Each party to this Agreement shall give prompt notice in writing to the other party of any Claims.

29.2 In the event of any Claims, Publisher shall have the right to suspend payments otherwise due to Author under the terms of this Agreement as security for Author's obligations under this section.

29.3 Author's warranties, representations, and indemnities as set forth in this Agreement shall extend to any person or entity against whom any Claims are asserted by reason of the exploitation of the rights granted by Author in this Agreement, as if such warranties, representations, and indemnities were originally made to such third parties.

29.4 All such warranties, representations, and indemnities shall survive the termination or expiration of this Agreement.

30.     **Insurance.** Publisher, at its own expense, shall name Author as an additional insured on any policies of insurance that Publisher, in its sole and absolute discretion, may maintain during the term of this Agreement.

## OPTIONS, NONCOMPETITION, AND OTHER RIGHTS AND RESTRICTIONS

31.     **Option on Author's Next Work.** Publisher shall have the right to acquire Author's next book-length work on the same terms and conditions set forth in this Agreement. Author shall submit a detailed outline and sample chapter of such work to Publisher before submitting the work to any other publisher, and Publisher shall have a period of thirty (30) days in which to review the submission and determine whether or not to exercise the option. The thirty (30)-day period described above shall not begin to run earlier than sixty (60) days after the publication of the Work. If Publisher declines to exercise its option, then Author may submit the work to other publishers or otherwise dispose of the work.

32.    **Author's Next Work.** Author acknowledges and agrees that the Work shall be Author's next published work in book form, and Author shall not publish or permit the publication of any other work in book form prior to publication of the Work by Publisher under this Agreement.

33.    **Reservation of Rights.** All rights in the Work not expressly granted to Publisher under this Agreement are wholly and exclusively reserved to Author.

34.    **Author's Noncompetition.** During the duration of this Agreement, Author shall not prepare, publish, or participate in the preparation or publication of, any competing work that is substantially similar to the Work, or which is likely to injure the sales of the Work.

35.    **Title and Series Rights.** Publisher reserves all rights in and to the title (including series title, if any), logotype, trademark, trade dress, format, and other features of the Work as published and promoted by Publisher. Publisher shall have the sole right to develop sequels or prequels, new or additional titles in a series, or related works using any and all such elements, and shall be free to commission or contract with any other person(s) for the preparation of such sequels, series, or related works.

# CESSATION OF PUBLICATION

36.    **Remainders.** If Publisher determines that there is not sufficient demand for the Work to enable it to continue its publication and sale profitably, the Publisher may dispose of the copies remaining on hand as it deems best. In such event, Author shall have the right, within two (2) weeks of the giving of written notice by Publisher, to a single purchase of some or all of such copies at the best available price, and the purchase of film and plates at Publisher's actual cost of manufacture. If Author declines to purchase such copies or other materials, Publisher may dispose of them and shall pay Author, in lieu of royalties or any other amounts otherwise payable under this Agreement, a sum equal to 5% of the amounts actually received by Publisher in excess of the cost of manufacture.

37.    **Reversion of Rights.** If the Work goes out of print in all Publisher's editions, Author shall have the right to request that Publisher reprint or cause a licensee to reprint the Work. Publisher shall have twelve (12) months after receipt

of any such written request from Author to comply, unless prevented from doing so by circumstances beyond Publisher's control. If Publisher declines to reprint the Work as described above, or if Publisher agrees to reprint the Work but fails to do so within the time allowed, then Author may terminate this Agreement upon sixty (60) days' notice in writing. Upon such termination, all rights granted under this Agreement, except the rights to dispose of existing stock, shall revert to Author, subject to all rights which may have been granted by Publisher to third parties under this Agreement, and Publisher shall have no further obligations or liabilities to Author except that Author's earned royalties shall be paid when and as due. The Work shall not be deemed out of print within the meaning of this section so long as the Work is available for sale either from stock in Publisher's, distributor's, or licensee's warehouse, or in regular sales channels.

38.     **Rights Surviving Termination.** Upon the expiration or termination of this Agreement, any rights reverting to Author shall be subject to all licenses and other grants of rights made by Publisher to third parties pursuant to this Agreement. Any and all rights of Publisher under such licenses and grants of rights, and all warranties, representations, and indemnities of Author, shall survive the expiration or termination of this Agreement.

## GENERAL PROVISIONS

39.     **Right to Withdraw Offer.** Publisher shall have the right to withdraw its offer of agreement at any time prior to delivery of this Agreement to and execution of this Agreement by Publisher.

40.     **Counterparts.** This Agreement may be signed in counterparts, and if so, the counterparts bearing the signatures of all parties shall be deemed to constitute one binding agreement.

41.     **Advice of Counsel.** Author acknowledges that Publisher has explained that he or she is entitled to seek the advice and counsel of an attorney or other counselor of Author's choice before agreeing to the terms set forth in this Agreement, and Publisher has encouraged Author to do so. Author acknowledges that, in the event Author signs this Agreement without seeking the advice of an attorney or other counselor, it is because Author has decided to forego such advice and counsel.

42.   **Entire Agreement.** Publisher and Author acknowledge that they have communicated with each other by letter, telephone and/or in person in negotiating this Agreement. However, Author acknowledges and agrees that this Agreement supersedes and replaces all other communications between Author and Publisher, and represents the complete and entire agreement of Author and Publisher regarding the Work.

43.   **Modification and Waiver.** This Agreement may not be modified or altered except by a written instrument signed by the party to be charged. No waiver of any term or condition of this Agreement, or of any breach of this Agreement or any portion thereof, shall be deemed a waiver of any other term, condition, or breach of this Agreement or any portion thereof.

44.   **No Employment or Other Relationship.** The parties acknowledge and agree that this Agreement is an arm's length transaction between independently contracting parties, and no partnership, joint venture, trust, employer-employee relationship, or other legal relationship is created between them.

45.   **Multiple Authors.** Whenever the term "Author" refers to more than one person, such persons will be jointly and severally responsible for all duties, obligations, and covenants under this Agreement, and shall share equally in all royalties and other amounts to be paid under this Agreement, unless otherwise specified in a writing signed by all parties.

46.   **Force Majeure.** Publisher's obligations under this Agreement shall be extended by a period equal to any period of force majeure that prevents Publisher from performing such obligations.

47.   **Notices.** Any written notice or delivery under any of the provisions of this Agreement shall be deemed to have been properly made by delivery in person to Author, or by mailing via traceable mail to the address(es) set forth in the Recitals and General Provisions above, except as the address(es) may be changed by notice in writing. Author and Publisher agree to accept service of process by mail at such addresses.

48.   **Binding on Successors.** This Agreement shall be binding on the heirs, executors, administrators, successors, and assigns of Author, and the successors, assigns, and licensees of Publisher, but no assignment by Author

shall be made without prior written consent of Publisher.

49.     **Applicable Law.** Regardless of the place of its physical execution, this Agreement shall be interpreted, construed, and governed in all respects by the laws of the state of [*Insert name of applicable state*].

50.     **Arbitration.** If any dispute shall arise between Author and Publisher regarding this Agreement, such dispute shall be referred to binding private arbitration in [*Insert city and state where arbitration will take place*] in accordance with the Rules of the American Arbitration Association, and any arbitration award shall be fully enforceable as a judgment in any court of competent jurisdiction. Notwithstanding the foregoing, the parties shall have the right to conduct reasonable discovery as permitted by the arbitrator(s) and the right to seek temporary, preliminary, and permanent injunctive relief in any court of competent jurisdiction during the pendency of the arbitration or to enforce the terms of an arbitration award.

51.     **Attorneys' Fees.** In any action on this Agreement, including litigation and arbitration, the losing party shall pay all attorneys' fees and costs incurred by the prevailing party.

52.     **Headings.** Headings and footers are for convenience only and are not to be deemed part of this Agreement.

53.     **Bankruptcy.** If a petition in bankruptcy or a petition for reorganization is filed by or against Publisher, or if Publisher makes an assignment for the benefit of creditors, or if Publisher liquidates its business for any cause whatsoever, Author may terminate this Agreement by written notice within sixty (60) days after any of the foregoing events, and all rights granted to Author by Publisher shall thereupon revert to Author.

54.     **Riders and Exhibits.** This Agreement consists of Paragraphs 1 through [*Insert number of last numbered paragraph*], and the following Exhibit(s) and Rider(s), if any:

---

[*Insert identifying name, number and/or letter of all attached exhibits and riders, or strike out if not applicable.*]

55.     **Signature Block.**

IN WITNESS WHEREOF, Author and Publisher have executed this Agreement as of the Effective Date.

"AUTHOR"                              "PUBLISHER"
[ *Insert full name of Author*]        [ *Insert full name and legal*
                                       *description of Publisher*]


By: _____

_____

(Signature of AUTHOR)                 Title: _____

# 1

## INTRODUCTORY CLAUSES

A contract will generally begin with introductory clauses where the contracting parties are identified, the subject matter of the contract is described, and the reasons why the parties are entering into the contract are set down. The sample introductory clause set forth below includes some important "defined terms"—that is, a series of definitions of what the contracting parties mean by certain capitalized words and phrases that will be used throughout the contract, e.g., "Agreement," "Author," "Publisher," "Work," etc. A defined term is always given the same meaning wherever it appears in a contract or other legal document, thus clarifying and simplifying the document at the same time.

### AN EXAMPLE OF AN INTRODUCTORY CLAUSE IN A BOOK PUBLISHING CONTRACT

This Publishing Agreement ("Agreement") is entered into as of [*Insert date here*] ("Effective Date") by and between [*Insert name, address and legal capacity of Publisher here*] ("Publisher"), and [*Insert name, address, Social Security number, date of birth, and citizenship of Author here*] ("Author") concerning a work presently titled [*Insert title here*] ("Work") and described as [*Insert description of subject matter, length, etc.*]

*Effective Date.* It's a good practice, although not a legal necessity, to specify a date when the contract is effective. This avoids any ambiguity about when the contract went into effect, and establishes a benchmark date for all the other time-related obligations in the contract. (As a general rule, and in the absence of an agreed-upon "Effective Date," a contract goes into effect when the *last* of the required signatures is placed on the contract.) And, since the contract actually may be signed before or after the "Effective Date," the phrase "effective as of" (or "dated as of") makes it clear that the parties are agreeing to a particular date as the operative date. Sometimes, the phrase "effective as of" or "dated as of" is used to establish a retroactive effective date for a contract that has been signed after the author and publisher started working together on a project.

*Identity of Parties.* When a single book is co-written by more than one author, then it is appropriate for all of the co-authors to be parties to the book contract. For the convenience of the publisher, whose standard contract form probably refers to the author in the singular, a contract with several authors will list the names and addresses of the various co-authors but identify all of them as "Author," i.e., John Doe and Jane Roe (collectively "Author"). Many publishers also include a clause elsewhere in the contract that establishes the principle that all of the co-authors are equally responsible for performing the obligations of "Author"—and, unless the contract specifies otherwise, all are entitled to equal shares of the compensation. (➤*Multiple Authors, Page 250; Compensation for Co-Authors and Collaborators, Page 130*)

A different issue arises, however, when the principal author of a book works with a ghostwriter or other collaborator who is not entitled to full participation in the book project as a co-author. One of two approaches can be used: The principal author can enter into a collaboration agreement with a ghostwriter by which the author acquires all rights in the ghostwriter's work, and then the author alone enters into a contract with the book publisher. (➤*Acquiring Rights from Contributor, Page 52*) Alternatively, both the author *and* the ghostwriter can jointly enter into the book contract, which then must address the additional question of the rights and responsibilities of the ghostwriter. The first approach is generally favored by the author, the second approach by the publisher, but either one is acceptable as long as the rights and duties of all parties—author, collaborator, and publisher—are defined in one or more signed contracts.

If the author uses a pseudonym, then both her legal name and the pseudonym should be specified, i.e., "Samuel L.

Clemens writing under the pseudonym 'Mark Twain' ('Author')." (➤ *Ownership of Title, Character, and Pseudonyms, Page 232*)

**Recitals.** Some contracts, especially older ones, include a set of formal "recitals"—that is, a series of declarative sentences in which the assumptions and purposes of the contracting parties are "recited." Recitals often begin with the word "Whereas," although the word is less commonly used nowadays because it sounds so fussy. Formal recitals are increasingly rare in publishing contracts, but it still makes sense to use them when it is important to create a written record of the facts on which the parties are relying in entering into the contract.

*Legal Capacity of Parties.* The legal capacity of the author and publisher should be described with specificity and in formal terms. The author, of course, is usually a living person acting in her individual capacity and should be identified as, for example, "Erica Jong, an individual." But the heirs of a deceased author might be acting through an estate or a trust: "The Estate of Henry Miller," for example, or "The Bruce Chatwin Family Trust."

The publisher, too, should be identified according to its legal status, whether it is a sole proprietorship, a partnership or joint venture, a corporation, a limited liability company, and so on. The actual legal name of the publisher, rather than its imprint, should be specified: "Simon & Schuster, Inc., a New York corporation," for example, is preferred over "Simon & Schuster." If the publisher is an individual, a partnership, or a joint venture "doing business as" a publishing house or press name, this fact should be specified, e.g., "Virginia Woolf and Leonard Woolf, joint venturers doing business as Hogarth Press."

---

✍ **Choice of Imprint.** A publishing house may have more than one imprint or division, and the contract will usually include a clause that reserves to the publisher the right to choose which one will actually publish the book. The same clause of the contract usually entitles the publisher to choose the "style and manner" of publication, including the title of the work. If the imprint, title or other particulars are deal points, then care should be taken to specify them in the contract. (➤ *Time and Manner of Publication, Page 160*)

---

*Addresses, Birthdates, Citizenship, Etc.* For obvious reasons, it makes sense to include the current addresses of the publisher and the author. However, it may be important for the publisher to know the birthdate, place of birth, citizenship, and Social Security number of the author for reasons of copyright registration, tracking down a missing author, or—in the worst case—tracing the assets of an author against whom the publisher has obtained a judgment. Sometimes the addresses of the parties to a contract are given in a separate clause that prescribes the procedure for giving formal notices (➤ *Notices, Page 251*), but, in all cases, the addresses of both the author and publisher ought to appear *somewhere* in the contract!

> ✍ **Author's Address**. If the contract is negotiated by the author's literary agent, it is not unusual to see the *agent's* office listed in the recitals as the mailing address for the *author*, e.g., "Herman Melville, c/o Starbuck Literary Agency, 1234 High Street, Nantucket, MA." Although the publisher is usually instructed to send checks, royalty statements, notices, and correspondence to the agent by a separate clause of the contract known as the "agency clause" (➤ *Agency, Page 203*), it's in the best interest of both the author and publisher for the author's address to appear in the contract. Then the publisher can maintain direct contact with the author if, for example, the agent is later terminated or the publisher needs to find the author for other reasons. (➤ *Notices, Page 251*)

*Description of the Work.* Most publishing contracts identify the work to be written by the author in informal and highly abbreviated terms, sometimes only by a title, a thumbnail description, and perhaps a specified word length: "A manuscript of approximately 100,000 words on the life and music of Van Morrison." But if the author and publisher ever find themselves in disagreement about what the book was intended to be, then a more detailed definition will be crucial to avoiding a dispute or even a lawsuit. If necessary, the book proposal itself—or, at least, a more detailed description of the book—can be attached to the contract as an exhibit and "incorporated by reference." It's a simple approach to avoiding the problem that sometimes arises when the manuscript is actually delivered and the publisher announces: "This is not the book we expected."

✍ **Description of Book Project.** Misunderstandings between an author and publisher over "the book we expected" often come to light only when a book is "orphaned," that is, the editor who originally acquired the book later leaves the publishing house, and a new editor takes over the project. That's why a detailed description of the work in the book contract may prevent a new editor from simply dumping a predecessor's projects on the pretext that the author's manuscript does not meet with the publisher's expectations.

# 2

## $

# TRANSFER OF RIGHTS

The transfer of rights in an author's work to the publisher is the single most fundamental deal point in any book contract. Here, the "bundle of rights" that make up the author's copyright in a work of authorship is defined and allocated between the two parties. The precise phrasing of the clause will determine how and by whom the author's work may be exploited far into the future and potentially well after the death of the author!

**The "Bundle of Rights" in a Copyrighted Work.** The transfer of rights in a work of authorship can be a subtle and complex matter because of the unique nature of copyright, which is often likened to a bundle of sticks and can be broken down into an almost infinite number of sticks, each one representing a right that can be separately owned and exploited. For example, the right to publish a manuscript as a book is only one stick in the bundle, and it can be divided into a number of separate rights. The right to publish the book in hardcover is one, the right to publish the book in softcover is another, and each foreign-language edition of the book is yet another. Other sticks in the bundle include the right to make the book into an audiocassette recording, a motion picture, a television series, a multimedia product on-line or on CD-ROM, and so on. (➤*Primary and Secondary Rights, Page 59*)

Under most circumstances, copyright in a work of authorship springs into existence when the author creates the work, and he owns *all* of the rights in the work. If a single work is created by more than one author, then each author owns an equal share of the copyright unless they have agreed to some other allocation of rights. And the author (or authors) may divide up and grant the various rights in the work of authorship exactly as he chooses. For example, the author may agree to grant hardcover and softcover publication rights to a book publisher but hold back (or "reserve") the motion picture and television rights so that these rights can be optioned or sold to a studio, a network, or a producer. So it's crucial for both the author and the publisher to understand and agree to the specific rights that are being granted in the book contract.

## BASIC APPROACHES TO THE TRANSFER OF RIGHTS UNDER COPYRIGHT

The various rights in a copyrighted work can be conveyed in three basic ways, and sample clauses are given below to illustrate each one.

*Grant of Rights.* The most common mechanism for conveyance of rights in a copyrighted work in a book publishing contract is a grant of rights. Here the author grants some or all the rights in his work to the publisher, who thereafter owns and controls the specified rights. Two sample clauses are given below: one version for the grant of *all* rights in the author's work, and another version for the grant of limited and specified rights. In both instances, ownership of the rights is transferred by the author to the publisher.

*License of Rights.* Another way to convey rights in a work of authorship is by means of a license rather than an outright grant of rights. A copyright license is roughly analogous to a lease of real property—the license, like the lease, does not convey *ownership* but only the right to *use* the property for a specified period of time.

*Work-for-Hire.* "Work made for hire" is a "legal fiction" under the copyright law of the United States that vests both ownership *and* authorship of a copyrighted work in the party that employed or commissioned the actual individual who actually created the work. When an author signs a work-for-hire agreement that complies with the requirements of the copyright law—or if the author creates a work within the "course and scope" of employment, whether or not he has signed *any* work-for-hire agreement—the employer or commissioning party is deemed to

**Acquiring Rights From Contributors.** The same principles that apply to the transfer of rights by an author to a publisher may be used to define how rights are acquired by a principal author, a group of co-authors, or a publisher from the various collaborators or contributors who may provide material for a book project—and care should be taken to enter into signed agreements to confirm the acquisition of such rights. For example, if the principal author of a book engages the services of a ghostwriter—or, for that matter, an editor, a researcher, even a clerical assistant—then the author must secure the right to use the work product of the ghostwriter or other contributor of copyrightable work. Similarly, if the publisher acquires a cover illustration, a preface, a map, an index, or any other work of authorship from a freelance contributor for use in connection with the author's work, then rights in the material ought to be secured in a separate agreement. If the contributors are willing and if the circumstances permit, both the principal author and the publisher will probably prefer to acquire such contributions as on a work-for-hire basis, but some form of signed agreement ought to be obtained in every instance.

be the "author" of the work for all purposes! Although work-for-hire is still a rarity in a conventional book publishing, it is a fixture of motion picture and television production and is becoming increasingly popular in journalism and multimedia products. The advantage of a work-for-hire to the copyright owner is that it rules out any future claim of authorship (or co-authorship) by someone who contributed some element of a published work a claim that is sometimes made by informal collaborators, artists who contribute illustrations to a published work, and even editors who work on a manuscript!

## GRANT OF RIGHTS

### A CLAUSE FOR GRANTING "ALL RIGHTS" TO THE PUBLISHER

Author, on behalf of himself and his heirs, executors, administrators, successors, and assigns, exclusively grants, assigns, and otherwise transfers to Publisher and its licensees, successors, and assigns, all right, title, and interest in and to the Work, throughout the world, in perpetuity, and in any and all media and forms of expressions now known or hereafter devised, including but not limited to all copyrights therein for the full term of such copyrights (and any and all extensions and renewals thereof), including but not limited to all primary and secondary rights therein.

This sample clause conveys *all* of the rights in the "bundle" from the author to the publisher, and only the publisher is entitled to exploit the rights during the term of the contract. The author's financial and creative participation in the exploitation of his work will be defined elsewhere in the contract (➤*Chapter 3: Author Compensation; Author's Rights of Consultation and Approval, Page 161*), but the publisher will be the owner of all rights in the author's work.

*"Author, on behalf of himself and his or her heirs, executors, administrators, successors, and assigns..."* A contract signed by the author will usually bind anyone who acquires rights in the same work from the author at a later date, whether by contract, by will, or by operation of law. The language here simply makes it clear that the author's rights and duties under the contract will also apply to the author's successors. Thus, for example, if the author assigns his publishing agreement to his wife, she will receive nothing more and nothing less than the author would have received, and the heirs of a deceased author will have the same rights that the author owned during his lifetime. Similarly, the publisher's successors (*"...its licensees, successors, and assigns..."*) will be bound by the terms of the contract.

*"...exclusively grants, assigns, and otherwise transfers..."* As noted above, the standard publishing agreement is generally structured as an outright grant of rights by the author to the publisher, rather than a license (which gives permission to the publisher to make use of a copyrighted work for only a limited period of time) or a work-for-hire agreement (which creates the legal fiction that the publisher is, as a matter of law, the author of the work). (➤*A "Work-for-Hire" Clause, Page 98*)

Even under an outright grant of rights, some or all rights may revert (i.e., go back) to the author later on, either under a reversionary clause (➤*Reversion of Rights, Page 238*) or by the author's statutory right to terminate the transfer of rights. (➤*A Work-for-Hire Clause, Page 98*). But the grant-of-rights language means that the publisher (and *not* the author) is the owner of important rights in the work once the contract is signed.

A typical grant-of-rights clause will be exclusive to the publisher, so that the rights are conveyed to the publisher alone and may not be used by the author or conveyed by the author to any other publisher. The only significant exception is found in the definition of the territory in which the publisher will exploit the rights—a U.S. publisher may be willing to share rights in the author's book in foreign markets as long as rights in the domestic market are exclusive. (➤ *Territory, Page 92*)

*"...to Publisher and its licensees, successors, and assigns..."* The rights are granted not only to the publisher, but also to its *"licensees, successors, and assigns,"* which makes it clear that the publisher is entitled to license or sell its rights in the author's work to another publisher. ("Assigns," which is often used as a noun in contracts, refers to anyone to whom the rights may be assigned.) By the same token, the publisher is binding its licensees, successors, and assigns to the terms of the contract with the author. If the publisher is acquired or merges with another company, or if the publisher licenses one of the subsidiary rights in the author's work to another publisher, then the publisher's "successor" and "licensee" are bound by the terms of the original contract, too.

*"...all right, title, and interest in and to the Work, throughout the world, in perpetuity, and in any and all media and forms of expressions now known or hereafter devised, including but not limited to all copyrights therein for the full term of such copyrights (and any and all extensions and renewals thereof), including but not limited to all primary and secondary rights therein."* The author is granting *all* rights in the work to the publisher without any limitations or reservations. In fact, the sample clause extends not only to the copyright in the author's work, which is limited in duration by statute, but to other rights that may belong to the publisher indefinitely. For example, the sweeping grant of rights arguably includes rights to ideas, characters, settings, plot lines, and other elements as well as titles and other elements that may be protected under trademark law.

An "all-rights" clause such as the one set forth above is increasingly rare in trade publishing, especially among the larger houses, but some publishers still seek to acquire complete ownership of the author's work. In fact, some publishers seek an even more comprehensive form of copyright ownership by using a work-for-hire agreement rather than a grant of rights. (➤*A Work-for-Hire Clause, Page 98*) More often, however, the scope of the grant-of-rights clause will be negotiated, and the publisher will acquire only limited and specified rights.

### A CLAUSE FOR GRANTING LIMITED AND SPECIFIED RIGHTS TO THE PUBLISHER

Author, on behalf of himself and his heirs, executors, administrators, successors, and assigns, exclusively grants, assigns, and otherwise transfers to Publisher and its licensees, successors, and assigns, the following specified rights in the Work for the full term of copyright in the Work and throughout the world.

1. The right to print, publish, distribute, sell, and generally exploit the Work in volume form, including both hardcover and softcover editions.

2. The right to use and generally exploit the Work in the form of abridged and/or unabridged sound recordings of the verbatim text of the Work, without the use of any other or additional material of any kind except incidental musical interludes and spoken introductory and explanatory segments, in the form of audiocassettes, compact discs, or similar audio products.

3. The right to use and generally exploit the Work in the form of an abridged and/or unabridged "electronic book," without the use of any additional material of any kind, in any and all electronic and/or digital media, including, by way of example only, portable digital storage media such as disks and diskettes and on-line computer services on the Internet or other computer-based networks.

Here is a sample clause in which the publisher acquires only a few specified rights—the right to publish the author's work in "volume" form (that is, in the form of a book, both hardcover and softcover), and in certain (but not all) audio and electronic formats. The clause is a grant of rights, and the ownership of the specified rights is conveyed outright by the author to the publisher, who is entitled to exploit the rights *"for the full term of copyright in the Work and throughout the world."*

The list of rights in the sample clause is only one highly simplified example of how the bundle of rights in the author's work can be defined and divided up between author and publisher. Typically, the book publisher will seek to acquire a great many more rights in the author's work, and the book contract will include a long list of "subsidiary" or "secondary" rights that are being transferred from the author to the publisher. (➤*Primary and Secondary Rights, Page 59*)

Note, by the way, that the sample clause defines the rights being acquired by the publisher by reference to the *media* through which the publisher may exploit the author's work (i.e., books and certain forms of audio and electronic media) but does not limit the *where* or *how long* the publisher may exploit these rights. As noted, the publisher is entitled to exploit the specified rights in the author's work *"in perpetuity"* and anywhere in the world. Some book contracts, however, will include clauses that limit the publisher's right to specific territories and specific periods of time. (➤*Term, Page 95; Territory, Page 92*)

The sample clause, by the way, illustrates one approach to audio and electronic rights in a book, but more elaborate clauses are preferable when defining and allocating these and other subsidiary rights. (➤*Audio Rights, Page 72; Electronic Rights, Page 76*).

> ✍ **Reservation of Rights.** The sample clause grants limited and specified rights to the publisher and, by implication, reserves all other rights in the book to the author, but it is common practice (and a good idea!) to include a clause that expressly says so: **"All rights not expressly granted to Publisher are hereby reserved exclusively by Author."**
>
> ✍ **Hard-Soft Deals.** Hardcover and softcover editions of a book were once regarded as separate rights in most publishing deals, and softcover rights to a book that reached bestseller status in hardcover

might command a spectacular price if the book went to auction among softcover publishers. Nowadays, however, an increasing percentage of book contracts are structured as "hard-soft" deals that is, the publisher acquires both hardcover and softcover rights at the same time. A hardcover publisher may treat softcover rights as a subsidiary right and license a paperback edition to another publisher.

📖 **Minimum Package of Rights.** A few publishers are content to acquire only the rights in the author's work that the publisher itself is able to exploit. For example, a publisher of hardback books may ask for hardcover rights only. Other publishers demand *all* rights in the author's work, including rights that will certainly be licensed to third parties if and when they are actually exploited. As a general proposition, publishers are likely to argue that they are entitled to acquire, at a minimum, the right to publish all versions of the book that will end up on the shelves of the same retail bookstore—that is, hardcover rights, softcover rights, audio rights and electronic rights. As a practical matter, of course, the question will always be answered in the course of negotiation between author and publisher since there is no "standard" allocation of rights in a book deal.

## LICENSING OF RIGHTS

Another way to convey rights in a work of authorship is to authorize the *use* of the work for specified purposes without conveying *ownership* of rights in the work, a legal mechanism that can be likened to a lease rather than a sale of real property. Like a lease, a license is often granted for a specified term of years rather than "duration of copyright" or "in perpetuity," and a license almost invariably limits and specifies the rights that the licensee is permitted to use during the term of the license. Licenses are rare in trade book publishing in the United States, especially between an author and a publisher, but they are commonly used in contracts with audio publishers and, especially, in transactions with foreign publishers for the right to translate and publish a book in another country. As with a limited grant of rights, a license must specify exactly which rights are being licensed to the publisher. (➤*Primary and Secondary Rights, Page 59*)

## A CLAUSE FOR LICENSING LIMITED AND SPECIFIED RIGHTS TO THE PUBLISHER

Author, on behalf of himself and his heirs, executors, administrators, successors, and assigns, grants an exclusive license to Publisher and its licensees, successors and assigns to exploit the following specified rights in the Work for a period commencing on the Effective Date of this Agreement and continuing for five (5) years, whereupon the license will expire, all rights will revert wholly and automatically to Author, and Publisher and its licensees, successors, and assigns shall make no further use of the Work

1. The right to prepare a translation of the Work in the Spanish language ("the Translation"), which translation shall be accurate, complete, and subject to the Author's reasonable right of review and approval; and

2. The right to print, publish, and sell the Translation in print publication form throughout the world during the term of this agreement.

*"Author...grants an exclusive license to Publisher..."* The sample clause uses the language of licensing rather than a grant of rights. What is being granted by the author to the publisher is a license to use certain rights, and not outright ownership of those rights.

*"...to exploit the following specified rights in the Work..."* Although it is theoretically possible to license *all* rights in a work of authorship, the more common practice is to license specified and limited rights, i.e., the right to publish an audio version, a foreign language edition and/or an edition in a foreign country, and so on. The rights that are being licensed should be carefully defined in the licensing clause; only one illustration is given in the sample clause (*"...The right to prepare a translation of the Work in the Spanish language..."* and *"...The right to print, publish, and sell the Translation..."*), but the same principle applies no matter what specific rights are being licensed.

*"...for a period commencing on the Effective Date of this Agreement and continuing for five (5) years, whereupon the*

*license will expire, all rights will revert wholly and automatically to Author, and Publisher and its licensees, successors, and assigns shall make no further use of the Work..."* By their very nature, licenses tend to be limited to a specified period of time, usually a specified term of years. The sample clause sets a term of five years, and specifically provides that the license will expire—and the licensed rights will revert to the author—at the end of the term. It is not unusual for licensing agreements to include a renewal mechanism by which the term is either extended automatically unless the license is terminated, or else the term is extended if the publisher meets certain specified sales or revenue benchmarks. Upon expiration of a license, the publisher will often enjoy a "sell-off" period a specified period of time during which the publisher may continue to sell stock on hand but may not manufacture new copies. (➤ *Term, Page 95*) But *some* method for determining the expiration or termination date of the license should always be provided, and the rights of the parties on expiration or termination should be defined.

## PRIMARY AND SECONDARY RIGHTS

Publishing contracts sometimes distinguish between "primary" rights, on one hand, and "secondary" or "subsidiary" rights, on the other hand. As a general proposition, the primary rights in a book contract are the rights that the publisher itself intends to exploit, and secondary or subsidiary rights are the rights that the publisher intends to license to third parties. Thus, for example, the right to publish the author's work in the form of a book is one of the primary rights in a contract with a book publisher, and the right to publish the same work as an audio product is a secondary right—but audio rights would be primary in a contract between an author and an audio publisher! For all practical purposes, "secondary" and "subsidiary" are interchangeable, and I will generally adopt the term "subsidiary" in *Kirsch's Guide* to define the rights that the publisher intends to license to third parties since it is more commonly used in publishing as well as the entertainment industry in general.

The technical distinction between primary and secondary is much less crucial in book publishing contracts nowadays because so many corporate publishers are conglomerates that engage in *all*

**Strike Outs**. If the grant-of-rights clause in a publishing contract is followed by a "laundry list" of primary and subsidiary rights, but the author and the publisher agree to reallocate the rights between them, it is a simple matter to mark up the contract form to show the allocation of rights by ~~striking out~~ the rights that are *not* being transferred to the publisher and writing **"Reserved to Author"** next to each such clause. All such modifications to a printed, typed or word-processed form should be initialed by both parties to avoid any misunderstanding later on.

aspects of publishing—hardcover, softcover, audio, electronic, multimedia, and more. Indeed, when it comes to the various sticks in the bundle of rights, what really counts in the negotiation and drafting of a book contract are the basic questions of how the various rights in the author's work are defined in terms of specific media and markets, who owns and controls the rights, and how the author is compensated for the exploitation of the rights that are transferred to the publisher.

Thanks to recent and rapid developments in publishing technology, entertainment media, and international markets, the bundle of rights in an author's work is ever-changing and ever-expanding. Not long ago, for example, the phrase "motion picture and television rights" was perfectly adequate to describe the one set of subsidiary rights in a book: the right to turn the book into a movie or television program, exhibit the movie in theaters and/or broadcast the program on television. Nowadays, however, a book publishing contract that refers only to "motion picture and television rights" creates an ambiguity about who owns the rights to exploit a movie or TV version of the author's work by means of cable television, satellite television, home video, in-flight movies, closed circuit television in hospitals and other institutions, and so on. Great care needs to be taken in negotiating and drafting the list of rights that are transferred from the author to the publisher, both in defining the rights and in making sure that the author is compensated for the exploitation of each right. (➤*Chapter 3: Author Compensation*)

Set forth below are some examples of the various rights in the bundle of rights in a work of authorship as they are commonly defined in contracts now in general use in the publishing industry.

## VARIOUS CLAUSES DEFINING
## TYPICAL PRIMARY AND SECONDARY RIGHTS

Here are typical examples of clauses that define the various rights in an author's work, each of which can be used in a grant-of-rights agreement or a licensing agreement to define and allocate rights between author and publisher. Whether the rights are "primary" or "subsidiary," as we have noted, depends on whether the publisher will exploit them itself or license them to a third party—but the more fundamental question is whether they are transferred to the publisher or reserved to the author.

The grant-of-rights clause in a publishing contract is typically followed by a long list of rights, all of which are transferred by the author to the publisher. If the publisher agrees to relinquish any of these rights in the course of negotiations, the contract form can be readily modified to indicate the listed rights that are being transferred to the publisher and the ones that are being reserved by the author.

---

✍ **Automatic Reversion.** If the author seeks to reserve one or more specific subsidiary rights but the publisher insists on acquiring them, a fallback position in negotiation is to ask for an automatic reversion if the publisher fails to exploit the right within a stated period of time. By way of example, a reversionary clause for audio rights might read: **"If Publisher fails to exploit audio rights in the Work by publishing or causing to be published an audio edition of the Work in the United States within eighteen (18) months after the delivery and acceptance of the Work, then all such audio rights will wholly and automatically revert to Author, who may freely exploit such rights without obligation to Publisher."**

✍ **Author's Right of Approval.** Once a subsidiary right is conveyed by the author to the publisher, it is generally up to the publisher to decide when and how to exploit it, subject only to the author's right to receive royalties or other compensation if the publisher does so. Some authors demand a say in the exploitation of subsidiary rights that have been transferred to the publisher—and a few authors with clout may actually get it! Here's an example of a clause that requires the publisher to obtain the author's approval: **"Publisher shall not enter into an agreement with a third party for exploitation of any of the subsidiary rights in the Work without the prior written consent of Author."**

---

## HARDCOVER RIGHTS

"Hardcover Rights," including the exclusive right to print, publish, distribute, sell, and generally exploit the Work, in the form of hardcover editions of the Work, distributed primarily through book trade channels such as bookstores and libraries.

Hardback editions are still the most prestigious and, for a fortunate few, the most profitable format for publication of a book. Still, the high costs of production, shipment, and storage may make hardback editions a much less common form of publication in the future. Even now, many books appear in simultaneous hardback and paperback editions, or—even more often—as paperback originals only. And the growing importance of "new media," including audio and electronic technologies, may further endanger the hardcover first edition in the publishing industry. Still, hardcover rights are still "primary" in most book publishing contracts.

## TRADE PAPERBACK RIGHTS

"Trade Paperback Rights," including the exclusive right to print, publish, distribute, sell, and generally exploit the Work, in the form of "trade paperback" or "quality paperback" editions of the Work distributed primarily through book trade channels such as bookstores and libraries.

Generally, a "trade" or "quality" paperback is the same size as a hardback, and may even be printed from the same plates and on the same paper stock, but the publisher is able to save money (and charge the consumer a lower price) by using a "soft" cover and a less expensive binding. Trade paperbacks and hardbacks are sold and promoted through the same channels of distribution, and when a book is published simultaneously in paperback and hardback, the paperback edition will usually be in a trade paperback format.

## MASS-MARKET PAPERBACK RIGHTS

"Mass-Market Paperback Rights," including the exclusive

right to print, publish, distribute, sell, and generally exploit the Work, in the form of softcover editions of the Work, whether as original editions or reprints, distributed primarily through the book trade, independent magazine wholesalers, direct accounts, and other customary channels of distribution.

A "mass-market" or "rack-size" paperback is smaller in overall size than a trade paperback, more cheaply printed and bound. Mass market paperbacks are also known as "rack-size" because they are displayed and sold on racks that are found outside the ordinary channels of the book trade, i.e., supermarket check-out displays, magazine stands, airport shops, and so on. (For that reason, mass-market paperbacks are often distributed to these outlets by magazine distributors rather than book distributors.) Mass-market paperbacks are often (but not always) reprints of books that originally appeared as hardback or quality paperback books, and, of course, are much cheaper than hardbacks or quality paperbacks.

## TRANSLATION RIGHTS

"Translation Rights," including the exclusive right to translate the Work, in whole or in part, into foreign languages, and to use, adapt, or otherwise exploit any and all of the rights in and to such translation(s) anywhere in the world.

A publishing contract in which the publisher acquires specified and limited rights in a book usually identifies the original language of the work and, whether by implication or by express provision, limits the publisher's rights to the original language. Thus, for example, the typical book contract between a U.S. publisher and a U.S. author contemplates the publication of the book in English, and the right to translate the work from its original language into other languages is a subsidiary right that may be transferred or reserved by the author.

*"...the exclusive right to translate the Work, in whole or in part, into foreign languages..."* The sample clause conveys translation rights in *all* languages of the world, but each language represents a separate subsidiary right and can be granted

**Foreign Rights.** "Translation rights" and "foreign rights" are sometimes used interchangeably during the negotiation of a book contract and even in the book contract itself. But a crucial distinction must be made between the two concepts. "Translation rights," as discussed above, define the right to prepare and publish the author's work in one or more foreign languages, but say nothing about where the translations may be distributed. Strictly speaking, "foreign rights" define *where* the author's work may exploited, but say nothing about the languages in which they will be published. Thus, for example, the term "foreign rights" may include the right to publish an English-language edition of a book in Mexico, while "Spanish-language rights" may include the right to publish a Spanish-language edition of the same book in the United States. Care must be taken in drafting a book contract to distinguish between these two concepts. (➤ *Territory, Page 92*)

or reserved separately, i.e., French rights, German rights, Spanish rights, and so on.

*"...and to use, adapt, or otherwise exploit any and all of the rights in and to such translation(s)..."* The broad language of the sample clause suggests that the owner of translation rights may freely exploit the translated work in any medium. A cautious author may wish to add a limiting phrase to make it clear that the translation may be exploited only in specified media, i.e., the addition of the phrase *"print publication"* to qualify *"any and all of the rights in and to such translation(s)"* would prevent the use of the translation in electronic media or audio products

*"...anywhere in the world."* The sample clause places no limits on *where* the owner of translation rights may sell copies of the translated work. But the *territories* in which translation rights may be exploited represent a right that can be separately allocated. For example, a publisher might acquire the right the translate the work into the Spanish language *and* the right to sell the Spanish translation worldwide, including not only Spain and Latin America but the United States, too. Or, as another example, a publisher may acquire the right to translate the work into German and sell the German-language edition only in specific countries where German is spoken such as only Germany, Austria, and Switzerland. Thus, a distinction must be made between *translation* rights, which includes the right to translate the

work into one or more foreign languages, and *foreign* rights, which includes the right to sell the book, regardless of language, in foreign countries. (➤ *Territory, Page 92; Foreign Rights, Page 64*)

---

✍ **Review and Approval of Translations.** Some translation clauses include a promise by the publisher that the translation of the author's work "**shall be accurate, complete, and subject to the Author's reasonable right of review and approval,**" or like phrases. Such promises are reassuring, of course, but it is the rare author who is able to make a meaningful judgment as to whether the translation of his novel into a foreign language is "accurate and complete."

---

### PERIODICAL PUBLICATION RIGHTS

"**Periodical Publication Rights,**" including the exclusive right to use and generally exploit all or any portion of the Work, in the form of excerpts, condensations, abridgments, or selections of the Work, in newspapers, magazines, and other periodicals, both in print and other media of publication, whether directly or through syndicates, either before ("First Serial Rights") or after ("Second Serial Rights") first publication of the Work in book form.

The sample clause broadly defines "periodical publication rights" to include, among other things, the right of the book publisher to authorize the use of the author's work in magazines, newspapers, and other periodicals, whether by selling such rights directly to the publisher of the periodicals or by using a "syndicate" that acts as a broker or distributor in offering periodical rights to publishers. The rights to publish a portion of the author's work in a magazine, newspaper, or other periodical are sometimes referred to as "serial rights," since magazines and newspapers are generally published as a series of consecutively numbered issues. As noted in the sample clause, "first serial rights" refers to publication of an excerpt from a book in a periodical *before* the book itself is published, and "second serial rights" refers to publication *after* the book is published; the sample clause assigns both first and second serial rights to the publisher. Like other subsidiary rights in a book, however, each of these rights may be granted or reserved by the author as a separate right, and if the publisher acquires any of them, the contract should include some form of compensation to the author for use of these rights. (➤*Chapter 3: Author Compensation*)

---

📖 **On-Line Periodicals.** Since many periodicals are also published in digital form and made available through on-line databases, computer services, and the Internet, the sample clause includes the key phrase "*both in print and other media of publication.*" If no such phrase appears in the periodical rights clause, then it is important for the publisher to secure electronic rights in the author's work, too. (➤*Electronic Rights, Page 76*)

---

## BOOK CLUB RIGHTS

"Book Club Rights," including the exclusive right to sell copies of the Work to book clubs, or to authorize book clubs to print and sell copies of the Work.

Most book publishers seek to own and control book club rights in the author's work, which is generally considered one of the primary rights in a book deal. Although the typical clause allows the publisher to authorize the book club to print its own edition of the book, the fact is that many book clubs will simply buy printed and bound copies directly from the publisher, although the book club edition will typically bear a cover and other editorial features that distinguish it from the publisher's edition of the same book.

---

✍ **Book Club Editions.** Authors are sometimes surprised and disappointed to find that book club editions are licensed by their publishers to book clubs on very modest financial terms, sometimes not much more than the cost of manufacture. Publishers generally defend the practice by pointing out that a book club edition serves to publicize and promote the author's work and, at least in theory, encourages the sales of the publisher's editions in bookstores. But a book club deal is also advantageous to the publisher, who achieves some economies in printing costs when a book club orders a supply of books from the publisher—an advantage that does not benefit the author!

---

## PHOTOCOPYING AND FACSIMILE RIGHTS

"Photocopying and Facsimile Rights," including the exclusive right to grant or withhold permission for the duplication and transmission of all or part of the Work by photocopying, facsimile, or other like means.

The right to make and sell copies of an author's work—or, more likely, some portion of the work—in the form of a photocopy or a faxed copy is not likely to generate much revenue. Indeed, an argument can be made that ready availability of a photocopied chapter from a book might discourage a book buyer from actually buying the book itself. Still, the publishing industry is increasingly vigilant when it comes to the casual photocopying of books, which is especially commonplace (and especially damaging to the author's royalty income) when a series of chapters from different books are photocopied, bound, and sold to students in a college class.

> ✍ **Photocopying.** Authors may ask for an additional provision that places certain restrictions on the use of photocopies, e.g., "**Publisher shall not make available photocopies or facsimile copies of more than a single chapter or a total of 2,500 words of the Work, and all such uses shall be revenue-generating.**" Recent innovations in collecting royalties for photocopying, notably through a private company called the Copyright Clearance Center, offer a practical way for a publisher to discourage casual photocopying while generating a modest source of revenue. The Copyright Clearance Center collects a modest fee on behalf of copyright owners in exchange for giving formal permission to make a limited number of photocopies of a published work. For that reason, some provision should be made in the contract for the sharing of revenue between author and publisher on the sale of photocopies and faxed copies.

## MICROFILM RIGHTS

"Microfilm Rights," including the exclusive right to use, adapt, or otherwise exploit the Work, or any portion thereof, in the form of microfilm, microfiche, slides, transparencies, filmstrips, and like processes attaining similar results.

Once a common way of storing and using books in reference libraries, microfilm and microfiche are less important than computer-based technologies nowadays, but many book contracts still identify them as separate subsidiary rights. Filmstrips and transparencies, too, are near-obsolescent teaching tools that are still invoked in some book contracts. But narrow definitions should be used in defining microfilm rights, and older contract forms should be approached with great caution, as they tend to lump photography-based technologies like microfilm and filmstrips with other technologies under the label "Transcription Rights." Indeed, the heading itself is a danger sign that recommends a careful reading and some thoughtful redrafting!

---

✍ **Transcription Rights**. Some publishers still use creaky "Transcription Rights" clauses that refer to old and even obsolescent technologies, including, by way of example, "phonographic, tape, wire, magnetic, electronic, light wave amplification, photographic, microfilm, microfiche, slides, filmstrips, transparencies [and] programming for any method of information storage or retrieval now known or hereafter devised." A better practice is to address these technologies elsewhere in the contract under the clauses that define and allocate audio rights, electronic rights, and so on. Sometimes, however, publishers are so wedded to their beloved contract forms that they refuse to delete the transcription clause. During a recent negotiation with the publisher, for example, an agent was unable to convince the publisher to delete or redraft the clause, but succeeded in adding the clarifying phrase: "...but excluding any uses encompassed under electronic rights, audio rights, video rights, motion picture rights or television rights."

---

## GENERAL PRINT PUBLICATION RIGHTS

"General Print Publication Rights," including the exclusive right to use and generally exploit all or any portion of the Work, in the form of condensed or abridged editions; bulk sales and other special sales, including but not limited to premium, promotional, corporate, and institutional sales; excerpts or selections of the Work in anthologies, compilations, digests, textbooks, and other similar works; Braille, large type, and other editions for the handicapped; book fairs; school editions and cheap editions; and unbound sheets.

The sample clause is a "catch-all" that assigns to the publisher a miscellaneous assortment of other print publication rights. Some of these rights are obsolete, or very nearly so; others are still regarded as valuable and sometimes appear as separate subsidiary rights in some book contracts. Each of these rights may be granted or reserved by the author as a separate right, but most publishers will expect to own and control at least these print-related rights in the author's book.

*"...to use and generally exploit all or any portion..."* The sample clause gives the publisher the right to exploit the entirety of the author's work in any of the specified formats or channels of distribution, or to select and use only portions of the author's work.

*"...condensed or abridged editions..."* The right to prepare and publish a shortened edition of the author's work for sale in book form, a rarity in today's book market but one that older contracts still invoke and publishers sometimes still seek to acquire.

*"...bulk sales and other special sales, including but not limited to premium, promotional, corporate, and institutional sales..."* The right to sell the author's work in bulk quantities to purchasers outside the ordinary channels of distribution in the book trade, usually at a deep discount to a single buyer in a large transaction, whether it is a discount store, a catalog publisher, a corporation, or institution. "Premium" and "promotional" sales often include the use of the author's work to promote the sales of merchandise or other goods and services, and "corporate" or "institutional" sales may include the preparation of a special edition imprinted with a cover, preface or other material especially designed for the bulk purchaser. Bulk and other special sales are usually "nonreturnable," a fact that justifies the drastic reduction in wholesale price. (➤*Returns, Page 113; Other Royalty Categories, Page 121*)

*"...excerpts or selections of the Work in anthologies, compilations, digests, textbooks and other similar works..."* The sample

clause broadly addresses the right of the publisher to authorize the use of excerpts from the author's work in a variety of formats, a right that is sometimes called "selection rights," "quotation rights," or "permissions," especially in older contracts. The sample clause makes a distinction between books, which are covered here, and periodicals, which fall under a different clause. (➤ *Periodical Publication Rights, Page 65*)

"*...Braille, large type, and other editions for the handicapped...*" Publishers often authorize the use of an author's work in Braille editions on a royalty-free basis, and if so, the contract should specify what uses are royalty-free. Large-type and certain audio-based products for use by the handicapped, however, are often published on a for-profit basis, and the distinction between royalty-free and royalty-paid uses should be carefully defined in the contract.

---

✍ **Audio Editions for the Handicapped**. The author may wish to ask for a definition that distinguishes between audio editions that are specially prepared for the handicapped and given away without charge, and audio editions that are prepared and published in ordinary course of trade, i.e., "**Audio editions prepared and published for ordinary commercial distribution are excluded from this clause and shall be governed by the Audio Rights clause.**"

---

"*...book fairs...*" Some publishers take the trouble to reserve the right to sell the author's work at book fairs, but the right is probably implicit in the general grant of publication rights and does not add much to the rights already controlled by the publisher in a conventional book contract.

"*...school editions...*" The sample clause confirms the right of the publisher to prepare and publish separate editions of the author's work for the schoolbook market, which is distinct from "trade" channels of distribution.

"*...and cheap editions...*" The phrase still appears in some older contract forms, where it was used to designate one or more edition of the book printed and bound with lower-quality materials than the customary trade book and sold at reduced price. Nowadays, a "cheap edition" may be regarded as functionally equivalent to mass-market paperbacks. In any event, the publisher generally reserves the right to determine the "style and manner" of publication, including paper and binding, elsewhere in the contract. (➤ *Time and Manner of Publication, Page 160*).

"*...unbound sheets...*" If the publisher licenses the right to publish an edition of the author's work to another publisher especially a book club, a foreign publisher, or an institutional buyer that wishes to include its own message on the cover or inside pages of the book it is often more cost-effective to sell and ship printed but unbound sheets rather than finished books, and this clause expressly grants the publisher the right to do so. Nowadays, however, a publisher will send only film—or, even more likely, a digital file contained on a single diskette—to another publisher that is licensed to produce its own edition of the author's work.

---

✍ **Author Approval of Premium Sales.** The use of the author's work as a premium by a corporation or other institution may arguably imply some kind of affiliation or endorsement by the author himself. For that reason, the author may wish to negotiate for the right to approve any such premium sales.

---

## DIRECT-RESPONSE MARKETING RIGHTS

"Direct-Response Marketing Rights," including the exclusive right to sell copies of the Work in any edition or medium authorized under this Agreement, through any form of direct-response marketing, including but not limited to any form of television, electronic media, direct mail, and catalogs.

The sample clause addresses the right to sell copies of the Work through various forms of direct-response marketing. The most familiar form of direct-response marketing is direct-mail advertising, but catalogs, "infomercials," and "home-shopping" television programs also fall into this category. Whether the direct-marketing right extends only to the sale of books or includes other products based on the book, such as audiocassettes, depends on the specific grant of rights in the book contract. Here, the sample clause specifies that the publisher is entitled to sell its products in *"any edition or medium authorized under this Agreement."*

> 📖 **Direct-Response Marketing**. Publishers might reasonably assume that the right to publish a book includes, by implication, the right to sell copies of the book through channels of direct-response marketing, but it is a good precaution to say so in the book contract, especially when the publisher acquires less than "all rights" in the author's work.

> ✍ **Sale of Author's Copies**. Many authors find it profitable to sell their own books, especially at public-speaking and teaching venues. Some authors even conduct their own mail-order businesses by sending out solicitations to their own mailing lists. If the author wishes to ensure the right to sell his books directly to the consumer, then the direct-marketing clause should be made "non-exclusive" and the author's right to engage in direct marketing should be reserved.
> (➤ *Author's Copies, Page 174*)

## Audio Rights

"Audio rights" generally include the right to prepare and publish a sounding recording of some or all of the contents of a book, and many publishers use audio rights clauses that make no distinction among various kinds of audio products. But it is possible—and, from the author's point of view, desirable—to make some finer distinctions between the various audio rights in a single work of authorship.

For example, the right to make a sound recording of the verbatim reading of the text of a book can readily be divided into two very different products that are generally exploited by different publishers in different markets. One is the *abridged* version of the book, which might include musical interludes, multiple readers, and introductory and explanatory material that does not appear in the book itself. The other is the *unabridged* version of the same book, which is likely to be nothing more than a single voice reading the text of the book aloud.

A further distinction may be made between a sound recording of the verbatim text of the book as it is read aloud by a reader, whether in an abridged or unabridged version, and a sounding recording of the *dramatization* of the book—that is, turning the text into narration and dialogue to be performed by one or more actors.

The first sample clause set forth below is an "all-rights" audio rights clause that is typical of clauses in general use in publishing contracts. The second sample clause proposes several sub-categories of audio rights and allows for these various rights to be separately allocated between author and publisher.

### AN ALL-INCLUSIVE AUDIO RIGHTS CLAUSE

"Audio Rights," including the exclusive right to adapt, use, or otherwise generally exploit the Work or any portion thereof in any form of sound recording and reproduction, including but not limited to audiocassettes, compact discs, or similar audio products of any kind or configuration whatsoever, whether now in existence or hereafter devised.

The sample clause does not distinguish between the various forms of audio publishing—abridged and unabridged—and does not rule out the use of material from the book in conjunction with other audio elements such as music, sound effects, and voice-over narration. For that reason, the second sample audio rights clause, set forth below, ought to be used when the author and the publisher agree to define and allocate the audio rights with more precision.

*"...the exclusive right to adapt, use, or otherwise generally exploit the Work or any portion thereof..."* The sample clause gives the publisher unlimited discretion in choosing material from the author's work and adapting it for use in an audio product, which implies the right to dramatize the work, add sound effects and musical interludes, and otherwise manipulate the content of the author's work. Audio rights, however, can be and usually are more narrowly and carefully defined. (➤*A Clause Defining Specific Audio Rights, Page 74*)

*"...any form of sound recording and reproduction, including but not limited to audiocassettes, compact discs, or similar audio products of any kind or configuration whatsoever, whether now*

*in existence or hereafter devised..."* Audio technologies are among the most diverse and fast-changing of all. The last few decades have seen the obsolescence of vinyl records and eight-track tapes, the diminishing importance of audiocassettes, the emergence of compact discs, and the introduction of digital audio tape (DAT). The sample clause makes it clear that *"audio products of any kind or configuration whatsoever"* are granted to the publisher, regardless of any future changes in audio technologies.

### A CLAUSE DEFINING SPECIFIC AUDIO RIGHTS

"Audio Rights," as the term is used in this Agreement, include the following specific applications and uses of sound recordings of the Work in any form of audio reproduction, including but not limited to audiocassettes, compact discs, or similar audio products of any kind or configuration whatsoever, whether now in existence or hereafter devised.

*Unabridged Sound Recordings.* The exclusive right to prepare and generally exploit unabridged non-dramatic sound recordings of the verbatim contents of the Work in its entirety without the addition of any other material whatsoever.

*Abridged Sound Recordings.* The exclusive right to prepare and generally exploit abridged non-dramatic sound recordings of the contents of the Work, or any portion thereof, without the use of any other or additional material whatsoever except incidental musical interludes and/or spoken introductory and/or explanatory segments.

*Dramatized Sound Recordings.* The exclusive right to adapt and use the Work, or any portion thereof, in preparing and generally exploiting dramatized sound recordings of the Work, including scenes, dialogue, and additional material, whether based upon the Work or otherwise.

The second sample audio rights clause proposes a distinction between abridged and unabridged sound recordings, which are regarded as separate and distinct products in the publishing industry. The sample clause also defines a third category of audio rights in which the author's work is "dramatized" that is, turned into scenes, dialogue, and narration that resembles a stage play. Dramatic rights are usually treated as a separate subsidiary right in publishing contracts, and care should be taken to avoid an overlap of audio rights, motion picture rights, television rights, and dramatic rights. (➤*Dramatic Rights, Page 84*)

"*...the following specific applications and uses of sound recordings...*" The sample clause sets up various categories of audio rights, each of which can be granted to the publisher or reserved by the author according to the agreement reached during negotiations.

"*...The exclusive right to prepare and generally exploit unabridged non-dramatic sound recordings...*" One specific and distinct category of audio rights is the unabridged reading of an author's work in its entirety. The sample clause confirms that the audio product must be complete and word-for-word ("*the verbatim contents of the Work in its entirety*") and that nothing may be added to the work. Unabridged recordings, because they are generally so lengthy, represent a separate and distinct market, and it is not unusual for a book to be issued in both abridged and unabridged audio versions by different audio publishers.

"*...abridged non-dramatic sound recordings of the contents of the Work, or any portion thereof...*" Abridged readings of an author's work in the form of a sound recording represent a separate market and, therefore, a separate subsidiary right. The demands of the market for abridged recordings makes it desirable for the publisher to be able to dress up the recording with "*incidental musical interludes and/or spoken introductory and/or explanatory segments,*" and the sample clause so provides. However, no "*other or additional material whatsoever*" may be added to the author's work in the audio version.

"*...The exclusive right to adapt and use the Work, or any portion thereof, in preparing and generally exploiting dramatized sound recordings of the Work, including scenes, dialogue, and additional material...*" A third and entirely distinct form of audio rights is the dramatized sound recording, an audio product in which an author's work is turned into *"scenes* [and] *dialogue"* and enhanced with *"additional material,"* including music, sound effects, and the like. Dramatized sound recordings are closely allied to dramatic rights (➤*Dramatic Rights, Page 84*) and may overlap with certain "allied and ancillary rights" in motion picture and television deals. Thus, the definition and allocation of these rights should be addressed with care in the other clauses of the contract. (➤*Allied and Ancillary Rights, Page 89*)

---

✍ **Adaptations.** Whenever the book contract permits the publisher to "adapt" the author's work, or to make any other decisions about how the author's work is used in another format or medium, the author may wish to ask for a right of consultation and/or approval to make sure that the publisher's decisions about changes to the work are acceptable. (➤*Author's Rights of Consultation and Approval, Page 161*)

✍ **Author as Audio Performer.** Some authors wish to perform the spoken-word recording of their own work, although the decision is usually reserved to the audio publisher. In the rare event that the publisher is willing to *guarantee* that the author will be used as the audio performer, then the contract ought to say so—and some form of compensation should be prescribed. More likely, however, the publisher will only agree to *consider* the author and to pay some additional compensation *if* the author is chosen to perform the work. In either case, the compensation should be *in addition to* the author's royalties or share of revenue for exploitation of the audio rights.

---

### Electronic Rights

"Electronic rights" is a loose and rather poorly understood term that refers generally to the right to adapt and use the author's work in computer-based media. Electronic rights are still too new and changing too fast to allow for settled legal definitions. The challenge to both the author and the publisher—or, more importantly, the attorneys representing them—is to come up with words and phrases that are sufficiently flexible to anticipate and describe the new media and technologies that are certain to emerge while avoiding conflicts and confusion with other subsidiary rights.

Older contract forms are especially treacherous when it comes to defining and allocating electronic rights. "Transcription rights" is an antiquated and obscure term that is sometimes still used in publishing contracts to refer to what are more accurately called electronic rights. Some contracts still refer to technologies that are already obsolete or may soon become so; e.g., magnetic tape, punch cards, programs for machine teaching, and ephemeral screen flashing. Other contracts refer to technologies that were on the horizon when the contract was first drafted but were ultimately unsuccessful in the marketplace: for example, a short-lived proprietary home-entertainment product called CD-Interactive (or CDI). Even the most recent contracts may go quickly out of date as markets, media, and technologies continue to change.

For these reasons, there is no such thing as a "standard" electronics rights clause in common use in the publishing industry, and the words and phrases to be found in various contracts do not yet have a common definition in the publishing industry. Some contracts lump all electronic rights into a single broad category. Other contracts make a distinction between computer-based products and services in which the contents of a book are simply reproduced in a digital form for on-screen reading— "electronic books," as they are called in some contracts—and those "interactive" or "multimedia" products and services in which some or all of the contents of the book are adapted and used in conjunction with words, images, and sounds from other sources, which are sometimes called "electronic versions." The same distinction between word-for-word reproduction of a book in a computer-based format and the adaptation of the book for use in a multimedia product is sometimes defined by reference to "linear" and "nonlinear" electronic rights.

Another emerging issue in the definition and allocation of electronic rights in a book publishing contract is the merger of entertainment and communication technologies. Today, for example, electronic rights on one hand, and motion picture and television rights on the other hand, are treated as separate and distinct sets of subsidiary rights although what is meant by "motion picture and television rights" has already changed in fundamental ways. (➤*Motion Picture and Television Rights, Page 86*) But the day may soon come when a single video monitor in the consumer's home will play audio and audiovisual programming on compact discs; permit direct access to on-line computer services such as America Online and LEXIS, the World Wide Web and the Internet; and display network television, cable television, and satellite television. On that day, a contract that fails to distinguish among the various sources of programming available on a single home video monitor may prompt a free-for-all among the owners of various subsidiary rights. One approach to solving the problem is suggested in the second sample clause below; but the book contracts in general use in the publishing industry today do not yet address the issue.

Finally, the computer is already beginning to change the way books are distributed and sold. "Publish-on-demand" technologies allow a consumer to order a book from a bookstore, a publisher's catalog, or an on-line service; then the book is retrieved from an electronic database, transmitted to a remote location, printed out, bound and handed or shipped to the consumer. Such systems are already in limited use in the book industry, but publishing contracts rarely address the question of who owns and controls the right to exploit a book through a computer-based "publish-on-demand" system. Since the end product is a book that is printed on paper and bound between covers, but the technology for producing the book is computer-based, the distinction between print publication rights and electronic rights begins to fade. (➤ *"Out of Print" in the Computer Age, Page 242*)

The first sample clause set forth below provides a broad definition of electronic rights that allows the publisher to acquire or the author to reserve *all* such rights without distinction or exception. The second sample clause distinguishes among various categories of electronic rights and thus allows the author and publisher to separately allocate each right to one or the other party. As there is not yet a "standard" electronic rights clause in general use in the publishing industry, the clauses set forth below, unlike most other sample clauses in *Kirsch's Guide*, may not closely resemble the electronic rights clauses found in other contract forms. Both the author and publisher should carefully evaluate what actually appears in a book publishing contract under consideration and evaluate how electronic rights are defined and allocated.

### AN ALL-INCLUSIVE ELECTRONIC RIGHTS CLAUSE

"Electronic Rights," including the exclusive right to use, adapt, or otherwise exploit the Work, or any portion thereof, alone or in conjunction with other matter, in computer-based and similar electronic media and technologies for data entry, storage, retrieval, transmission, display, and output of any and all kinds, and/or like media and technologies attaining similar results, whether now known or hereafter devised. Without limiting the generality of the foregoing, "Electronic Rights" includes but is not limited to electronic, digital, and computer-based media and technologies of all kinds, and the storage, retrieval, transmission, display, output, and reproduction of data through such any such media and technologies, including, by way of example only, interactive media and multimedia in which the Work may be adapted and used in conjunction with other matter, whether such data is stored on hard drives or other fixed storage media, disks and diskettes, and other portable storage media, and/or remote on-line databases.

The sample clause represents an effort to define electronic rights in the broadest possible manner without relying on references to specific technologies or proprietary computer products and services that may change in the future.

*"...the exclusive right to use, adapt, or otherwise exploit the Work, or any portion thereof, alone or in conjunction with other matter..."* A distinction needs to be made in an electronic rights clause between use of an author's work in its original and literal form and the use of the work in conjunction with other words, images, and sounds to create a "multimedia" or "interactive" electronic product. Because the sample clause is intended to be all-inclusive, it has been drafted to include *both* kinds of electronic products, but the second sample clause given below distinguishes between them.

*"...computer-based and similar electronic media and technologies for data entry, storage, retrieval, transmission, display, and*

*output of any and all kinds, and/or like media and technologies attaining similar results...*" Electronic rights are defined in the sample clause as "computer-based," but an effort is made to define these rights even more broadly by reference to the concrete processes and results: "*...data entry, storage, retrieval, transmission, display and output of any and all kinds....*" And the sample clause goes still further by referring to media that may "*[attain] similar results*" by use of different technologies.

"*...whether now known or hereafter devised...*" The sample clause seeks to capture rights in technologies that have not yet been invented, an effort that is sometimes upheld by the courts and sometimes not. As a general rule, such a "future technologies" clause will allow the publisher to acquire rights in technologies that were already in existence or reasonably anticipated at the time the contract was signed, but will not reach genuinely novel technologies that create an entirely new product or service. (➤*Future Media and Technologies, Page 92*)

"*...Without limiting the generality of the foregoing, "Electronic Rights" includes but is not limited to electronic, digital, and computer-based media and technologies of all kinds...*" The phrase "without limiting the generality of the foregoing" may strike the layperson as a clunky and even laughable example of legalese. It is often used by attorneys, however, to make it clear that an example of how a clause is intended to work in real life is illustrative only, and does not define the outer limits of the right that is being transferred or reserved. The clause goes on to cite a miscellaneous assortment of computer-related media and technologies, but only as examples and not as a comprehensive list of the rights covered by the clause. In other words, the phrase "*...without limiting the generality of the foregoing...*" is intended to blur the lines that define a specific contractual right or duty. If, on the other hand, the drafter of the contract wishes to sharply define and limits the rights or duties that are being described, then the phrase should *not* be used.

Precisely because the definition in the first sample clause is so broad, it is only suitable for contracts in which *all* electronic rights in the author's work are either transferred to the publisher or reserved to the author. If the author and publisher wish to break up the bundle of electronic rights and allocate the various rights between them, then the following clause (or one like it) must be used.

A CLAUSE DEFINING SPECIFIC ELECTRONIC RIGHTS

"Electronic Rights," as the term is used in this Agreement, include the following specific applications and uses of the Work in computer-based and similar electronic media and technologies for data entry, storage, retrieval, transmission, display and output of any and all kinds, and/or like media and technologies attaining similar results, whether now known or hereafter devised.

*Electronic Books.* The exclusive right to use and generally exploit all or any portion of the contents of the Work, but without the addition of any other material whatsoever, in electronic versions of the Work that are reproduced in the form of portable storage media and offered for sale or license to the consumer.

*Publishing-on-Demand.* The exclusive right to store, reproduce, transmit, and generally use and exploit all or any portion of the Work, but without the addition of any other material whatsoever, in the form of "Publishing-on-Demand" products and services. By way of illustration only, and without limiting the generality of the foregoing, "Publishing-on-Demand" refers to the manufacture and sale of copies of the Work by means of storage, transmission, and output of the Work in which the end product is a single printed copy of the Work for sale to a consumer.

*Databases, Networks, and On-line Services.* The exclusive right to store, reproduce, transmit, and generally use and exploit all or any part of the Work, but without the addition of any matter whatsoever, in a remote electronic database, network, or other on-line computer service, or similar system attaining like results, for use by consumers who are licensed to access the database, network, or service, and display and/or download the Work for their own personal use only.

*Interactive and Multimedia.* The exclusive right to adapt and generally use and exploit all or any part of the Work, whether alone or in conjunction with other material, in an interactive or multimedia product or service in any of the media or technologies described above.

The second sample clause distinguishes among the various special applications that fall within the broad category of electronic rights, and allows the author and publisher to allocate the various rights between them. The basic definition of electronic rights given in the first paragraph ("....*applications and uses of the Work in computer-based and similar electronic media and technologies for data entry, storage, retrieval, transmission, display and output of any and all kinds...*") generally applies to all these special applications, but the subparagraphs that follow the introductory paragraph are designed to permit the author to reserve or transfer each right separately.

*Electronic Books: "....exploit all or any portion of the contents of the Work, but without the addition of any other material whatsoever..."* The sample clause applies only to the literal and verbatim reproduction of an author's work in the form of an "electronic book" rather than a "multimedia" or "interactive" product. For that reason, the publisher is not permitted to combine the author's work with material from other sources, a fact that probably limits the value of the right to create an electronic version. As a practical matter, electronic books that consist only of text on a computer screen have proven to be mostly unsuccessful in the marketplace; only reference works such as dictionaries, encyclopedias, map books, and the like are especially useful in electronic versions. Still, the right to produce an electronic version of a book is regarded by some publishers as a primary right in a book contract.

📖 **Publisher's Right to Add Incidental Text and Images.** Even when the publisher agrees *not* to use the author's work in conjunction with other material to create a multimedia product, it is still reasonable and appropriate to reserve the right to include graphics, introductory or explanatory text, musical interludes, and the like in the end product. For that reason, the publisher may prefer to add one more sentence to the sample clause: "**Nothing in this Agreement shall prevent the Publisher from incorporating incidental text, images or sounds as introductory, explanatory or transitional material in conjunction with the Work.**"

*Publish on Demand: "...the manufacture and sale of copies of the Work by means of storage, transmission, and output of the Work in which the end product is a single printed copy of the Work for sale to a consumer."* The sample clause proposes a definition of the right to publish a book "on demand" through computer-based technologies, but a standard definition is not yet in common use. If and when publishing-on-demand becomes a routine form of marketing in the book industry, publishers will surely claim it as a primary right—and, since the end product in publishing-on-demand is a print product, it may not always be regarded as something that belongs in the electronic rights clause.

🖋 **Publish-on-Demand.** If "publish-on-demand" bookselling is put into general use in the publishing industry, then the question of when a book goes out of print becomes an especially troublesome issue for the author. The rights granted to a publisher under a book contract generally revert to the author when the book is no longer in print, but the out-of-print definitions in general use ought to be carefully reviewed to make sure that the rights do not fall into limbo if the book is still available for single-copy purchases through "print-on-demand" technologies. (➤*Reversion of Rights, Page 238*)

*Databases, Networks, and On-line Services: "...a remote electronic database, network, or other on-line computer service, or similar system attaining like results..."* Few, if any, books are made available in their entirety on-line, but the publisher generally wishes to secure the right to do so, if only to display portions of a newly published book for promotional purposes.

> ✍ **Databases.** The author may wish to negotiate for a clause that limits the on-line use of his work to short excerpts only, especially if the publisher does not intend to pay him for the use. If so, the following sentence might be added to the electronic rights clause: "**Use of the Work in databases, networks, and on-line services is limited to excerpts of no more than 5,000 words for promotional and publicity purposes only unless the proposed use generates revenue for the Author under this Agreement.**"

*Interactive and Multimedia: "...whether alone or in conjunction with other material, in an interactive or multimedia product or service..."* The right to create an "interactive" or "multimedia" product based on the author's work is potentially the most valuable electronic right in a book, at least according to the conventional wisdom of the publishing industry nowadays. However, since the market for interactive computer products based on books is still uncertain and rapidly changing, the right to create such products is probably less valuable to authors *and* publishers than either of them are willing to admit. Still, interactive and multimedia rights are so different in kind from other electronic rights that, as proposed in the sample clause, an effort should be made to distinguish and allocate such rights separately.

### DRAMATIC RIGHTS

"**Dramatic Rights,**" **including the exclusive right to use, adapt, or otherwise exploit the Work or any element thereof (including but not limited to characters, plot, title, scenes, settings, attire, and physical characteristics) in one or more live theatrical or stage presentations.**

"Dramatizing" a work of prose, as we have already noted, means turning the prose into scenes and dialogue, a process that is used not only in playwriting but also motion pictures, television programs, and even certain audio products. The sample clause narrowly defines "dramatic rights" as the right to turn a book into a stage play for *live* presentation on the stage. Thus, the sample clause avoids any conflict with motion picture and television rights, which are treated as entirely separate subsidiary rights in the same work. Similar clauses in general use in book contracts, however, do not always make such distinctions, and care should be taken to make sure that the grant of dramatic rights to one buyer does not conflict with the grant of motion picture and television rights to a different buyer.

## READING RIGHTS

"Reading Rights," including the exclusive right to authorize the public reading of all or any portion of the verbatim text of the Work before a live audience, but without dramatization of any kind or the making of any audio, audiovisual, or other recording of the reading.

Public readings of a book are rare outside the promotional efforts of the author himself, and do not represent a significant source of revenue for either author or publisher. Still, reading rights are sometimes still included as a separate subsidiary right in older contracts. The

**Ownership of Characters and Title.** The sample clauses that define dramatic, motion picture and television rights may be read to suggest that the buyer of such rights is entitled to use the *characters* and *title* of the original work apart from the other elements of the book. But characters and title are potentially valuable elements that a vigilant author may wish to reserve and protect, especially when the author has written (or may wish to write) a series of related books in the same series. For example, the producer who acquires the right to make a play, movie or television series based on a single best-selling mystery novel featuring a distinctive character may also claim the right to use the same character to create prequels and sequels. The question of who owns the title and characters in a book is generally addressed with precision in motion picture and television option and purchase agreements—but the cautious author may wish to reserve such rights in the publishing contract to avoid selling the character and title along with the rights to a single book. At the very least, the author should negotiate for additional compensation for additional uses of a character or title. (➤ *Title and Series Rights, Page 231*)

sample clause makes it clear, however, that reading rights do *not* include the right to record and re-use the live performance in any other medium.

## MOTION PICTURE AND TELEVISION RIGHTS

"Motion Picture and Television Rights," including the exclusive right to use, adapt, or otherwise exploit the Work, or any element thereof (including but not limited to characters, plot, title, scenes, settings, attire, and physical characteristics) in the form of one or more motion pictures and/or television programs of any kind, including but not limited to the right to disseminate such motion pictures and/or television programs by means of distribution and exhibition in theaters or otherwise, broadcasting, cable, satellite, telephone or other land lines, pay-per-view, closed-circuit, videocassettes, laser discs, digital video discs, and/or any other form of video transmission, exhibition, reproduction and sale, including but not limited to both analog and digital technologies and all other similar audiovisual media, whether now in existence or hereinafter devised.

The right to turn a book into a motion picture or a television program are separate distinct subsidiary rights, and each of these two broad categories—motion picture rights and television rights—can be further subdivided into a great many other sub-rights. For example, an author might sell one producer the right to make his book into a TV special, a movie-of-the-week or a mini-series, and sell another producer the right to make the same book into a theatrical feature. The right to broadcast a movie over network television is theoretically separate and distinct from the right to license the same movie to a cable channel like HBO or a pay-per-view service. And the right to reproduce and sell the same movie to consumers in the form of a videocassette, laser disc or DVD is yet another distinct right.

At least in theory, each of these subsidiary rights in a book may be separately defined, allocated, and exploited—and sometimes it happens that a documentary film producer or an independent television production company is willing to buy only the specific right that is required for a single project and leave the other rights in the hands of the author or publisher. As a practical matter, however, motion picture and television rights are usually bundled together at some point in the development of a project for the simple reason that most producers expect to control "ancillary" markets in order to recoup their investment and maximize their profit. Although some book contracts address motion picture rights and television rights in separate clauses, the sample clause is a broad and all-inclusive approach to defining *all* of the related subsidiary rights in a single clause.

*"...the exclusive right to use, adapt, or otherwise exploit the Work, or any element thereof (including but not limited to characters, plot, title, scenes, settings, attire, and physical characteristics)..."* The owner of motion picture and television rights under the sample clause is free to use or discard *any* element of the book, including not only the basic plot but also the characters and title. When the book is part of a series, or the central character is one that the author has used or intends to use in other books, the cautious author will negotiate for limitations on the use of the character and title for sequels and prequels. (➤ *Ownership of Characters and Title, Page 85*)

*"...one or more motion pictures and/or television programs of any kind..."* No limits are placed in the sample clause on the *number* of movie and TV projects that may be produced on the basis of the book. Thus, the owner of the motion picture and television rights under the sample clause, whether it is the author or the publisher, controls the right to produce not only a theatrical motion picture based on the book, but also a sequel or prequel to the movie, a TV movie or mini-series, or a TV series. When defining motion picture and television rights in a *book* contract, it is probably premature to divide up these rights between author and publisher. After all, it makes no commercial sense for the publisher to control the right to make the initial movie version of a book and reserve to the author the right to make a sequel. But the author should bear in mind that the sample clause embodies the ownership and control of *all* aspects of motion picture and television production. If the author reserves these rights, then he will be able to decide on how to exploit them in the future, but if he conveys them to the publisher, then it will be the publisher's decision.

*"...including but not limited to the right to disseminate such motion pictures and/or television programs by means of distribution and exhibition in theaters or otherwise, broadcasting, cable, satellite, telephone or other land lines, pay-per-view, closed-circuit..."* The sample clause addresses the conventional form of movie distribution (*"...exhibition in theaters..."*) *and* the various media and markets for video-based products including not only broadcast, cable, and satellite television but even closed-circuit television of the kind found in hospitals and airplanes. Again, the clause attempts to define a comprehensive package of motion picture and television rights, and each of these various markets and media is potentially more valuable in the aggregate than as a separate right. If, for some reason, motion picture rights are defined and allocated separately from television rights, then a distinction ought to be made between the applicable media and markets for each right.

*"...videocassettes, laser discs, digital video discs..."* The right to release a motion picture in the home video market in the form of a videocassette or a laser disc is one of the "ancillary" rights that producers deem essential to the profitability of a motion picture project. Only rarely will the buyer of movie rights be willing to forego the home video rights. A few books, however, lend themselves to home video products that can be readily distinguished from movie and TV projects and separately exploited in the home video market.

*"...any other form of video transmission, exhibition, reproduction and sale, including but not limited to both analog and digital technologies and all other similar audiovisual media, whether now in existence or hereinafter devised."* Because it is intended to cover *all* rights in motion picture and television media, the sample clause includes an effort to capture "future technologies," too. A truly new technology that is developed in the future probably falls outside the reach of the sample clause, but if it is merely a refinement of an existing technology, the owner of motion picture and television rights is likely to end up owning the rights to the new media, too.

## RADIO RIGHTS

*"Radio Rights," including the exclusive right to use, adapt, or*

*otherwise exploit the Work or any element thereof (including but not limited to characters, plot, title, scenes, settings, attire, and physical characteristics) for any form of radio programming, including but not limited to dissemination by broadcasting, cable, satellite, telephone or other land lines, pay-per-view, digital, closed-circuit or other forms of radio transmission, whether now in existence or hereinafter devised.*

Since an original radio program based on a book is a rarity nowadays outside National Public Radio and the BBC, radio rights are marginal in financial value. Nevertheless, radio rights are still defined as a separate subsidiary right in many book contracts, and a decision must be made on how to allocate the rights between author and publisher. As a practical matter, radio rights are probably most valuable if bundled with motion picture and television rights.

📖 **Allied and Ancillary Rights**. Some book contracts—and most agreements for motion picture and television rights in a book—refer to "allied and ancillary rights," i.e., "**Author grants publisher all motion picture and television rights, including allied and ancillary rights, in the Work.**" But the phrase does *not* have a clear and well-settled meaning. Arguably, an "allied" or "ancillary" right is one that is so closely related to another right in the bundle that the two rights are linked. For example, the right to make a book into a theatrical motion picture is probably "allied" and "ancillary" to the right to broadcast the movie on network television, or to make it available on a "pay-per-view" basis on a cable service, or to sell the movie for home-viewing in the form of a videocassette. But, unless one party or the other is seeking to gain some advantage by using hazy definitions, it is far better practice to avoid terms like "allied" and "ancillary," and to spend some time and effort in defining exactly what rights are being granted and what rights are being reserved. (➤ *Clarity and Confusion in Contracts, Page 9*)

📖 **Performance Rights**. The contract now used by one major publisher seeks to address one specific problem of overlapping subsidiary rights by lumping together motion picture, television, video, radio, dramatic rights, and "allied merchandising rights derived therefrom"

approach is useful only when performance rights are allocated to the author or publisher as a package. Otherwise, care must be taken to define each of these rights as a separate and distinct right and to allocate them with precision between author and publisher.

## COMMERCIAL RIGHTS

"Commercial Rights," including the exclusive right to manufacture, sell, and otherwise distribute products, by-products, services, facilities, merchandise, and other commodities of every nature or description, whether now in existence or hereafter devised, including but not limited to photographs, illustrations, drawings, posters, and other artwork, toys, games, wearing apparel, foods, beverages, cosmetics, toiletries and similar items, which may refer to or embody the Work, or any derivative works based on the Work, including but not limited to characters, plot, title, scenes, settings, attire, and physical characteristics.

Commercial (or merchandising) rights in a book figure ever more importantly in the negotiation of a book contract because they are regarded as increasingly valuable, especially if the book turns out to be a bestseller or generates a motion picture or television spin-off. A doll or an "action figure" based on a character from a best-selling book is one example of merchandising rights, and so are posters, T-shirts, and lunch boxes.

**Spin-Offs.** The "bundle of rights" under copyright grows ever larger as the publishing industry explores new markets, new media, and new product lines. One publisher, for example, includes "Theme Park Ride Rights" and "Calendar Rights" in its standard contract, and the long-running bestseller *Midnight in the Garden of Evil* spun off a line of cookies that are packaged in an old-fashioned tin that bears the familiar cover design of the book. Some of the more exotic subsidiary rights in a book may fall into a familiar category for example, "Cookie Rights" are probably included in commercial or merchandising rights but it is a rare contract that covers the right to turn a book into a theme park ride!

*"...the exclusive right to manufacture, sell and otherwise distribute products, by-products, services, facilities, merchandise, and other commodities of every nature or description..."* Although commercial rights are sometimes referred to as "merchandising" rights, the sample clause includes both goods and services *"of every nature or description."* The most familiar examples are enumerated (*"...photographs, illustrations, drawings, posters and other artwork, toys, games, wearing apparel, foods, beverages, cosmetics, toiletries and similar items..."*), but the list is only illustrative. Of course, the various commercial uses to which a book might be put can be separately defined and allocated in a book contract, but most contracts simply lump all commercial rights into a single clause.

*"...which may refer to or embody the Work, or any derivative works based on the Work, including but not limited to characters, plot, title, scenes, settings, attire, and physical characteristics."* The merchandising uses of a book, unlike a derivative work such as an audio or electronic version, may be only loosely connected with the book itself. A product such as a T-shirt, a poster, or a lunch-box is likely to use only the title, characters, or settings of a book, as the sample clause suggests, rather than the text itself. But the commercial rights in a book are expansively defined to include just about any element of the author's work that *"refer[s] to or embod[ies] the Work."*

> 📖 **Bundling.** Sometimes a publisher will be asked for the right to package a book with other merchandise, or the publisher itself may wish do so. For example, a manufacturer of vitamins might want to include a copy of a book on health and nutrition as a premium in a single shrink-wrapped package, or a publisher might want to "bundle" a book with an audio or video product and offer the two items as a single item of merchandise. Such uses *may* be adequately covered under a given commercial rights clause or a direct-marketing clause (➤*Direct-Response Marketing Rights, Page 71*), but the point can be clarified with one additional sentence: **"Publisher shall have the right to package, promote, and sell the Work in any format authorized under this Agreement together with products, services, facilities, merchandise, and other commodities of every nature or description, whether now in existence or hereafter devised."**

## FUTURE MEDIA AND TECHNOLOGIES

The right to disseminate, use, adapt, or otherwise exploit the Work, or to authorize others to do so, by any means or medium of communication now in existence or hereafter devised.

Thanks to the velocity of technological change in the 20th century, publisher and producers have sought to capture rights in media that have not yet been invented, and the "future technologies" clause is an effort to do so. As a general rule, however, the courts have refused to enforce such clauses to wholly new and novel technologies and markets that were not even contemplated when the contract was signed. Thus, for example, a future technologies clause in an "all-rights" book contract drafted in the 1960s would have applied to compact discs because they were simply a technological improvement on existing sound recordings such as vinyl records and audiocassettes, but the clause would *not* have reached a genuinely new technology such as videocassettes and laser discs for home use or a CD-ROM product for use on a personal computer.

## TERRITORY

A book contract should specify not only *what* rights in the author's work are being conveyed to the publisher, but also *where* the rights may be used by the publisher. When the publisher acquires *all* rights in a book, the territory is usually defined in the grant-of-rights clause, where the publisher is specifically empowered to exercise the rights in the author's work "throughout the world" or even "throughout the universe," according to some book contracts. ("World rights" is the shorthand phrase customarily used in negotiations). (➤*A Clause for Granting "All Rights" to the Publisher, Page 52*). More commonly, however, the territory in which the publisher is entitled to exploit the author's work is defined and limited in some manner, whether by reference to one or more countries, a geographical region, or a language.

Thus, for example, a book contract might include a long list of specific countries in which the publisher will enjoy rights, sometimes so long that it is attached to the contract as a separate rider. Or the publisher's territory might be defined by a generalized political or geographical phrase: "North America," "the British Commonwealth," or "the countries of the European Union." And sometimes the territory is defined by reference to a *language* rather than a geographical description, especially in a contract for foreign rights in an author's work. A contract for Spanish rights might define the territory as "all countries of the world where Spanish is an official language," and a contract for German rights might define the term as "Germany, Austria, Liechtenstein, Luxembourg, Switzerland, and other German-speaking countries throughout the world. (➤*Foreign Rights, Page 64*)

The sample clause below illustrates one common definition of territory in a contract between an author and a U.S. publisher. However, the publisher's territory is a fundamental deal point in a book contract:

**The Value of Foreign Rights.** Authors are often inclined to hold back foreign rights from their U.S. publishers on the theory that they would prefer not to share the revenues from foreign book deals with the publisher. (➤*Sharing of Revenues from Subsidiary Rights, Page 125*) The decision, however, should take into account two issues. First, who is better positioned to actually sell foreign rights? If the author is not represented by a capable foreign rights agent, then the publisher is probably more likely to succeed in selling the foreign rights than the unrepresented author. Second, even if the author is represented by a foreign rights agent, what commissions will be paid on the deals made by the agent? By carefully evaluating the split of foreign revenues between author and publisher with the commissions paid to the author's foreign rights agent, it may turn out that a foreign rights deal made by the publisher actually yields more money for the author.

the larger the territory assigned to the publisher, the greater the opportunity to make money on the author's work. Conversely, if the author reserves foreign rights in his book, he will be able to sell the territories without sharing the revenues with the publisher. (➤*Sharing of Revenues From Subsidiary Rights, Page 125*) Thus, the publisher is generally willing to pay a larger advance and more generous royalties for world rights than it would offer for the same book in the U.S. market only, and some publishers might not be interested in publishing a given book at all unless world rights were available. The actual formulation of a territory clause, therefore, depends entirely on the deal struck between the author and the publisher.

# TERRITORY

The rights granted to Publisher in this Agreement may be exploited during the Term in the United States, its territories and dependencies, including but not limited to Guam, Puerto Rico, and the U.S. Virgin Islands, and its military bases wherever located, Canada, and the Philippines.

*"The rights granted to Publisher in this Agreement..."* Only the rights actually conveyed by the author to the publisher, as defined elsewhere in the agreement (➤*Basic Approaches to the Transfer of Rights Under Copyright, Page 51*), may be exploited by the publisher, and so the territory clause addresses only the question of where in the world those rights may be exploited.

*"...during the Term..."* Similarly, the duration of the publisher's rights is defined elsewhere in the contract (➤*Term, Page 95*), and the territory clause does not ordinarily affect how long the rights in the author's work may be exploited by the publisher.

*"...in the United States, its territories and dependencies, including but not limited to Guam, Puerto Rico, and the U.S. Virgin Islands, and its military bases wherever located, Canada, and the Philippines."* The sample clause illustrates one common approach to defining the exclusive territory of a U.S. publisher. Note, for example, that overseas military bases are generally regarded as part of the U.S. market. By tradition, U.S. publishers have come to regard Canada as so closely linked to the domestic book industry that it is often included in what is otherwise a domestic book contract, and the same is sometimes true of the Philippines, where English is commonly spoken.

📖 **Exclusivity.** The grant-of-rights clause will usually specify that various specific rights in the author's work are owned "exclusively" by the publisher, but the territory clause may specify places where both the author *and* the publisher are entitled to exploit the rights on an equal basis. For example, a contract for hardcover rights in a book may include the phrase: "**The rights in the Work are exclusive to Publisher in the United States and Canada, and non-exclusive throughout the rest of the world.**" A better practice, however, is to carefully define exclusivity both in the grant-of-rights clause *and* the territory clause, and make sure the two are consistent.

📖 **Geographical Terminology.** Care should be taken in defining the territory in terms that may be rendered obsolete in our tumultuous world. Older contracts that define the publisher's territory as "the British Empire," for example, now raise fundamental questions about where the publisher actually enjoys exclusive rights, and recent history gives us plenty of examples of political entities that simply no longer exist!

## TERM

A typical book contract based on an outright grant of rights entitles the publisher to exploit the specified rights in the author's work "for the full term of copyright, including any and all extensions and renewals thereof." Some contracts, including the various grant-of-rights clauses in *Kirsch's Guide*, go even further and convey rights to the publisher "in perpetuity." So the duration (or "term") of a grant-of-rights contract is not ordinarily measured in years: either the contract remains in effect as long as the work is protected under contract, or the contract remains in effect forever. For that reason, it is rare to find a separate clause that defines the term of a grant-of-rights contract; the term is usually defined in the clause in which the author grants rights to the publisher.

Nevertheless, a grant-of-rights contract is subject to early termination under a number of circumstances. Generally, a book contract will terminate if the author fails to deliver a satisfactory manuscript of the work (➤*Termination for Nondelivery or Unsatisfactory Delivery, Page 151*) or if the book goes out of print. (➤*Reversion of Rights, Page 238*) And, regardless of how the term of a book contract is defined—a specified number of years, the duration of copyright, or even "in perpetuity"—the fact remains that the Copyright Act guarantees the right of the author (and his heirs and successors) to terminate the transfer of rights at some point in the future. (➤*Author's Right of Termination, Page 100*)

By contrast, a licensing agreement almost always defines the term of the contract as a period of time, usually a specified number of years, during which the publisher is entitled to exploit the licensed rights.

A work-for-hire agreement need not and should not mention a term of years at all, since the party acquiring rights under a work-for-hire agreement is deemed to be the author of the work for purposes of copyright ownership. The flesh-and-blood human being who actually created the work of authorship does *not* enjoy the right to terminate the transfer of rights, which is the principal benefit of a work-for-hire agreement.

Only rarely will a publisher agree to acquire rights for a limited period of time, and such clauses commonly appear only in a licensing agreement. Indeed, by definition, a grant-of-rights clause conveys ownership of rights to the publisher, and a term of years is generally inapplicable to the transaction, even if the contract provides for a reversion of rights under certain circumstances. (➤ *Reversion of Rights, Page 238*) If the publisher's rights are limited to a specified number of years, then the transaction is best characterized as a license rather than a grant of rights.

The specified term of years is often embodied in the clause that defines what rights are being licensed to the publisher, i.e., the author licenses the specified rights to the publisher "*for a period commencing on the effective date of this agreement and continuing for five (5) years, whereupon the license will expire.*" (➤ *A Clause for Licensing Limited and Specified Rights to the Publisher, Page 58*) Some licensing agreements, however, will include a separate clause in which the term of years is defined.

### A CLAUSE FOR SPECIFYING THE TERM OF RIGHTS IN A LICENSING AGREEMENT

Publisher may exploit the rights in the Work licensed under this Agreement for a term of five (5) years, commencing on the date of first publication by Publisher, and upon the expiration or other termination of this Agreement, all rights will revert wholly and automatically to Author.

"*...exploit the rights in the Work licensed under this Agreement...*" The sample clause is limited to defining the *term* of the licensing agreement, and the definition of the rights that are being licensed is set forth elsewhere in the Agreement.

*"...commencing on the date of first publication..."* According to the sample clause, the publisher's specified term of years does not begin to run until the author's work has actually been published by the publisher. Thus, the publisher enjoys the benefit of the full term even if publication is delayed.

*"...and upon the expiration or other termination of this Agreement, all rights will revert wholly and automatically to Author."* Because a license conveys only the right to use a work of authorship, and not ownership of copyright, the rights *"will revert wholly and automatically to Author"* when the term has expired or the Agreement has been otherwise terminated. Some licensing agreements include roll-over provisions that will automatically extend the term if, for example, neither party gives notice of termination to the other or the publisher pays a certain minimum royalty to the author.

## WORK-FOR-HIRE

"Work-for-hire," as we have already noted, is a legal mechanism that vests complete ownership of copyright in a work of authorship in the employer or commissioning party of the flesh-and-blood individual who actually created it. Such works are called "works made for hire" or "commissioned works" in the U. S. Copyright Act, and the "author" of a work-for-hire is considered the employer or commissioning party. For that reason, the sample clause below refers to the creator of the work of authorship as "Contractor" rather than "Author." Not every work of authorship is eligible for treatment as a work-for-hire under the Copyright Act, and even when it is, the author and publisher are required to strictly adhere to rigorous standards and procedures.

But once a work of authorship has been successfully acquired on a work-for-hire basis, then the acquiring party enjoys substantial and enduring rights in the work. As noted, the acquiring party is considered to be the author of the work for all purposes. The person from whom the work was acquired does not enjoy the statutory right to terminate the transfer of copyright at a later date (➤ *Termination of Transfers, Page 235*) and cannot argue that he still owns rights in media and technologies that have not yet been invented. (➤ *Future Media and Technologies, Page 92*) For these reasons, authors who work with ghostwriters or other collaborators, and publishers that acquire work from a number of contributors to a single work, often prefer to use the work-for-hire approach when it is available.

Of course, work-for-hire status is not always available. As a general rule, any work of authorship that an employee creates within the course and scope of employment belongs to the employer as work-for-hire, whether or not a written agreement exists between employer and employee. Work-for-hire by independent contractors, by contrast, must fall within certain categories specified in the Copyright Act. One story contributed to an anthology of short stories might be acquired on a work-for-hire basis, for example, but a novel written in its entirety by a single freelance author can never be work-for-hire, even if the author and publisher agree otherwise. And even when a particular work falls within one of the statutory categories, the parties must have entered into a written work-for-hire agreement before the completion of the work in order to achieve work-for-hire status. (See *Kirsch's Handbook, Chapter 2: Co-Authorship and Copyright*).

### A WORK-FOR-HIRE CLAUSE

To the extent that Contractor's Work includes any work of authorship entitled to protection under the laws of copyright, Contractor and Publisher acknowledge and agree that (i) Contractor's Work has been specially ordered and commissioned by Publisher as a contribution to a collective work, a compilation, a supplementary work, or such other category of work as may be eligible for treatment as a "work made for hire" under the United States Copyright Act; (ii) Contractor's Work shall be deemed a "commissioned work" and "work made for hire" to the greatest extent permitted by law; (iii) Contractor is an independent contractor and not a partner, joint author or joint venturer of Publisher, and (iv) Publisher shall be the sole author of Contractor's Work and any work embodying the Contractor's Work pursuant to the United States Copyright

Act, and the sole owner of the original materials embodying Contractor's Work, and/or any works derived therefrom. Contractor waives all moral rights in Contractor's Work to the greatest extent permitted by law. Publisher shall have the right but not the obligation to acknowledge or credit Contractor in a style and manner to be determined by Publisher in his sole discretion.

*"...Contractor's Work..."* The sample clause refers to the author as "Contractor" (and his work product as "Contractor's Work") because the word "author" has a special (and highly artificial) meaning in a work-for-hire agreement. For purposes of works made for hire, the author of the work—and the owner of copyright—is either the employer of the individual who actually creates the work of authorship, or else the one who commissions the individual to create the work. Thus, it is legally inconsistent and inappropriate to use the term "author" to describe the person who creates a work-for-hire.

*"...a collective work, a compilation, a supplementary work, or such other category of work as may be eligible for treatment as a 'work made for hire'..."* Only certain categories of work are eligible for treatment as work-for-hire under the U.S. Copyright Act when the creator of the work is an independent contractor rather than an ordinary employee. Some (but not all) of them are specified in the sample clause: a contribution to a collective work, such as a story that appears in a collection of short stories; a supplementary work such as a foreword, an afterword, an illustration, a map, a chart, a table, a bibliography, an appendix, or an index; and a compilation, such as a phone directory or a dictionary. The statutory list of eligible works is short and highly specific. An atlas or a set of questions and answers for a test may be treated as a work made for hire, but a novel written by a single author is not. For this reason, work-for-hire made *not* be available for certain works of authorship, and such works *must* be acquired by some other mechanism for transfer of rights. (➤*A "Safety Net" Clause for Use in Conjunction With a Work-for-hire Clause, Page 101*)

📖 **Author's Right of Termination**. One of the chief advantages of acquiring a work of authorship on a work-for-hire basis is the fact that ownership of copyright will vest in the publisher forever. If, on the other hand, the publisher acquires the same work under a grant of rights, even if the grant is for "all rights" and the term is "in perpetuity," the U.S. Copyright Act bestows upon the author (and his heirs and successors) the right to terminate the transfer of rights to the publisher and recover copyright ownership at a point between 35 and 40 years after signing the book publishing contract or publication of the book. Thus, the publisher is always at risk of losing rights at some point in the distant future unless the work was acquired on a work-for-hire basis! (See *Kirsch's Handbook, Chapter 8: Remaindering, Reversion and Copyright*)

*"...Contractor's Work shall be deemed a 'commissioned work' and 'work made for hire' to the greatest extent permitted by law..."* The clause repeats the words and phrases that actually appear in the section of the U. S. Copyright Act that defines when a work of authorship may be characterized as a work for hire.

*"...Contractor is an independent contractor and not a partner, joint author or joint venturer of Publisher..."* The sample clause characterizes the creator of the work as an independent contractor rather than an employee. Although the work of an employee can be a work-for-hire, too, most publishers prefer to make it clear that the creator of the work is *not* an employee and thus is ineligible for employment benefits. At the same time, the clause seeks to prevent the assertion of any other or greater legal rights by ruling out any other legal relationship, such as partnership or joint authorship, between the publisher and the creator of the work.

*"...the sole owner of the original materials embodying Contractor's Work, and/or any works derived therefrom."* Under the sample clause, the publisher owns not only the copyright in the work of authorship but also the physical object in which the work is embodied. If the work is a photograph, for example, the publisher would own the negatives and prints as well as the intangible right called copyright. The publisher also claims the right to create new and derivative works based upon the work.

*"...Contractor waives all moral rights in Contractor's Work to the greatest extent permitted by law..."* The sample clause asks the author to give up his "moral rights," a set of legal rights in a work of authorship that are recognized under European law but only vaguely and obliquely protected under U. S. law. Moral rights include the right to be identified as the author of a work of authorship and the right to prevent any substantial changes in the work even after the copyright has been transferred to another person. *"[T]o the great extent permitted by law,"* these rights are waived.

*"...Publisher shall have the right but not the obligation to acknowledge or credit Contractor in a style and manner to be determined by Publisher in his sole discretion."* The sample clause holds out the possibility that the owner of rights in a work-for-hire will *"acknowledge or credit"* the writer who actually created the work. Whether or not to do so, however, is left to the *"sole discretion"* of the person acquiring rights, and so is the *"style and manner"* of any such credit.

## A "SAFETY NET" CLAUSE FOR USE IN CONJUNCTION WITH A WORK-FOR-HIRE CLAUSE

Work-for-hire is a narrow and highly technical legal mechanism that must strictly comply with the statutory provisions of the U. S. Copyright Act. Sometimes, despite the clear intention and best efforts of the publisher, a work is later deemed *not* to be a work made for hire after all, usually because the author (or the author's heirs and successors) have experienced a change of heart and seek to recover ownership of the work. That is why a publisher ought to include a "safety net" clause like the one set forth below. The clause simply provides that if a work turns out to be ineligible for treatment as a work-for-hire for any reason, then the publisher may fall back on a conventional grant of rights.

**To the extent that all or any portion of Contractor's Work is not properly characterized as "work made for hire," then Contractor hereby irrevocably grants to Publisher all right, title and interest in and to such Contractor's Work (including but not limited to the copyright, trademark and other**

intellectual property rights therein), and any and all ideas and information embodied therein, in perpetuity and throughout the world.

Just in case it turns out that the work is *not* eligible for treatment as work-for-hire, the "safety net" clause uses the language of a comprehensive grant of rights in order to vest in the publisher the outright ownership of rights in the work. In fact, the grant of rights goes beyond the scope of copyright and includes "trademark and other intellectual property rights" as well as "all ideas and information embodied therein," which are *not* ordinarily protected under copyright. The duration of the grant of rights is "in perpetuity" and the scope is "throughout the world." But ownership of copyright under the safety net clause is still *not* as comprehensive as work-for-hire, because the transfer of rights will be subject to termination at some later date and will not reach rights in technologies not yet invented at the time of the contract.

**3**

**$**

# AUTHOR COMPENSATION

Ideally, a book contract will specify some form of compensation for every right that an author conveys to a publisher, and the contract ought to be carefully drafted and reviewed to make sure that none of the rights in the "bundle of rights" have been overlooked. (➤*Chapter 2: Transfer of Rights*) The most common approach to author compensation consists of three elements: an advance (➤*Advances, page 104*), a royalty on sales of the author's work as published by the publisher (➤*Royalties, Page 109*), and a share of revenue from the publisher's exploitation of rights in the author's work by licensing the rights to third parties. (➤*Sharing of Revenues From Subsidiary Rights, Page 125*)

Nothing in the law of copyright or the "custom and practice" of the publishing industry *requires* any of these forms of compensation. A book contract is fully enforceable as long as something of value—"consideration" is the technical term used by attorneys—is promised or paid by the publisher to the author. Thus, for example, a publisher might offer to pay a freelance author a weekly or monthly stipend or a lump sum of money for the task of writing a book, and an employee of the publishing house who writes a book within the "course and scope" of employment need not be paid anything above and beyond her ordinary wages. However, the conventional book contract will include an advance, a royalty, and a mechanism for sharing of revenues from subsidiary rights. Sample clauses illustrating these various forms of compensation are given below.

## ADVANCES

An advance is a sum of money paid to an author by the publisher as a prepayment of royalties that may be earned on the actual sales of the book or the exploitation of other rights in the author's work. (➤*Royalties, Page 109*) Sometimes the advance is paid in a lump sum but more often in installments as the book is written and published. Once the book starts to generate sales or other income, the publisher is entitled to pay itself back out of the money otherwise due to the author on actual sales of the book. Only when the book has "earned out"—that is, the publisher has recouped the advance out of royalties—is the publisher obligated to make further payments to the author.

To illustrate how an advance against royalties actually works, let us consider a highly simplified book deal in which the author is paid an advance of $1,000 and a royalty rate of 10% of the retail price for a book that is ultimately published and sold at a suggested retail price of $10.00. (➤*Royalties, Page 109*) For each book that is actually sold and paid for, the author earns a royalty of $1.00. Since the publisher has already paid the author an advance of $1,000, which is equivalent to earned royalties on the sale of 1,000 books, it is entitled to retain the first $1,000 as a recoupment of the advance. When the royalties on actual sales equal the advance already paid to the author, the book is said to have earned out, and the publisher is obligated to start paying royalties. On the sale of the 1,001st copy, the publisher owes the author $1.00, and the author owes the publisher nothing.

As a general practice in the publishing industry, an advance is considered to be "recoupable" but "nonrefundable." In other words, the publisher is entitled to recoup the advance out of earned royalties and other income from the exploitation of rights in the book that have been conveyed to the publisher, but if the book fails to sell a sufficient number of copies to earn out, the author is *not* obliged to pay back the rest of the advance. However, the advance is almost always "returnable" under certain specified circumstances, including nondelivery of the manuscript or rejection of a completed manuscript as unsatisfactory. (➤*Preparation and Delivery of the Manuscript, Page 134*)

Nothing in the law or tradition of publishing *requires* a publisher to pay an advance. Indeed, the advances offered by some publishers nowadays are so modest as to be strictly nominal—advances of $1,000 to $5,000 are not unusual among independent publishers—and many small presses do not offer any advances at all. Even a major publisher may consider an advance of $20,000 to $50,000 to be generous, especially for a first novel or an unproven writer. The tantalizing "six-figure" advances that motivate so many aspiring authors are increasingly rare in today's highly competitive publishing industry. Only a best-selling author with a long track record—or, sometimes, a newcomer whose project catches the imagination of a few big-spending publishing houses—will be offered an advance

**Grants.** Some publishers, especially in the field of professional and technical publishing, offer to underwrite a portion of the author's expenses in the form of a lump-sum payment known as a "grant." Unlike a conventional advance, a grant is *not* considered to be an advance against royalties and is *not* recouped by the publisher out of the author's earned royalties; rather, it is a way for the publisher to share in expenses that the author incurs in developing and producing a book. For example, grants are often used to pay for specialized research, charts and illustrations, and other specific tasks related to the book itself. Some deals include both an advance against royalties and a grant; one is recoupable by the publisher, the other is not. Since grants are not always offered by the publisher as part of a standard book contract, the grant is often described in a "rider"—that is, an attachment that is incorporated by reference into the contract itself.

measured in six figures or more. No formula or standard exists for determining the size of the advance that a book will command when offered to a publisher. Essentially, the advance is a measure of how many publishers want a particular book and how much they want it. If a book generates only a few offers from publishers, then the publisher with the high bid sets the market value! (▶*Clout, Page 14*)

Still, the advance *is* a crucial factor in most publishing deals. The conventional wisdom in the publishing industry is that the larger the advance, the more the publisher wants to protect its investment by supporting the book with advertising and promotion, an author tour, and the other resources of the publishing house. As a practical matter, a book with a big advance is more likely to command the attention of the sales and marketing department than a book with a modest one. And the author may be tempted to give up more rights in her work or accept a less favorable royalty rate in exchange for a larger advance. After all, the advance is money in the author's pocket *now*, while the other deal points in a book contract are highly speculative. Above all, since the hard reality of publishing is that most books do *not* earn out, the advance is often the only money the author will actually receive in exchange for the blood, sweat, and tears that go into the writing of a book.

> ✍ **Tax Planning**. Authors whose work commands a large advance ought to consult a qualified advisor such as a certified public accountant or tax attorney before signing a book contract, especially if the money to be paid by the publisher represents a sudden windfall after years of struggle. Under certain circumstances, the author may achieve a significant tax savings if a large advance is paid out over a period of years rather than in a lump sum. On the other hand, given the vagaries of the publishing industry and the risk that a publisher will suffer a change of heart about a pending book project, the typical author is likely to "take the money and run."

## ADVANCE AGAINST ROYALTIES

Publisher shall pay to Author, as an advance against royalties and any other amounts owing by Publisher to Author under this Agreement, the sum of [*Insert amount here*] to be paid as follows: One-third upon signing of this Agreement, one-third upon delivery and acceptance of the complete Manuscript, and one-third upon publication of the Work in the first Publisher's edition.

*"...as an advance against royalties and any other amounts owing by Publisher to Author under this Agreement..."* The publisher is generally entitled to recoup the advance out of *all* money otherwise owing to the author, including not only royalties on sales of the book itself but also out of the author's share of other

income generated by the book. For example, if the publisher sells the audio rights or foreign rights to the author's work, the publisher is entitled to pay itself back out of the author's share of the money paid for these rights. (➤*Sharing of Revenues From Subsidiary Rights, Page 125*)

*"...to be paid as follows: One-third upon signing of this Agreement..."* A portion of the advance is almost always paid to the author on signing, but the publisher will usually divide the total amount of the advance into installments. Two obvious motives are at work: first, the publisher wants to keep the author hard at work on the book project by holding out the promise of a "payday" when specified deadlines are met; second, the publisher wants to protect itself against paying out money for a manuscript that is later deemed to be unsatisfactory. That's why certain important deadlines and decisions are commonly used as the typical triggering events for payment of additional portions of the advance. Delivery of the manuscript, completion of revisions, and

**Bonuses.** Some of the seven-figure advances in the biggest publishing deals are actually based on a complex series of bonuses and incentives, sometimes in the form of lump-sum payments but more often as additional advances against royalties. The most common example is the so-called "bestseller clause," which triggers the payment of additional advances if the author's book appears on a specified bestseller list, i.e., **"In the event the Work appears on the *New York Times* Bestseller List during the first year after publication, the Publisher shall pay to the Author, as additional advances against royalties and other sums accruing to Author under this Agreement, $25,000 for the first appearance of the Work and $5,000 for each subsequent appearance of the Work up to a total of $50,000."** More exotic bonus clauses may obligate the publisher to make additional payments if, for example, the author appears on a major radio or television show such as *Oprah*, *Larry King Live*, or *Fresh Air*, or if the book wins a major literary prize. Among the more creative approaches was one adopted by a publisher that promised to pay the author a specified sum of money for each theater in which the movie version of her novel was screened.

formal acceptance of the manuscript by the publisher are the usual benchmarks in an advance clause.

Other triggering events are based on the publisher's cash flow rather than on the author's work product. For example, some portion of the advance might not be paid until the book is actually published, an event that might come months or even years after the manuscript has been formally accepted. (➤ *Time of Publication, Page 172*) When the publisher acquires both hardcover and softcover rights to the same book, a portion of the advance might be deferred until the book is actually published in a paperback edition.

---

📖 **Payment and Acceptance.** Installments of the advance are sometimes paid on *acceptance* of a portion of the manuscript (i.e., **"upon acceptance by Publisher of one-half of the manuscript of the Work..."**) and other times on *delivery* rather than on acceptance of the manuscript. The cautious publisher will make it clear that payment on delivery or payment upon acceptance of *less* than the entire manuscript will not preclude the publisher from rejecting the entire manuscript later on, i.e., **"The making of a payment upon Author's delivery of all or any portion of the manuscript, or upon the acceptance of a portion of the manuscript, shall not be deemed to indicate Publisher's acceptance of the complete manuscript."**

📖 **Minimum Guaranteed Royalty.** At least one independent publisher of my acquaintance has come up with an ingenious approach to the sometimes nettlesome question of advances. Instead of an advance, the publisher offers a "minimum guaranteed royalty," that is, a specified payment in each of the first several royalty periods after actual publication of the author's work, whether or not the author is entitled to a royalty based on sales of the book. As the publisher points out to its authors, the money saved on the advance can be applied to advertising and promotion of the book on publication!

---

✍ **Deadlines for Payment.** When some portion of the advance is paid on paperback publication, the author should ask for a specified deadline by which the advance will be paid in full in case the paperback edition is delayed or canceled, i.e., **"...on first publication of the Work in any paperback edition, or twelve months after first hardcover publication, whichever is earlier."**

✍ **"Most Favored Nation."** The author with enough clout to command the very best deal available from a particular publisher may ask for a "most-favored-nation clause" to make sure that no one else ever gets a better deal later on: **"Publisher acknowledges and agrees that Author shall be paid advances and royalties no less advantageous than those offered to any other author whose work is now or hereafter published by Publisher, and in the event that Publisher shall later enter into a contract with one or more authors on more advantageous terms than those set forth here, then this Agreement shall be modified and amended to provide that any such more advantageous terms shall be paid to Author under this and any other agreement between Author and Publisher."** Such clauses are common enough in the motion picture industry but rare indeed in publishing, and it is only the exceptional author who carries enough clout to extract such a promise.

## ROYALTIES

### Royalties Based on Retail Price

A royalty is a payment of money by the publisher to the author based on the sales of the author's book or the exploitation of other rights in the author's work. Although some contracts, especially in merchandising and in the recording industry, state the royalty as a specified amount of money per unit, royalties in book publishing contracts are usually expressed as a *percentage* of either the suggested retail price of the book (➤*A Clause for a Fixed Royalty Based on Retail Price, See below*) or the publisher's net income, i.e., the wholesale price of the book. (➤*A Clause for a Fixed Royalty Based on Publisher's Net Income, Page 119*) Similarly, the author's share of money from the exploitation of subsidiary rights is expressed in the typical book contract as a *percentage* of the total amount of money received by the publisher. (➤*Sharing of Revenues From Subsidiary Rights, Page 125*)

A CLAUSE FOR A FIXED ROYALTY BASED ON RETAIL PRICE

For each copy of the Work published by the Publisher under this Agreement, Publisher shall credit Author's account with a royalty of ____% of the Invoice Price on all Net Copies Sold.

"Invoice Price," as the term is used in this Agreement, means the price shown on Publisher's invoices to wholesalers and retailers from which the Publisher's discounts are calculated. The difference between the Invoice Price and the suggested retail price or cover price as such price may be printed on the dust jacket or cover of the Work shall not exceed 5% without Author's consent.

"Net Copies Sold," as used in this Agreement, means the sale less returns of any and all copies of the Work sold by Publisher through conventional channels of distribution in the book trade, and does not include promotional and review copies, Author's copies (whether free or purchased by Author), or copies for which a royalty rate is otherwise set forth in this Agreement.

*"For each copy of the Work published by the Publisher under this Agreement..."* The royalty described in the sample clause is paid only on the publisher's editions of the author's work, and a different royalty mechanism applies to editions that may be published by third parties under license from the publisher. (➤*Sharing of Revenues From Subsidiary Rights, Page 125*)

*"...Publisher shall credit Author's account..."* The author's royalties are not paid outright by the publisher. Rather, the publisher opens and maintains an account in the name of the author, and both debits and credits will be applied to the author's account from time to time. For example, the advance against royalties paid to the author is treated as a debit (➤*Advances, Page 104*), the royalties earned by the author from the sales of her book are treated as credits, and the publisher will strike a balance at each accounting. Thus, the first royalties earned by the author are always applied by the publisher to the recoupment of the advance, and even when the book has earned out and the advance is fully repaid, there may be additional debits against which the royalties may be applied. For example, if the publisher charged the author's account for the preparation of an index (➤*Artwork, Permissions, Index, and Other Materials, Page 137*) or the purchase of additional copies of her book (➤*Author's Copies, Page 174*), the publisher will pay itself back out of royalty income before issuing a check to the

author. Only when the credits to the author's account actually exceed the debits will the publisher be obligated to make a payment to the author. Even then, the publisher is generally under no obligation to actually write a check except at the time prescribed in the contract for the rendering of accounts, usually quarterly or semiannually. (➤*Accounting, Page 193*)

"*...with a royalty of _____%...*" The sample clause sets the author's royalty as a *fixed* percentage, which means that the same royalty rate will be apply for the duration of the contract, whether the publisher succeeds in selling a few hundred copies or a few million copies. A more typical approach, especially among major publishers, is a royalty rate that increases as the sales of the book increase. An example of an escalating royalty is set forth below. (➤*A Clause for Escalating Royalties Based on Retail Price, Page 115*)

"*...of the Invoice Price...*" Just as crucial as the royalty *rate* is the dollar figure to which the percentage is actually applied, whether the suggested retail price or the actual wholesale income. The sample clause set forth above states the author's

**"Standard" Royalties.** Once upon a time, the "standard" royalty in a hardcover book contract was 10 percent of the suggested retail price, escalating to 12½ percent and then 15 percent as total sales of the book reached specified levels, and the breakpoints were often expressed in increments of 5,000 copies. (➤*A Clause for Escalating Royalties Based on Retail Price, Page 115*) Nowadays, however, there is simply no such thing as a "standard" royalty rate. Royalties of 10 to 15 percent of suggested retail price are not unusual in hardcover book contracts, 7 to 10 percent are common in trade softcover deals, and 6 to 8 percent are used in many mass market paperback contracts. But the royalty is always subject to negotiation and is ultimately defined by what the publisher is willing to pay. A mass market paperback by an untested author might command a meager 4 or 5 percent royalty, while a bestselling author like Stephen King will command a kingly 50 percent royalty.

royalty as a percentage of the retail price, but a highly technical term—"*Invoice Price*"—is used to define exactly how the royalty shall be calculated. In order to understand how the sample clause works, we need to pause and consider the subtle but real difference between "cover price" and "invoice price."

The "cover price" is the price actually printed on the cover or dust jacket of the book itself and indicates the price that the publisher recommends to the bookstore or other book retailer for sale of the book to the consumer. That's why the cover price is sometimes also called the "retail price" or, more accurately, the "suggested retail price," since United States antitrust law generally prevents the publisher from dictating the price at which the book is sold.

The "invoice price" is the base price actually printed on the invoice that the publisher sends to wholesalers, distributors, bookstores, and other retailers. Then the publisher calculates the wholesale price by subtracting from the invoice price an amount defined as the "wholesale discount," which is usually expressed as a percentage of the invoice price. The wholesale discount offered by publishers to the book trade is generally 40% off the invoice price, although the discounts in certain transactions and channels of distribution may be higher or lower. (➤ *Other Royalty Categories, Page 121*) As a simple example of a wholesale transaction in the book industry, if the invoice price of a book is $10.00, and the wholesale discount is 40%, then the amount subtracted from the invoice price is $4.00 (40% of $10.00), and the price actually paid by the wholesale-level customer to the publisher is $6.00.

The cover price and the invoice price of a particular book, however, are not always identical. The cover price may include a small additional sum that is meant to defray the costs of shipping books from the publisher to the wholesaler or retailer, an amount known as "Freight Pass Through" or "FPT." Since the FPT is meant to pay for an item of overhead, the publisher does not want to include it in the base price of the book when calculating the author's royalty. That's why the sample clause carefully specifies that the royalty will be a percentage of *"the price shown on Publisher's invoices to wholesalers and retailers from which the Publisher's discounts are calculated,"* which excludes the FPT. At the same time, the sample clause also protects the author against an excessive FPT by providing that *"[t]he difference between the Invoice Price and the suggested retail price...shall not exceed 5% without Author's consent."*

Suppose, for example, that the suggested retail price printed on the dust jacket of a book is $10.50, including fifty cents earmarked by the publisher as a FPT charge. (The dust jacket, by the way, will often signal the fact that the cover price includes a Freight Pass Through with the telltale letters "FPT" next to the price.) On the publisher's invoice, the FPT will be deducted from the retail price, and so the wholesale discount will be calculated on the invoice price of $10.00 rather than the cover price of $10.50. Likewise, the sample clause provides that the author's royalty will be calculated as a percentage of the invoice price rather than the cover price.

Not every book contract distinguishes between cover price and invoice price for purposes of the author's royalty. If the contract specifies a royalty based on "cover price," "retail price," "suggested retail price," or "suggested customer's price," rather than invoice price, as the term is generally used in the book trade and defined in the sample clause, then the author's royalty will be marginally greater than the one in the sample clause.

*"...'Net Copies Sold'... means the sale less returns of any and all copies sold by Publisher..."* No royalties are paid on "returns," as the sample clause carefully notes. (➤*Returns,* See sidebar) The initial order from the bookstore will be recorded as a sale in the publisher's accounting system even though the bookseller may ultimately return the book; however, the publisher is not obligated to pay a royalty if the book is later returned. For this reason, the publisher is entitled to hold back a portion of the author's royalties until it is certain that a book that has been sold will not be returned. (➤*Reserve Against Returns, Page 199*)

**Returns**. A long and often-lamented practice in the book industry permits a bookseller to order a book from a publisher, put it on the shelf, leave it on display for a while, and then return the book to the publisher if no one buys it. If and when an unsold book is returned to the publisher, the bookseller is entitled to a refund or, more commonly, a credit for another wholesale purchase. Books are sometimes returned because they are defective or damaged in shipping, but most returns are simply unsold books. Although a book is generally considered to have been sold when shipped, the sale is strictly conditional in most transactions, and the bookseller's right of return means that a sale credited to the author's royalty account may disappear when returns are counted.

*"...through conventional channels of distribution in the book trade..."* The sample clause specifies that the author's full royalty is not paid on *every* copy of her book that is sold. Only books that are sold *"through conventional channels of distribution in the book trade,"* which generally refers to bookstores and other retail outlets where books are commonly sold, are entitled to the full royalty. The contract will specify a different—and, as a general rule, lower— royalty for sales outside "conventional channels." (➤*Other Royalty Categories, Page 121*)

*"...and does not include promotional and review copies, Author's copies (whether free or purchased by Author)..."* As a rule, the publisher pays a royalty only when a book is sold and not when it is given away to promote and publicize the book. Thus, the author does not earn a royalty on the hundreds and sometimes thousands of copies that are customarily sent to book reviewers, columnists, and others in the press and the publishing industry. However, the sample clause also rules out payment of a royalty on copies purchased from the publisher by the author herself, even though the author is generally obliged to pay for such copies at the same wholesale price as the one paid in the ordinary course of trade. (➤*Author's Copies, Page 174*)

---

✍ **Royalties on Author's Copies**. Since the publisher is making money when the author buys a copy of her own book, the author may wish to negotiate for the payment of royalties on such sales. A certain number of copies will always be given to the author free of charge (➤*Author's Copies, Page 174*), and no royalties will be paid on these free copies, but the author is generally obliged to pay for additional copies at a price that is equal to, or sometimes even higher than, the wholesale price of the book. Thus, the author may argue that the same royalty should be paid whether the book is sold to a bookstore or to the author herself—or, if no royalty is to be paid, then the price of the author's copies should be reduced.

---

*"...or copies for which a royalty rate is otherwise set forth in this Agreement."* The sample clause notes that the full royalty described here does not apply to all categories of sale. Indeed, the full royalty is paid only on sales to bookstores and other customary wholesale-level customers. A separate—and, generally,

much lower—royalty mechanism is prescribed for various other categories of sale, each of which is set forth in a separate clause of the contract. (➤ *Other Royalty Categories, Page 121*)

---

📖 **Safety Net on Royalties.** A royalty rate should be specified for *all* categories of sale and *all* rights that belong to the publisher, and some publishers favor a catch-all provision that sets a kind of safety net on royalties: **"For all other categories of sales and exploitation of rights for which a royalty rate is not specified elsewhere in this Agreement, Publisher shall credit Author's account with a royalty of ___% of Publisher's Net Revenues."**

---

## A CLAUSE FOR ESCALATING ROYALTIES
### BASED ON RETAIL PRICE

For each Edition of the Work published by the Publisher under this Agreement, Publisher shall credit Author's account with the following royalties on Net Copies Sold:

1. ___% of the Invoice Price on the first 5,000 Net Copies Sold of any Edition;

2. ___% of the Invoice Price on the next 5,000 Net Copies Sold of any Edition; and

3. ___% of the Invoice Price on sales in excess of 10,000 Net Copies Sold of any Edition.

"Edition," as used in this Agreement, refers to the Work as published in any particular content, length, and format. If the Work is materially revised or redesigned in any manner, or changed in length or content, then the Work as revised shall be considered a new "Edition" for purposes of this Section.

"Invoice Price," as the term is used in this Agreement, means the price shown on Publisher's invoices to wholesalers and retailers from which the Publisher's discounts are calculated. The difference between the Invoice Price and the suggested retail price or cover price as such price may be printed on the dust jacket or cover of the Work shall not exceed 5% without Author's consent.

"Net Copies Sold," as used in this Agreement, means the sale less returns of any and all copies sold by Publisher through conventional channels of distribution in the book trade, and does not include promotional and review copies, Author's copies (whether free or purchased by Author), or copies for which a royalty rate is otherwise set forth in this Agreement.

The crucial difference between the sample clause for an *escalating* royalty and the clause for a *fixed* royalty (➤*A Clause for a Fixed Royalty Based on Retail Price, Page 109*) is that the author's royalty rate will increase as the sales of the book reach certain specified levels or "breakpoints." The specific percentages and breakpoints, however, are always subject to negotiation and may vary significantly from publisher to publisher and from deal to deal. (➤*"Standard" Royalties, Page 111*)

**Royalties, Hard and Soft.** If the publisher is entitled to issue various editions of the author's work—a hardback edition, a trade paperback edition, a mass-market edition, and so on—it is customary to specify a separate royalty rate, whether fixed or escalating, for each edition. As a general proposition, the highest range of royalties are paid for hardcover editions, the middle range for trade paperbacks, and the lowest range for mass-market paperbacks. Thus, a book contract might have a separate royalty clause for each edition.

*"For each Edition of the Work..."* As the sample clause illustrates, an escalating royalty obliges the publisher to pay the author a greater percentage of the retail price as the sales of the book increase. For that reason, the publisher typically reserves the right to "reset the clock" on the calculation of royalties when a new edition is published. For example, once the publisher has sold 10,000 copies of the book, the author will be entitled to the maximum royalty rate of 15 percent on all sales thereafter. But if the publisher revises the book or issues some other new edition, then the

royalty rate goes back to 10 percent!

Precisely because the publication of a new edition allows the publisher to pay a lower royalty rate, the sample clause carefully defines the term "edition" to clarify the circumstances under which the publisher is entitled to go back to the base royalty rate. According to the sample clause, "*the Work as published in any particular content, length, and format*" is an edition, and the royalty rate will go back to 10 percent if the publisher issues a new edition, i.e., "*If the Work is materially revised or redesigned in any manner, or changed in length or content.*"

(For a discussion of the other elements of the sample clause, including the defined terms "Net Copies Sold" and "Invoice Price," see *A Clause for a Fixed Royalty Based on Retail Price, Page 109.*)

**Front-Loaded.** The rationale for an escalating royalty rate is the simple fact that a publisher's investment in a book is "front-loaded" and, therefore, the sale of the 10,000th copy of a book is far more profitable than the sale of the first copy. The initial costs of publication—the author's advance, cover and page design, editing, typesetting, proofreading, permissions, plate-making expenses, the first round of advertising and promotion, and so on—must be paid by the publisher in the early stages of developing and publishing a book. Once these start-up costs are recouped, however, the basic expense of the publisher is limited to "paper, printing and binding" ("PPB")—a phrase that is sometimes rendered as "plant, paper, printing and binding"—and the profit margin increases dramatically. Escalating royalties allow the author to share in the profits—and "resetting the clock" for a new edition reflects the fact that the publisher will once again bear the new start-up costs.

---

✍ **Reduced Royalties.** Even when a "standard" royalty of 10%–12½%–15% of the suggested retail price is promised in a contract, much lower royalties are likely to be paid for various specific categories of sale specified elsewhere in the contract. (➤*Other Royalty Categories, Page 121*) For that reason, a book contract must be read thoroughly and carefully—and the reduced royalties must be taken into account—in order to determine its real economic value.

### Royalties Based on Publisher's Net Income

Royalties based on retail price were once the norm in publishing, but nowadays it is increasingly common for publishers to calculate royalties on net income, i.e., the money actually received by the publisher from the sale of the author's books. "Net royalties"—as royalties based on net income are sometimes called—are especially common among independent publishers, academic and technical publishers, and small presses. Even the major publishing houses, however, tend to offer a net royalty in many specific categories of sale.

A net royalty is substantially less valuable to the author than a royalty based on retail price because the publisher rarely, if ever, actually sells a book at the cover price unless it is selling to the consumer by direct mail or some other form of direct-response marketing. Rather, the publisher generally sells books at a wholesale discount of 40 percent or more off the retail price, and "deep discount" sales to some wholesale customers may be as high as 55 or 60 percent off the retail price. Thus, on a book with a suggested retail price of $10.00, the publisher is likely to collect no more than $6.00 per copy and sometimes much less. Hence, a 10 percent royalty based on the publisher's net income yields 60 cents (for each copy sold at the standard trade discount of 40 percent) rather than the $1.00 that would be due if the 10 percent royalty were instead based on the retail price.

Publishers favor a net royalty for obvious reasons. Since it is based on money actually received by the publisher, regardless of the category of sale, the accounting of royalties is simpler and more straightforward, and so are the royalty statements that the publisher prepares and sends to the author. (➤*Accounting, Page 193*). From the publisher's point of view, there is a certain sense of fundamental fairness about a net royalty: the publisher pays the author a percentage of what the publisher actually puts in its bank account, not a percentage of a suggested retail price that may or may not be paid to the bookseller by its customer. As the publishing industry grows ever more volatile, the net royalty is becoming increasingly common among publishers large and small.

The bottom line on royalties is, quite literally, a matter of dollars and cents, not percentages, price points, accounting convenience, or an intuitive sense of what is fair. The royalty, no matter how it is defined and calculated, is the amount of money that the publisher pays to the author for the right to exploit her work. So the author must "crunch the numbers"—figure out exactly how much will be paid under the various royalty mechanisms in a variety of typical transactions—and decide if the publisher is offering enough money to make it worthwhile.

## A CLAUSE FOR A FIXED ROYALTY
### BASED ON PUBLISHER'S NET INCOME

For each copy of the Work published by the Publisher under this Agreement, Publisher shall credit Author's account with a royalty equal to _____% of Net Revenues from the sale of any and all Net Copies Sold.

"Net Revenues," as used in this Agreement, refers to money actually received by Publisher from the sale of copies of the Work, net of returns, after deduction of shipping, customs, insurance, fees and commissions, currency exchange discounts, and costs of collection.

"Net Copies Sold," as used in this Agreement, means the sale less returns of any and all copies sold by Publisher through conventional channels of distribution in the book trade, and does not include promotional and review copies, Author's copies (whether free or purchased by Author), or copies for which a royalty rate is otherwise set forth in this Agreement.

*"....a royalty equal to _____% of Net Revenues from the Sale of any and all Net Copies Sold..."* A "net royalty," as illustrated in the sample clause, is not related in any way to the suggested retail price of a book. Rather, the royalty rate is applied to *"money actually received by Publisher from the sale of copies of the Work,"* which is generally at least 40 percent less than the cover price of the book.

Some net royalty clauses refer simply to "money actually received by Publisher," but the sample clause uses a defined term—"*Net Revenues*"—that permits the publisher to make certain specified adjustments and deductions before calculating the author's royalty. Exactly what may be netted out of the "money actually received by Publisher" is subject to negotiation and may vary from deal to deal. The definition used in the sample clause excludes returns from the calculation of the author's royalty—a standard feature in all virtually all royalty clauses—and goes on to specify that the publisher may deduct "*shipping, customs, insurance, fees and commissions, currency exchange discounts, and costs of collection.*" Other clauses in common use may adopt a different defined term for the same concept (i.e., "Amount Received") and a slightly different list of adjustments and deductions.

The sample clause for a royalty based on the publisher's net income sets a fixed royalty rate for the life of the contract, but the rationale for an escalating royalty rate applies whether the author's royalty is based on retail price or net income. (➤*A Clause for Escalating Royalties Based on Retail Price, Page 115*) As more copies of the author's book are printed and sold, and the publisher has recouped its start-up costs, the real cost per copy drops and the profits begin to rise dramatically. That is why the author may wish to argue for an escalating royalty rate based on the number of copies of sold, especially when the royalty is based on the publisher's net income.

(For a discussion of the other elements of the sample clause, including the defined term "Net Copies Sold," see *A Clause for a Fixed Royalty Based on Retail Price, Page 109.*)

> 📖 **Recoupment of Publisher's Costs**. A few publishers use a definition of net income that permits them to recoup some or all of the costs of development, production, manufacture, and sale of a book, and sometimes even a portion of their general operating overhead, out of gross revenues *before* starting to pay a royalty to the author. Such clauses are common in the recording and motion picture industries, where royalties and revenue participation may not begin until certain specified costs are recouped, but it is still unusual for a publisher to demand the same right in a book publishing contract.

## Other Royalty Categories

Even when a publishers offers to pay what seems to be a generous royalty—a royalty based on retail price rather than net income, for instance, or a royalty that escalates as sales increase over the life of the contract—the "fine print" will often provide for different and drastically reduced royalty rates for sales of the same book in various other specified categories. Typically, the highest royalty is usually reserved for sales of hardcover copies of the book through "ordinary channels of trade" and at conventional wholesale discounts. But a great many of the books actually sold by a publisher may fall into one or more categories for which only a reduced royalty is paid.

For example, one contract used by a major publisher provides for a "standard" royalty of 10%–12½%–15% of the "suggested customer's price"—that is, the retail price—for "all hardcover copies sold through ordinary channels of trade in the United States." But the royalty for "all hardcover copies sold in the United States at discounts higher than the Publisher's announced discounts for wholesale and retail accounts in the book trade" drops to "10% of the amounts received by the Publisher." The same reduced royalty applies to *all* sales on a "nonreturnable basis" or "outside the ordinary channels of the book trade," "special sales," "premium sales," and sales through "catalog accounts" and "book fairs."

Another major publisher uses a contract that initially provides for a royalty equal to 15 percent of the retail price for *all* hardcover sales. However, a careful reading of the subsequent clauses reveals that the royalty is only "one-half (½) of the prevailing royalty rate, based on the amount received by Publisher," when it comes to "copies sold as premiums to commercial purchasers for use in connection with other goods and services," sales to "governmental agencies" or "outside usual wholesale and retail channels," and sales "at a discount of more than sixty percent (60%) from the United States invoice price." In other words, the royalty *rate* drops by half, and the reduced royalty rate is applied against publisher's net income rather than the retail price of the price, a mechanism that substantially reduces the real economic value of the royalty.

The sample clause set forth below offers one typical approach to reduced royalties, but the contracts in common use in the publishing industry take a great many different approaches, and each contract must be carefully read and evaluated on its own unique terms. Indeed, the best way to analyze a reduced royalty clause is to plug a few numbers into the royalty provisions of a given clause—the full royalty rate, the suggested cover price of the book, the wholesale discount, the reduced royalty, and so on—and then measure the impact of a reduced royalty on the money actually paid to the author in any given transaction.

### A CLAUSE FOR REDUCED ROYALTIES ON SPECIFIED CATEGORIES OF SALE

For any and all sales of the Work in any Publisher's edition at discounts greater than the Publisher's announced wholesale discounts in the book trade; nonreturnable sales; direct sales; export sales; and bulk, premium and other special sales, Author's royalty shall be one-half of the full royalty specified for sales in ordinary channels of distribution in the book trade.

**"For any and sales of the Work in any Publisher's edition..."** The clause applies only to editions of the author's work actually issued by the publisher. As a general matter, publication of the author's work and exploitation of other rights by third parties under license from the publisher is covered under a separate clause. (➤*Sharing of Revenues from Subsidiary Rights, Page 125*)

**"...at discounts greater than the Publisher's announced wholesale discounts in the book trade..."** A publisher will almost always seek to reduce the author's royalties on so-called "deep discount" sales, which are understood to be sales at a wholesale discount that is substantially greater than the publisher's customary discount in the book trade. A wholesale discount of 40 percent off the retail price is common in trade publishing, but greater discounts are generally offered when the bookseller purchases a greater number of books. In contrast, the standard discounts in other publishing fields such as textbooks and technical books tend to be lower. As noted above, the definition of a deep discount sale may vary from contract to contract, and some contracts do not offer *any* precise definition, but a deep discount always means a reduced profit margin for the publisher and, therefore, it usually results in a reduced royalty for the author.

"...**nonreturnable sales**..." As we have already noted (➤*Returns, Page 113*), the standard terms of sale in the book trade allow a retail bookseller to order a book from the publisher and then return it for a refund or a credit if the book is not sold. However, if a wholesale purchaser is willing to give up its right to return an unsold book, the publisher is generally willing to give a much more generous discount to the purchaser—and, as a result, the publisher pays a much less generous royalty to the author. As a practical matter, deep discount sales and nonreturnable sales are sometimes one and the same thing.

"...**direct sales**..." When the publisher sells a copy of the author's work directly to a consumer, a reduced royalty is often paid. The reduction of royalties on direct sales strikes most authors as not only niggardly but counter-intuitive. Why, after all, would the publisher expect the author to accept a lower royalty on a direct sale, since the publisher is getting 100 percent of the retail price of the book rather than the retail price less the wholesale discount? Publishers argue that the real cost of a making a direct sale to the consumer, which generally requires the publisher to pay for advertising in magazines and newspapers, printing and mailing of catalogs or direct-mail pieces in bulk quantities, is much greater than a conventional wholesale transaction and thus justifies the lower royalty.

"...**export sales**..." When the publisher enjoys the right to sell its own editions of the author's work in foreign countries (➤*Foreign Rights, Page 64*), a reduced royalty is paid on the rationale that shipping costs, currency conversions, and other costs of sale make it less profitable than a domestic sale. The category is a narrow one, however, since few copies of printed and bound books are actually sold in this manner—precisely because of these high costs of doing business abroad.

"...**bulk, premium and other special sales**..." Reduced royalties are often paid on what some book contracts refer to as "special" sales, which is often another way of saying "sales outside usual wholesale and retail channels." Examples of special sales include "bulk" sales, where a single purchaser such as a discount chain buys copies of a book in bulk quantities in a single transaction; "corporate" or "institutional" sales, where a corporation or institution, such as a college, a hospital, or the like, buys copies in bulk for in-house or other special uses; and "premium" or "promotional" sales, where a quantity of books are purchased and used to promote the sale of other goods and services. As noted above, such sales are often made on a nonreturnable basis and at prices that are much lower than the conventional wholesale discount price.

**"...Author's royalty shall be one-half of the full royalty specified for sales in ordinary channels of distribution in the book trade."** The sample clause proposes one approach to reduced royalties in specified categories of sale: the author will be entitled to 50 percent of the *"full royalty specified for sales in ordinary channels of distribution."* Thus, for example, if the contract provides for a royalty of 10 percent of suggested retail price on the sale of a hardback copy of the author's work at an ordinary wholesale discount, then the same sale at a deep discount would earn a royalty of 5 percent of suggested retail price. But the actual mechanism for reducing the author's royalty varies from contract to contract, and each such clause must be carefully analyzed and evaluated to determine how it will be calculated and how deeply it reduces the actual royalty paid to the author.

---

✍ **Dangers of Reduced Royalties**. Deep discounting is a fact of life in the publishing industry nowadays, and the reduced royalties clause in the typical book contract is a kind of trapdoor that may cause a drastic drop in the real value of a book contract. For that reason, the royalty *floor*—the lowest royalty that the publisher may pay on any category of sale—may be as important as the upper range of an escalating royalty.

✍ **Stepped-Down Royalties**. The typical reduced royalty clause simply cuts the author's royalty by cutting the royalty rate by a large fraction—a reduction of one-half to two-thirds of the "prevailing" royalty rate is not uncommon—or by shifting from a royalty based on retail price to one based net income, or by doing both at once! However,

---

the author may be able to negotiate for a reduced royalty that steps down as the wholesale discount increases, which results in a much less precipitous drop in actual royalty income. One author of my acquaintance was able to persuade her publisher to add a deep discount schedule in which the royalty rate stepped down gradually as the wholesale discount increased, i.e., when the wholesale discount was greater than 40 percent but less than 45 percent off the retail price, the royalty rate decreased from 12 percent to 11 percent; a discount of 45 to 49 percent resulted in a royalty of 10 percent; and so on.

📖 **Royalty Accounting**. Some book contracts include a list of royalty rates, each one slightly or greatly different than the standard royalty, and each one applicable to a different category of sale; a single contract might specify as many as a dozen different rates. The sheer complexity of such royalty schedules results in accounting issues that may be as burdensome to the publisher that prepares the royalty statement as it is to the author who reads it. For that reason, some publishers favor a reduced royalty clause, such as the one used in *Kirsch's Guide*, which simply cuts the standard royalty by a fixed percentage (i.e., one-third, one-half, two-thirds).

📖 **Calculation of Escalated Royalties**. Publishers that agree to royalties that escalate according to sales are often inclined to *exclude* sales of books in reduced royalty categories from the calculation of total sales: **"Sales of the Work in any category for which a reduced royalty is paid shall be excluded from the calculation of total sales for the purpose of determining the escalation of royalties."** Suppose, for example, that the author is entitled to a base royalty of 15 percent of suggested retail price when total sales exceed 10,000 copies, but half of those sales are deep discount or direct-marketing sales. Under this example, the author would have to wait for another 5,000 copies to sell in the full royalty category before the escalated royalty would kick in.

## SHARING OF REVENUES FROM SUBSIDIARY RIGHTS

Royalties usually fall into one of two categories: first, the royalties that the publisher will pay the author for the rights that the publisher itself exploits; and, second, the royalties that the publisher will pay the author when the publisher licenses a specific right in the author's work to a third party. The first kind of royalty is usually expressed as either a percentage of the retail price of the book or of the publisher's net income from sales of the book (➤*Royalties, Page 109*), and the second kind of royalty is usually expressed as a percentage of the revenues paid to the publisher by the third party to whom the rights are licensed.

**Flow-Through.** One way to sweeten a book deal is a "flow-through" clause, which speeds up the payment of certain kinds of royalties to the author. Royalties on sales of the publisher's editions are generally calculated and paid on a quarterly or semiannual basis, which means that the author must wait three to six months or sometimes even longer before pocketing the royalty on a sale that took place at the beginning of a royalty period. A flow-through clause, which usually applies only to revenues from licensing of rights to third parties, obligates the publisher to pay the author her share of third-party payments promptly upon receipt by the publisher: **"Author's share of revenue from the exploitation of rights by third parties, after deduction of unearned advances and other charges against the Author's account, shall be paid within 30 days after receipt by Publisher."**

A very rough rule-of-thumb is a 50-50 split on revenues from the exploitation of subsidiary rights, half to the publisher and half to the author, but the actual splits may vary greatly from one subsidiary right to another and from deal to deal. For example, an author may seek to reserve motion picture, television, and dramatic rights in a novel, and if successful in doing so, the author will not be required to share *any* revenue from reserved rights with the publisher. Publishers are often most generous in sharing income from the least valuable rights. For example, the revenues from the publication of an excerpt from the author's work in a periodical is a right that may be granted to a magazine or newspaper free of charge or for a few hundred dollars; such revenues are often shared 90 percent to the author and 10 percent to the publisher. Yet the publisher's share of revenues from potentially more valuable rights in a book deal—foreign and translation rights, for example, or softcover rights in a hardback deal—might range from 20 to 50 percent.

As a general proposition, the sharing of revenues from third parties for the exploitation of subsidiary rights is always subject to hard and even heated negotiation between author and publisher. In any given book deal, as we have already seen, some rights will be wholly reserved by the author, some rights will be granted to the publisher, and the sharing of revenues from the exploitation of such rights may be as low as 10 percent or as high as 90 percent, all depending on the deal that has been struck.

### A CLAUSE FOR A FIXED SHARE OF REVENUES FROM LICENSING OF RIGHTS TO THIRD PARTIES

Publisher shall credit Author's account with a royalty equal to 50% of all Net Revenues actually received by Publisher for the exploitation or disposition of any and all rights in the Work by third parties under license from the Publisher.

"Net Revenues," as used in this Agreement, refers to money actually received by Publisher from the sale of copies of the Work, net of returns, after deduction of shipping, customs, insurance, fees and commissions, currency exchange discounts, and costs of collection.

*"Publisher shall credit Author's account..."* The sample clause provides that the author's share of revenues from rights licensed to a third party will be *"credit[ed to] the Author's account."* Thus, the author's share will be subject to recoupment of advances, overpayment of royalties, and other charges against the author's account, and then the remaining amount will be paid to the author when the publisher renders an accounting as required under the contract. (➤*Accounting, Page 193*)

*"...a royalty equal to 50% of all Net Revenues actually received by Publisher..."* The sample clause proposes an equal split of revenues between author and publisher, but only after deduction of specified costs and charges, i.e., fees and commissions paid to a foreign rights agent who places the author's work

with various foreign publishers. The precise definition of deductible costs and charges—and, crucially, the actual split or revenues between author and publisher—may be the subject of active negotiation and, therefore, may vary from deal to deal. (For a discussion of the definition of "Net Revenues" as used in the sample clause, see *A Clause for a Fixed Royalty Based on Publisher's Net Income, Page 119.*)

"*...for the exploitation or disposition of any and all rights in the Work by third parties under license from the Publisher.*" The sharing of revenues between author and publisher as provided in the sample clause applies to *all* circumstances in which the publisher licenses a right in the author's work to a third party, whether it is a primary right that the publisher chooses not to exploit itself or a "secondary" or "subsidiary" right that the publisher acquired but never intended to exploit in the first place. Exactly what constitutes a primary, secondary, or subsidiary right depends on a careful reading of other clauses in the contract, which may or may not include specific definitions (➤ *Primary and Secondary Rights, Page 59*). But the principle established in the sample clause is that the publisher and the author will share in the revenues generated whenever *any* of the rights in the author's work are licensed to a third party.

## A CLAUSE FOR A SHARING OF REVENUES FROM LICENSING OF RIGHTS TO THIRD PARTIES IN SPECIFIED PERCENTAGES

Publisher shall credit Author's account with a royalty equal to Author's share, as specified below, of all Net Revenues actually received by Publisher for the exploitation or disposition of any and all rights in the Work by third parties under license from the Publisher.

|  | Author's Share | Publisher's Share |
|---|---|---|
| Hardcover Rights | _____% | _____% |
| Trade Paperback Rights | _____% | _____% |
| Mass-Market Paperback Rights | _____% | _____% |

| | | |
|---|---|---|
| Translation and Foreign Rights | _____% | _____% |
| Periodical Publication Rights | _____% | _____% |
| Book Club Rights | _____% | _____% |
| Photocopying and Facsimile Rights | _____% | _____% |
| Microfilm Rights | _____% | _____% |
| General Print Publication Rights | _____% | _____% |
| Direct-Response Marketing Rights | _____% | _____% |
| Audio Rights | _____% | _____% |
| Electronic Rights | _____% | _____% |
| Dramatic Rights | _____% | _____% |
| Reading Rights | _____% | _____% |
| Motion Picture and Television Rights | _____% | _____% |
| Radio Rights | _____% | _____% |
| Commercial Rights | _____% | _____% |
| Future Technologies | _____% | _____% |

*"...a royalty equal to Author's share, as specified..."* As an alternative to a fixed split of revenues from third-party licensing, the sample clause allows the publisher to specify specific shares for each right in the author's work. A clause that enumerates the various rights and specifies a particular share for each one is more commonly used by publishers than the one that provides for a fixed split, since it allows more flexibility in negotiation and drafting. For example, the publisher may fill in the blanks with more generous percentages for some specified rights in exchange for less generous percentages for other rights. And if the author reserves one or more of the enumerated rights in the sample clause, the reserved rights can be stricken out and

initialed, but the clause remains in effect as to the other rights. (For a discussion of the other words and phrases in the sample clause, see *A Clause for a Fixed Share of Revenues from Licensing Rights to Third Parties, Page 127.)*

---

✍ **Licensing of Rights to a Related Company.** Nowadays, thanks to the number and velocity of mergers and acquisitions in the publishing industry, it is not unusual for a publisher to be a division or a subsidiary of a vast conglomerate. For that reason, a hardback publisher may find itself selling off subsidiary rights in an author's work to one of its sister companies, whether it's a paperback house, an audio publisher, an electronic publisher, or even a motion picture studio or television network. The author, of course, prefers an arm's length negotiation between unrelated parties on the fair assumption that it will produce a much higher price than a deal struck between two companies under the same corporate umbrella. Under these circumstances, the author may seek an additional clause that requires the author's prior written consent to transactions between the publisher and a related company, or—at a minimum—a clause that requires any such transaction to be "**on terms and conditions no less advantageous to Author than an arm's length transaction with a third party.**"

---

## COMPENSATION FOR CO-AUTHORS AND COLLABORATORS

Any of the forms of compensation discussed here, and a few others besides, can be adapted for use in compensating a co-author, collaborator, or other contributor to an author's work.

**Co-Authors.** As a general rule, co-authors of a single work of authorship are entitled to share equally in the proceeds from the exploitation of all rights in the work unless they have agreed otherwise among themselves. Still, the cautious publisher may include a clause to that effect in the contract for a project with multiple authors, using the defined term "Author" to refer collectively to all co-authors: "**The co-authors of the Work shall share equally in all rights and duties of Author under this Agreement, and all payments owed by Publisher to Author under this Agreement shall be paid in equal shares to each of the co-authors.**" (➤*Multiple Authors, Page 250*) If some other split is agreed upon by the co-author, the contract should specifically say so, i.e., "**All payments to Author under this Agreement shall be paid in the following shares: Author No. 1, Seventy Percent (70%) and Author No. 2, Thirty Percent (30%).**" If an agent is involved in the contract, then the agency clause will usually provide that *all* amounts are paid to the agent of record, who will be responsible for dividing up and disbursing the payments to the various co-authors. (➤*Agency, Page 203*)

**Ghostwriters and Other Collaborators.** If the principal author of a book engages the services of a ghostwriter or other collaborator, the manner and amount of compensation for the ghostwriter or collaborator should be negotiated in advance and embodied in a formal written agreement signed by both parties. Indeed, the publisher that deals with a principal author and a ghostwriter ought to insist on such a formal approach, if only for its own protection.

Great flexibility and creativity is often shown in the deals struck by authors and ghostwriters. If the principal value of a book project is found in the celebrity, notoriety, expertise or experience of the principal author—and the ghostwriter is merely a technician who puts words on paper—then the ghostwriter's compensation may be a small fraction of the total amount of author compensation. If, on the other hand, the ghostwriter is an accomplished "book doctor" with a string of bestsellers, then the ghostwriter might command half or even more of the author's compensation.

Often, it is the ghostwriter who is responsible for the early and intensive efforts in the research and writing of a book, especially when the principal author is, for example, a doctor, a scientist, or a business executive who brings expertise or life experience rather than writing skills to the project. Suppose, for example, that the principal author will continue to work at her profession while the ghostwriter devotes all of her time to the actual writing of the book. In such cases, it is not unusual or unfair for the ghostwriter to be allocated most or all of the advance, while the principal author waits until the book earns out before collecting any sizable amount of money. Indeed, I have written contracts in which the ghostwriter takes 75 percent of the advance and the principal author takes 75 percent of the earned royalties until each party has been paid the same amount of money, and thereafter the proceeds are shared equally.

By contrast, the principal author of a book may be willing and able to simply hire a ghostwriter or other collaborator, sometimes paying by the hour or by the week, sometimes offering a flat fee for a specified number of manuscript pages by a certain date. In such circumstances, the collaborator is paid on a fee-for-service basis and does not participate at all in advances, royalties, or other sharing of revenues between the principal author and the publisher.

Of course, the creative, financial, and legal relationship between an author and a collaborator can be a complex and potentially volatile one. Much more is at stake than money; so the agreement between author and collaborator should address, among other things, the following: ownership of copyright in the collaborator's work-in-progress and the finished book, authorship credit for the collaborator, the right of the author to terminate the collaborator, the right of the collaborator to withdraw from the project, and the impact of early termination on the ghostwriter's credit and compensation. (See *Kirsch's Handbook, Chapter 2: Co-Authorship and Copyright*)

# 4

## THE MANUSCRIPT

The paperless office is one of the broken dreams of the computer revolution, but the fact is that the writing, editing, design, and preparation of a book for publication takes place mostly and sometimes entirely in the form of screen displays and diskettes. The book you are reading right now was written on an IBM ThinkPad, submitted to the publisher by E-mail, typeset and designed on a PageMaker program, and delivered to the printer in the form of a single diskette. Yet the author's handiwork is still identified in most book contracts as "the manuscript."

The clauses devoted to the manuscript in the typical book contract are mostly logistical in nature—the date by which the manuscript must be delivered, the form in which it is to be delivered, the right and responsibility of the author to read and return proofs of the book after the manuscript as been set into type, and so on. But, hidden away among the dreary details of word counts and deadlines, are some crucial provisions that will literally determine whether the project will go further than the manuscript itself and actually see print.

The delivery (or, for that matter, the nondelivery) of the manuscript presents the publisher with its first opportunity to judge the quality of what the author has created, and its first opportunity to reject the author's work, call back the advance, and cancel the project if the author's work fails to meet with approval. Thus, the definition of when and how a publisher may reject a manuscript is a clause of such importance that it belongs with the more glamorous deal points of a book contract. Indeed, whether or not the author gets to keep the advance depends on what is written in the clauses on the handling of the manuscript.

## PREPARATION AND DELIVERY OF
## THE MANUSCRIPT

### DELIVERY OF MANUSCRIPT

Author agrees to deliver the manuscript of the Work in the English language in its entirety ("the Manuscript") to the Publisher not later than [*Insert date of manuscript delivery*] ("the Initial Delivery Date") in the form of (a) a computer-readable file stored on one or more disks in such format(s) and word-processing program(s) as Publisher may specify, and (b) two (2) computer-generated printouts of the Work, double-spaced on 8½-by-11-inch white paper, which Manuscript shall be approximately [*Insert word or page count*] in length and shall otherwise be acceptable to Publisher in form and content.

*"Author agrees to deliver the manuscript of the Work in the English language in its entirety ('the Manuscript')..."* Here is the first and most fundamental duty of the author under a book contract—he must write the book and deliver it to the publisher! The sample clause provides that the manuscript is to be delivered "in its entirety," a caution to tardy authors who come up with only partial manuscripts on the due date. Technically, the author who delivers less than the complete manuscript on the deadline is in breach of contract. The sample clause carefully notes that the manuscript is to be written in the English language, an unusual detail but one that makes sense in what has become a multinational industry. As we have seen in other clauses, the fact that the phrase "the Manuscript" appears in quotations marks and parentheses indicates that it is now a "defined term" and will have the same meaning when used elsewhere in the contract.

*"...not later than* [*Insert date of manuscript delivery*] *(the Initial Delivery Date')..."* A firm and specific date must be inserted in the sample clause to establish a deadline for submission of the author's completed work. Some contracts provide for a series of due dates, i.e., *"One-third of the Manuscript not*

later than [Date], and the balance of the Manuscript not later than 60 days thereafter," or "The first ten chapters on or before [Date], and the last ten chapters on or before [Date]." The use of multiple deadlines allows the publisher to satisfy itself that the author is making progress toward completion of the manuscript; otherwise, the publisher might not find out until the final deadline that the author is behind schedule and struggling to catch up. When multiple deadlines are used, the delivery of each portion of the manuscript may trigger the payment of a portion of the advance. (➤*Advances, Page 104*) But the manuscript delivery clause *must* specify a final date by which the entire manuscript is be completed and delivered to the publisher.

The sample clause introduces a defined term ("*the Initial Delivery Date*") to identify the deadline for submission of the manuscript, but—as the term itself suggests—the author will be expected to make further submissions on subsequent deadlines that will appear in subsequent clauses of the contract. (➤*A Clause Providing for Author's Right to Revise Manuscript Prior to Rejection, Page 148*)

"*...in the form of (a) a computer-readable file stored on one or more disks in such format(s) and word-processing program(s) as Publisher may specify...*" Not every book contract requires delivery of the manuscript on disk, but it is an increasingly common practice in publishing because it allows the publisher to go directly from manuscript into page proofs in a single continuous process. No longer are manuscripts set in type, and if the author delivers the manuscript on disk, then the publisher need not even go the trouble of "keystroking" the manuscript into a computer. Once stored in the publisher's word-processing computer, the manuscript is typeset, the pages are designed, and the book designer can see on a computer screen what the final pages will look like. When printed out on paper, the typeset and designed pages can be used as page proofs for fact-checking, proofreading, and final editing changes.

"*...and (b) two (2) computer-generated printouts of the Work, double-spaced on 8½-by-11-inch white paper...*" No matter how much the publishing industry has come to rely on computers, however, the various editors who will work on the manuscript will probably prefer to put their comments and corrections on old-fashioned manuscript pages rather than on a document on the computer screen. So the sample clause makes it the author's responsibility to send two printouts of the work in a specified format. Some publishers will accept a manuscript delivery in the form of disks only and then print out the needed copies, but the sample clause shifts both the responsibility and cost of doing so, however minor, to the author. As a practical matter, the text editor and copy editor may send marked-up manuscript pages back to the author for the task of inputting changes into the computer where the manuscript resides.

*"...which Manuscript shall be approximately [Insert number word or page count] in length..."* The sample clause notes the contemplated length of the manuscript in the form of a word or page count. Many contracts, including the model contract in *Kirsch's Guide,* describe the author's work in considerably more detail in the introductory clauses (➤*Description of the Work, Page 48*), and the more detailed description of the work is an important benchmark for both the author and publisher. Still, the author should consider whether the manuscript length is reasonable and appropriate, if only because the delivery of a manuscript that is substantially longer or shorter than promised may be treated as a breach of contract by the publisher.

*"...and shall otherwise be acceptable to Publisher in form and content."* A fundamental principle in the publishing industry is that a publisher is not obligated to publish an unsatisfactory manuscript a concept that appears here for the first time in the Model Contract, but is typically expressed in several other clauses of a standard book contract. The phrase used in the sample clause is intended to establish the contractual obligation of the author to deliver a manuscript that is *"acceptable to Publisher in form and content,"* but we will explore the scope and substance of the publisher's right to reject an unsatisfactory manuscript in much greater detail in subsequent clauses of the model contract. (➤*A Clause Providing for Author's Right to Revise Manuscript Prior to Rejection, Page 148*)

---

📖 **Measuring the Manuscript.** Some contracts describe the length of the manuscript as a specified number of pages, which immediately

---

introduces a vexing ambiguity into the contract: does it mean manuscript pages or book pages? Even if the length is given in pages, the number of words that can be accommodated on a printed page will vary according to type size, paper size, and other design and production factors. Measuring the manuscript by specifying the number of *words* rather than pages is preferable.

✍ **Computer Formats for Manuscript Delivery.** The sample clause allows the publisher to specify the storage format (i.e., diskette, CD-ROM, etc.) and the word-processing program that the author is required to use, but the point can and should be negotiated to make sure that the author is using an acceptable program and storage medium. If the author will be required to purchase new computer equipment or a different word-processing program—a much more remote risk nowadays—the cost should be taken into account during the negotiation of other deal points.

### ARTWORK, PERMISSIONS, INDEX, AND OTHER MATERIALS

Author shall deliver to Publisher, at Author's sole expense, not later than the Initial Delivery Date or such other date(s) as may be designated by Publisher, each of the following:

1. Original art, illustrations, maps, charts, photographs, or other artwork (collectively "Artwork"), in a form suitable for reproduction.

2. An index, bibliography, table of contents, foreword, introduction, preface, or similar matter ("Frontmatter" and "Backmatter").

3. Written authorizations and permissions for the use of any copyrighted or other proprietary materials (including but not limited to Artwork, Backmatter, and/or Frontmatter) owned by any third party which appear in the Work and written releases or consents by any person or entity described, quoted, or depicted in the Work (collectively "Permissions").

**4. If Author fails or refuses to deliver the Artwork, Backmatter, Frontmatter, Permissions, or other material**

required to be delivered by Author under this Agreement, Publisher shall have the right, but not the obligation, to acquire or prepare any and all such matter, or to engage a skilled person to do so, and Author shall reimburse Publisher for all costs and expenses incurred by Publisher in doing so.

5. Author acknowledges and confirms that Publisher shall have no liability of any kind for the loss or destruction of the Manuscript, Artwork, Frontmatter, Backmatter, or any other documents or materials provided by Author to Publisher, and agrees to make and maintain copies of all such documents and materials for use in the event of such loss or destruction.

*"Author shall deliver to Publisher, at Author's sole expense, not later than the Initial Delivery Date or such other date(s) as may be designated by Publisher, each of the following..."* Writing and delivering a manuscript of the author's work is not the only responsibility of the author under a typical book contract. As discussed below, the author may be asked to prepare—or, more often, acquire and pay for—artwork, permissions, "frontmatter" and "backmatter" (the various materials preceding and following the primary manuscript title page, index, etc.), and other materials that will be used in connection with the book project.

The sample clause requires the author to deliver these materials at the same time as the initial manuscript unless the publisher designates some other date, whether earlier or later. Some of the materials to be delivered by the author—such as the various consents and approvals described in the sample clause as "Permissions"—might be required in advance of manuscript delivery. Others, such as an index, cannot be completed until long after the manuscript is delivered, edited, and set into type, and the pages are numbered.

The sample clause empowers the publisher alone to set the deadlines for all of these materials, but the scheduling is not always a unilateral decision: some book contracts set the deadlines in advance or provide that the delivery dates are subject to mutual agreement of the author and publisher.

*"...Original art, illustrations, maps, charts, photographs, and other artwork (collectively 'Artwork')..."* Authors are sometimes surprised to discover that they are expected to not only *write* their books but also to acquire the artwork to illustrate them. As a practical matter, the decision of whether or not and how to illustrate a book is made by the publisher sometimes with the author's consultation and sometimes not and it is often the publisher that actually does the work of locating, obtaining, and clearing the rights to use artwork. The sample clause, however, shifts both the burden and the cost of doing so to the author alone.

Of course, if the book consists of art and text by a single author, or a writer and an artist working together as co-authors, then the issue of artwork will generally be handled in the introductory clauses where the work itself is defined and described, rather than in the manuscript preparation clause. (➤ *Description of the Work, Page 48*)

*"...in a form suitable for reproduction..."* The artwork provided for use must be *"suitable for reproduction."* Thus, for example, a high-quality color print of a particular photograph, rather than a black-and-white print or a color photocopy, or a map drawn by a professional cartographer rather than the author's crude efforts with pen and paper, will be required if the publisher says so. As a result, the requirement that artwork be delivered in a form specified by the publisher may result in an unanticipated expense to the author.

---

✍ **Joint Approval of Artwork and Other Materials**. According to the sample clause, the publisher decides what artwork is necessary, but the author pays for it. A better approach from the author's point of view is one that provides for joint approval of artwork and/or a list that specifies in advance the artwork that is to be delivered by the author and the form in which it is to be delivered, i.e., **"The Artwork shall consist of the items described in Exhibit '__' to this Agreement and such other items as Author and Publisher may jointly agree upon and approve, and the expense of acquiring the Artwork shall be allocated between Author and Publisher according to their mutual agreement."** Ideally, of course, the publisher will bear some or all of the cost of acquiring the agreed-upon art, but the allocation of costs and expenses is always subject to negotiation. The

---

> same approach can be used in allocating the burden and expense of obtaining a preface or a foreword, permissions for the use of copyrighted materials, and indexing of the finished book.

*"...An index, bibliography, table of contents, foreword, introduction, preface, or similar matter ('Frontmatter' and 'Backmatter')..."* A finished book may include various elements that precede or follow the main text of the author's work, all of which fall into the category of "frontmatter" and "backmatter" in the jargon of the publishing industry. Some of these elements—a table of contents, for example, or a bibliography—are customarily prepared by the author during the process of researching and writing a book and do not represent an appreciable burden to the author. Others, such as the preparation of an index, are specialized tasks that are jobbed out to individuals or firms that specialize in indexing. Sometimes a foreword or preface will be solicited from a celebrity or an expert in order to heighten the appeal of the book or enhance its credibility. The sample clause, and most book contracts, allocate *all* of these responsibilities to the author, even though it is often the publisher that takes the initiative in obtaining them.

*"...Written authorizations and permissions for the use of any copyrighted or other proprietary materials...owned by any third party..."* Most works of authorship include at least some material that is quoted or copied from another source—a quotation from a book or magazine article, a photograph or an illustration, a chart or a graph. Some limited use may be made of copyrighted material without the permission of the copyright owner under the doctrine known as "fair use," but the fair use doctrine is so unpredictable in application that most publishers insist on seeking prior written consent for the use of materials from copyrighted sources. (See *Kirsch's Handbook, Chapter 5: Preparing the Manuscript*)

The sample clause applies not only to copyrighted works but also *"proprietary materials,"* which is broad enough to require formal clearance of any use of trademarks and trade secrets belonging to third parties. The contractual responsibility for securing such *"authorizations and permissions"* is assigned to the author in the sample clause, and extends not only to incidental quotations but to *everything* that falls under the defined terms "*Artwork, Backmatter and/or Frontmatter.*" Consent to use all such materials must be secured by the author in writing, a process that is known generally as "Permissions."

"*...written releases or consents by any person or entity described, quoted or depicted in the Work...*" The sample clause illustrates an especially strict approach to clearance because it extends beyond the use of materials protected under copyright or trademark and requires the author to seek permission from persons "*described, quoted or depicted in the Work.*" Interview releases and even the formal acquisition of "life story rights" are commonplace in motion picture and television production, but few book publishers are quite so demanding, and only rarely are "*written releases or consents*" obtained from individuals who, for example, agree to be interviewed by an author in connection with a book project. But the sample clause empowers the publisher to demand formal clearance of materials in the author's work that may raise the risk of a lawsuit for defamation or invasion of privacy by someone who is unhappy with his treatment by the author.

---

✍ **Preapproved Clearance and Consent Forms**. Some publishers are more demanding than others in their clearance policies, and the author is well-served by finding out in advance what kind of clearances, consents, and permissions the publisher will actually require *before* signing a book contract and embarking on research for his book. A useful approach is to attach pre-approved legal forms as exhibits to the contract, i.e., "**Publisher acknowledges and agrees that permissions and releases in the form of the attached sample forms will be sufficient to satisfy the Author's obligation to secure such permissions and releases under this Agreement.**"

---

"*...If Author fails or refuses to deliver the Artwork, Backmatter, Frontmatter, Permissions or other material...*" As a basic proposition, the author is contractually required to take the initiative in acquiring artwork, frontmatter and backmatter, permissions, and so on, even though many of these tasks are actually undertaken by the publisher in the typical book deal. Indeed, the sample clause contemplates precisely such a situation, and prescribes how the publisher will be compensated for completing the tasks that are assigned to the author in the contract itself.

However, as we have already noted, some tasks are best handled by the author, others by the publisher, still others by independent specialists. The author is best positioned to obtain interview releases from individuals who have been consulted in the course of research for his book, for example, and the publisher will enjoy a certain degree of professional courtesy in seeking permission to use materials from a copyrighted work issued by another publishing house. Indexing is probably best handled by a professional indexer. If the author and publisher agree in advance on how to divide up the various tasks, the clause should be modified to reflect the actual allocation of work.

*"...Publisher shall have the right, but not the obligation, to acquire or prepare any and all such matter, or to engage a skilled person to do so..."* The publisher is empowered—but not obligated—to acquire whatever additional materials are required for the completion of the book if the author *"fails or refuses"* to do so, whether by the efforts of its own art department, permissions department, etc., or by jobbing out the task to an outside specialist such as a clearance service, an indexer, or some other vendor or contractor.

However, the publisher is not *obliged* to step up and finish the work assigned to the author. Rather, the publisher may elect to hold the author in breach of contract if he does not live up to these obligations. Thus, the author who simply assumes that the publisher will worry about permissions, for example, and says nothing more about it faces the risk that the publisher will simply cancel the project. (➤ *Termination of the Contract for Defects in Delivery, Page 151*)

For that reason, it is preferable and perhaps even crucial to discuss and decide the allocation of work during the negotiation of the book contract, and the clause can and should be marked up to reflect the arrangements actually agreed upon by the author and publisher.

*"...and Author shall reimburse Publisher for all costs and expenses incurred by Publisher in doing so..."* If the author does not provide the materials specified in the sample clause, and the publisher elects to acquire them on its own resources and initiative, the costs will be charged to the author, usually in the form of a debit against the author's account but sometimes by an invoice that requires immediate payment. (➤*Accounting, Page 193*)

---

✍ **Caps on Costs and Expenses.** The sample clause sets no limits on the costs for which the publisher is entitled to reimbursement, and makes no distinction between actual costs paid by the publisher to a third party, such as a freelance researcher or an indexer, and cost items that represent some arbitrary charge for use of the publisher's in-house staff and facilities. The author can protect himself against such charges by asking for a fixed limit on such costs and charges ( *"...***not to exceed $_____ without Author's prior written approval...**"*) and a change in the wording of the sample clause from *"all costs and expenses incurred by Publisher"* to *"all cost and expenses paid to third parties by Publisher."*

✍ **Debits on Author's Account.** Whenever the author is required to pay or reimburse the publisher for some cost or charge, including the cost of acquiring materials that are the responsibility of the author, it is preferable for the item to be handled as a debit on the author's account, i.e., **"All such costs and expenses shall be charged to the Author's account and recouped out of earned royalties, if any."** Otherwise, the author may be obliged to come up with cash to pay such costs or charges.

---

*"...Publisher shall have no liability of any kind for the loss or destruction of the Manuscript, Artwork, Frontmatter, Backmatter, or any other documents or materials provided by Author to Publisher..."* The commonsense notion that the author should make and keep copies of *everything* that he sends to the publisher should go without saying, but it is such a crucial precaution that many book contracts make it a contractual responsibility of the author to do so. If the author sends his only copy of the manuscript, and the manuscript is lost or destroyed through the ineptitude of the mails or the publisher, he will find himself in the unhappy predicament that befell Thomas Carlisle, whose housekeeper accidentally burned the manuscript of *A History of the French Revolution* and

forced him to write it all over again! But the sample clause relieves the publisher of any legal responsibility for such a catastrophe by specifically obligating the author "*to make and maintain copies of all such documents and materials for use in the event of such loss or destruction.*"

## THE PUBLISHER'S RIGHT TO REJECT THE MANUSCRIPT

Generally, a book contract will provide for one of three approaches to defining the circumstances under which a manuscript may be accepted or rejected by the publisher. The unqualified right of the publisher to reject an unsatisfactory manuscript was once a commonplace of the standard book contract, and many contracts now in use still preserve the prerogative of the publisher to simply say "No" to an author's work. (➤*A Clause Providing for Publisher's Unqualified Right to Reject the Manuscript, Page 145*)

However, some precedent in publishing law suggests that a publisher must act reasonably and in good faith even when the contract reserves an unqualified right to reject the author's work. (See *Kirsch's Handbook, Chapter 4: The Book Publishing Contract*) By allowing the author an opportunity to fix what's wrong with the author's work, the publisher is fulfilling its implied obligation under the law of contract to "publish in good faith." Of course, many publishers are willing to give the author an opportunity to submit a revised draft of a manuscript out of a sense of fair play and collegiality, but the publisher that adopts a kinder and gentler approach to a flawed manuscript will enjoy some legal benefits, too. (➤*A Clause Providing for Author's Right to Revise the Manuscript Prior to Rejection, Page 148*)

A few publishers have begun to adopt clauses that significantly alter and expand their right to reject a manuscript on the basis of changes in the marketability and commercial appeal of the book between the time of signing a contract and the delivery of the manuscript. From a publisher's point of view, such clauses are ideal because the publisher enjoys the right to change its mind about publishing a book even if the author's work is soundly researched, well written and otherwise perfectly satisfactory. Authors, on the other hand, regard such clauses with well-justified horror and outrage. Essentially, a clause that permits the cancellation of a book because of changed market conditions turns the standard book contract into nothing more than an option—a fundamental and even revolutionary change in the basic structure of a book deal. (➤*A Clause Providing for Publisher's Right to Terminate Due to Changed Conditions, Page 154*)

## A CLAUSE PROVIDING FOR PUBLISHER'S UNQUALIFIED RIGHT TO REJECT THE MANUSCRIPT

**If Publisher, in its sole discretion, deems the Manuscript, Artwork, Frontmatter and/or Backmatter, Permissions and/ or any other materials delivered by Author under this Agreement to be unacceptable in form or substance, then Publisher shall have the right to terminate this Agreement without further obligation to the Author.**

*"If Publisher, in its sole discretion..."* Some book contracts permit the publisher to reject a manuscript when it is first submitted; some contracts permit the publisher to reject the manuscript only after the author has been given an opportunity to fix what the publisher finds unsatisfactory: but virtually all book contracts include a clause that permits the publisher to act *"in its sole discretion"* in rejecting the manuscript. In other words, the publisher is not ordinarily bound by an objective standard of what is and is not publishable in passing judgment on an author's work. However, the publisher that acts arbitrarily or capriciously in rejecting a manuscript—or who claims to reject a manuscript as unsatisfactory when, in fact, the publisher has simply changed its mind about publishing the author's work—may expose itself to a legal claim by the author. Reasonableness and good faith, according to the basic law of contracts, is expected of every publisher in exercising its discretion under a book contract.

*"...deems the Manuscript...and/or any other materials delivered by Author under this Agreement to be unacceptable in form or substance..."* Significantly, the sample clause does not establish any guidelines or criteria for rejection of the manuscript. The reason most often cited by publishers in rejecting a

book is: "I'm afraid you just haven't pulled it off," as more than one editor has said to more than one disappointed writer. Another frequently cited reason for rejection is that the manuscript is "not the book we bought" that is, the work as actually written by the author is substantially different from the work as promised in the original proposal. But the standard of acceptability in the sample clause (and in virtually all book contracts) is so broad and so general that almost any sense of dissatisfaction with the author's work on the part of the publisher will provide the legal grounds for declaring the work "unacceptable in form or substance."

However, the standard rejection clause does *not* permit the publisher to reject a book due to changed market conditions or other external factors. The flaws that justify rejection of a book as "unacceptable in form or substance" must be found within the manuscript itself or some other defect in the author's performance of his duties under the book contract. If the publisher wishes to reserve the right to cancel for other reasons, including changed market conditions, such grounds must be specified in the contract.

✍ **The Importance of a Well-Described Book**. The description of the author's work at the outset of a book contract often consists of only a few brief words or phrases and a word count, which raises the risk that the author and the publisher do not really share a common understanding of what the book is intended to be. That's why it is so important for the author's work to be described in some detail in the contract itself. Attaching the original book proposal as an exhibit, for example, is a good way to avoid a dispute between author and publisher over "the book we bought." (➤*Description of Book Project, Page 49; Description of the Work, Page 48*)

✍ **Designating a Formal Manuscript Delivery**. Authors will often submit chapters or other chunks of the manuscript as they write, a healthy form of creative collaboration and a good way for the author to find out if he is "on the right track" as he continues to work on the book. But it is often important to avoid confusion about what constitutes the final manuscript and when it is actually delivered, since delivery of the manuscript may trigger a payment by the publisher (➤*Advances, Page 104*) or set the starting date of a specified period for review and acceptance of the manuscript by the publisher. (➤ *Time Limits on Acceptance or Rejection, Page 151*) For this reason, the author should make it clear that a final and formal submission is being made with an appropriate cover letter, i.e., "I am now delivering the final manuscript in its entirety as described in Section __ of our contract."

*"...then Publisher shall have the right to terminate this Agreement without further obligation to the Author."* According to the sample clause, the delivery of an unsatisfactory manuscript (or other materials, including Artwork, Frontmatter and Backmatter, Permissions, etc.) entitles the publisher to simply terminate the contract *"without further obligation to the Author."* Thus, the publisher can walk away from the contract and the book project without any lingering legal duties toward the author. But the *author* may have some continuing obligations to the *publisher*, especially when an advance has been paid, and subsequent clauses will address the mechanics of termination, including the all-important issue of what happens to the advance and the rights granted by the author to the publisher. (➤ *Chapter 10: Cessation of Publication*)

📖 **The Danger of a Kind Word**. Publishers and their editors may find themselves in an awkward position when an author submits portions of a work in progress, whether informally or because the contract requires delivery in installments. The publisher, who wishes to encourage the author to keep working, may be tempted to utter a few words of praise as a morale booster. Yet the publisher's early encouragement may create a conflict later on if the completed manuscript is rejected. The publisher's attorney might recommend a formal reservation of rights in a comment letter (i.e., *"Nothing in this letter shall be deemed to constitute the acceptance of the manuscript by the publisher or a waiver of the publisher's right to reject the manuscript"*), but such brittle and off-putting phrases rarely find their way into informal correspondence, and rightly so! A better approach is to point out any problems in the partial manuscript, even if oblique language is used, and to add a few words to note that the formal manuscript has not yet been delivered and evaluated: *"Of course, we are looking forward to reading and commenting on the completed manuscript when it is finished and delivered in its entirety."*

## A CLAUSE PROVIDING FOR AUTHOR'S RIGHT
## TO REVISE THE MANUSCRIPT PRIOR TO REJECTION

If Publisher, in its sole discretion, deems the Manuscript, Artwork, Frontmatter and/or Backmatter, Permissions and/ or any other materials delivered by Author under this Agreement to be unacceptable in form or substance, then Publisher shall so advise Author by written notice, and Author shall have the opportunity to cure any defects and generally revise, correct, and/or supplement the Manuscript, Artwork, Frontmatter and/or Backmatter, Permissions and/or other materials to the satisfaction of Publisher, and deliver fully revised, corrected and/or supplemented Manuscript, Artwork, Frontmatter and/or Backmatter, Permissions and/or other materials no later than thirty (30) days after receipt of Publisher's notice ("the Final Delivery Date"). If such revised, corrected and/or supplemented materials are not delivered in a timely manner, or if they are deemed unsatisfactory in form or substance by Publisher, then Publisher shall have the unqualified right to terminate this Agreement without further obligation to Author.

Not every book contract entitles the publisher to flatly reject a manuscript on first submission and then promptly cancel the contract. The second sample clause illustrates a more generous and flexible approach to manuscript submissions, one that appears as a standard clause in some contracts and is almost always sought by authors and their agents in negotiations with publishers. Given the realities of the creative process, the inevitable differences of taste and style between authors and their publishers, and the notion that the law imposes at least some obligation on a publisher to act reasonably in rejecting a manuscript, the alternative approach is probably a preferable one for all publishers.

*"If Publisher, in its sole discretion, deems the Manuscript...to be unacceptable in form or substance, then Publisher shall so*

*advise Author by written notice..."* The sample clause sets up a two-step procedure for the rejection of a manuscript or other submissions and the termination of the book contract. If the publisher finds any of the materials submitted by the author to be unsatisfactory for any reason—e.g., the manuscript is poorly written, the artwork is poorly rendered, the author has failed to submit the frontmatter and backmatter required by the publisher, etc.—the publisher is obliged to *"so advise Author by written notice."* By implication, the written notice must give the author at least some idea of the problems that the publisher has detected in the author's work, since the clause goes on to give the author an opportunity to "cure" these defects. A *pro forma* letter of rejection is not enough to satisfy the publisher's duties under the sample clause, and the publisher ought to provide the author enough details and examples of what is wrong with the manuscript or other submissions to give him a reasonable and realistic opportunity to fix it.

*"...and Author shall have the opportunity to cure any defects and generally revise, correct and/or supplement the Manuscript, Artwork, Frontmatter and/or Backmatter, Permissions and/or other materials ..."* The author is given a second chance to satisfy his obligations under the contract, whether by revising the manuscript, providing a missing illustration or preface, obtaining formal permission for the use of a quoted passage from another work, or otherwise addressing the defects identified by the publisher. The sample clause implies that the publisher will have alerted the author to these problems, and it is now the author's obligation to address and resolve each of them by *"generally revis[ing], correct[ing] and/or supplement[ing]"* the materials that he has already delivered.

*"...to the satisfaction of Publisher..."* Of course, the sample clause makes it clear that the revisions, corrections, and additions to the author's work must be satisfactory to the publisher.

*"...and deliver fully revised, corrected and/or supplemented Manuscript, Artwork, Frontmatter and/or Backmatter, Permissions and/or other materials no later than thirty (30) days after receipt of Publisher's notice ("the Final Delivery Date")..."* A new deadline is established in the sample clause,

identified by the defined term "*Final Delivery Date*," and the author's right to cure the defects in the manuscript and other materials lasts only as long as the contract provides. Thirty days, of course, is probably long enough for only minor and cursory revisions, and the author may wish to negotiate for a significantly longer period. But *some* deadline is preferable from the publisher's point of view, since it prevents a book project from falling into limbo and provides a specific date at which the publisher enjoys the right to reject the author's work once and for all. Since the sample clause calculates the final delivery date from the "*receipt*" of the publisher's notice, the publisher should send the notice in some manner that confirms actual receipt, whether by messenger or some form of traceable mail. (➤ *Notices, Page 251*)

"*...If such revised, corrected and/or supplemented materials are not delivered in a timely manner...*" Once the publisher has fulfilled its duty to notify the author of the defects in the manuscript or other submissions, the burden shifts to the author to respond by revising and correcting his work—and the author must do so "*in a timely manner.*" If the revised and corrected submissions are not delivered according to the deadline in the contract, then the publisher will enjoy the right to reject the project and terminate the contract whether or not the revisions are otherwise acceptable.

"*...or if they are deemed unsatisfactory in form or substance by Publisher...*" Even if the revised and corrected submissions are delivered on time, the publisher still enjoys the right to reject the author's work if the new materials, too, are "*unsatisfactory in form or substance.*" Indeed, the publisher's right to reject is now "*unqualified*" that is, the publisher need not offer a detailed explanation for its decision and is free to simply declare the new submissions to be unacceptable.

"*...then Publisher shall have the unqualified right to terminate this Agreement without further obligation to Author.*" The author has no further right to revise the manuscript or other materials once the publisher has rejected the second submission. Now the publisher is free to terminate the book contract "*without further obligation to Author,*" although the author may have a few obligations to the publisher, especially if an advance has already been paid. (➤ *Chapter 10: Cessation of Publication*)

> ✍ **Time Limits on Acceptance or Rejection.** An author's work may fall into a kind of contractual black hole if no specific time limits are set for the publisher's acceptance or rejection of a completed manuscript or other submissions. Ideally, at least from the author's perspective, the contract will provide for *automatic* acceptance if the manuscript is not formally rejected within a specified time period, i.e., **"The manuscript and other submissions by Author under this Agreement shall be deemed accepted by the Publisher for all purposes unless rejected in writing within thirty (30) days after submission."**

## TERMINATION OF THE CONTRACT FOR DEFECTS IN DELIVERY

A typical book contract is subject to termination by author or publisher under various circumstances over the life of the contract. The first of these circumstances arises when the author delivers—or, in some cases, *fails* to deliver—the manuscript or other materials required under the contract. The publisher is generally entitled to terminate the contract if the author fails to deliver these materials on time or if the publisher is dissatisfied with what the author has delivered. The book contract will provide a mechanism for terminating the contract and a description of the specific legal and financial consequences of termination.

### TERMINATION FOR NONDELIVERY OR UNSATISFACTORY DELIVERY

If Author fails to deliver the Manuscript, Artwork, Frontmatter and/or Backmatter, Permissions, and/or other materials required under this Agreement, and/or any revisions and corrections thereof as requested by Publisher, on the dates designated by Publisher, or if Author fails to do so in a form and substance satisfactory to Publisher, then Publisher shall have the right to terminate this Agreement by so informing Author by letter sent by traceable mail to the address of Author set forth above. Upon termination by Publisher, Author shall, without prejudice to any other right or remedy of Publisher, immediately repay Publisher any sums previously paid to Author, and upon such repayment, all rights granted to Publisher under this Agreement shall revert to Author.

*"If Author fails to deliver the Manuscript...or other materials required under this Agreement..."* The sample clause contemplates and summarizes various defects in delivery of the author's work as required under the book contract, each of which entitles the publisher to terminate the contract. These defects include the failure of the author to deliver *"the Manuscript, Artwork, Frontmatter and/or Backmatter, Permissions and/or other materials required under this Agreement,"* the failure to deliver any of the foregoing materials *"on the dates designated by Publisher,"* the failure of the author to deliver *"any revisions and corrections...as requested by Publisher,"* and the failure to deliver any of the foregoing materials *"in a form and substance satisfactory to Publisher."* In other words, the clause applies to nondelivery, late delivery, or delivery of the author's work in unsatisfactory form or substance, and extends to both the initial submission of the author's work and, if applicable, any revised or corrected submissions by the author.

*"...then Publisher shall have the right to terminate this Agreement..."* Under any of the circumstances described above, the publisher has the fundamental right to terminate the book contract. The publisher, of course, is no longer required to publish the author's work, and owes no further legal or financial obligations of any kind to the author. However, as discussed below, the publisher must take certain formal steps to terminate the contract, and, even then, the author may owe some lingering obligations to the publisher.

*"...by so informing Author by letter sent by traceable mail to the address of Author set forth above..."* Under the sample clause, the contract remains in full force and effect unless and until proper notice of termination is given. The publisher is obliged to give notice of termination in a specified manner, i.e., *"by letter sent by traceable mail to the address of Author"*—the address is set forth in the introductory clauses of the book contract. (▶*Addresses, Birthdates, Citizenship, Etc., Page 48*) Not every contract

is quite so specific on the mechanics of termination, but it is always prudent for the publisher to give notice of termination in writing, and to convey the notice in a manner that confirms the fact that the author has actually received it. (➤*Notices, Page 251*)

"*...Upon termination by Publisher, Author shall... immediately repay Publisher any sums previously paid to Author...*" The formal termination of the contract obliges the author to "*immediately*" repay the advance or any other "*sums previously paid to Author,*" including any grants or expense allowances that the publisher may have provided to the author. (➤*Grants, Page 105*)

The obligation to repay the advance is always a crisis and sometimes a catastrophe for the author, especially if the advance was a generous one. As a practical matter, even the author who has not spent a penny of the advance on himself will not have the entire advance on hand; a portion of the advance has already been paid to the author's literary agent (➤*Agency, Page 203*), and an even bigger portion to the Internal Revenue Service. Even without a first proceeds clause, some publishers are willing to work out

**$ First Proceeds**. The obligation of an author to repay his advance to the publisher is sometimes softened by a so-called "first proceeds" clause, which allows the author to seek another publisher for his work and then repay the first publisher's advance out of the "first proceeds" paid to him by his new publisher, i.e., "**Upon termination of this Agreement by Publisher, Author shall repay Publisher any sums previously paid to Author out of the first proceeds of any sale or other disposition of rights to the Work.**" The most generous first proceeds clause will defer repayment for as long as it takes to resell the author's work, but the more typical clause sets a specific time limit on repayment out of first proceeds that is, if the author's work is not resold within a specific number of months or years, then the author is obliged to repay the advance out of his own resources, i.e., "**If the Work is not resold, and/or if the sums owing to Publisher are not repaid, within twelve (12) months after termination of this Agreement, then all such sums shall be payable in full by Author.**" As a technical matter, the rights to the author's work must revert to the author *prior* to repayment of the advance to the original publisher; otherwise, the author would not be entitled to resell the work.

payment terms or forego collection efforts for a limited period of time. But the obligation to repay the advance is legally enforceable and some publishers have resorted to the courts to collect what is owed to them.

*"...and upon such repayment, all rights granted to Publisher under this Agreement shall revert to Author."* Only when the advance is actually repaid will the rights to the author's work revert from the publisher to the author. Thus, the publisher continues to own and control the rights to the author's work even though it has been rejected, and the publisher's rights serve as a kind of lien to secure repayment of the advance. Once the advance is repaid, then the author once again owns the rights to his work and is free to resell them to another publisher. If, however, the author has succeeded in obtaining a "first proceeds" clause, then he is free to resell the work immediately and repay the advance out of the proceeds of the sale. (➤*First Proceeds, Page 153*)

## THE PUBLISHER'S RIGHT TO TERMINATE THE CONTRACT DUE TO CHANGED MARKET CONDITIONS

Here is something truly new in the publishing industry—an escape clause by which the publisher may cancel a contract for a book that is otherwise acceptable if the publisher decides not to publish the book because of a change in market conditions or circumstances that have nothing to do with the quality of the book itself. Only a few publishers are now using such termination clauses in their standard contracts, but it is so advantageous to the publisher that the sample clause (or something very much like it) is likely to be generally adopted and implemented in the publishing industry, although only over the protests of outraged authors!

The termination clause fundamentally changes the business structure and essential logic of a book deal. Once upon a time, the basic assumption of a book contract was that the author would invest his resources in the writing of a book, the publisher would invest its resources in publishing the book, and the shared goal of the two parties was putting the book on the bookstore shelf. Most authors and publishers, of course, still embrace these assumptions, and the contracts they sign oblige the publisher to publish the author's work if it is "acceptable in form and substance." By contrast, the sample clause permits the publisher to change its mind and back out of a book contract at any time if the deal is no longer quite so attractive as a business proposition.

The sample termination clause addresses a persistent problem that often presents itself when a book is rejected on the more conventional grounds that it is unacceptable in form or substance. The aggrieved author may argue that the publisher's supposed dissatisfaction with the author's work is merely a subterfuge, and the real reason for the rejection is that the publisher has simply changed its mind about publishing the book sometimes because of changed market conditions, other times because the acquiring editor has left the house and no one else wants to take over the project. On rare occasions, such arguments have ripened into lawsuits between authors and publishers, and the publisher is then forced to prove in court that it did not have an ulterior motive in rejecting the manuscript. So it is possible to conclude that a certain degree of courage and honesty is at work in a termination clause: the publisher is straightforwardly asserting the right to change its mind about a book, regardless of the quality of the author's work, and is warning the author in advance of its right to do so.

Authors, of course, regard such clauses with fear and loathing, and they will make every effort to remove them from the contracts in which they appear, sometimes successfully, more often not. Publishers that are vigilant enough to adopt such tough-minded clauses in the first place are unlikely to let them go in the course of negotiations. But the publisher that relies on the right to cancel a book contract due to changed market conditions must be careful to include at least some form of consideration—something of value promised or given by the publisher to the author—to compensate the author for the potential cancellation of the book deal, or else the entire contract may be regarded as "illusory" and thus unenforceable if challenged in court.

The sample clause is adapted from a contract form now in use by a major New York publisher. Although such termination clauses are still a rarity in the publishing industry—too rare to be called a standard clause—the likelihood is that publishers will come to rely on such clauses as a convenient way to extricate themselves from book deals long after the contract is signed.

## A CLAUSE PROVIDING FOR PUBLISHER'S RIGHT TO TERMINATE DUE TO CHANGED CONDITIONS

Publisher shall not be obligated to publish the Work, if, in its sole and absolute judgment, whether before or after acceptance of the Work, Publisher determines that supervening events or circumstances since the date of this Agreement have materially and adversely changed the economic expectations of the Publisher regarding the Work at the time of making this Agreement. Upon making such a determination, Publisher may terminate this Agreement without further obligation by notice in writing to Author, and Author may retain all payments previously made to Author under this Agreement.

*"Publisher shall not be obligated to publish the Work..."* Unlike the other clauses on rejection of the manuscript, the sample clause considered here is unrelated to the quality or timeliness of the author's work. Rather, the clause relieves the publisher of the legal obligation to publish the author's work at all, even if it is otherwise satisfactory in form and content. Thus, the sample clause establishes separate grounds for termination of a book project, and it may appear in conjunction with, *not* instead of, one of the other sample clauses on termination of a contract due to unacceptability of the manuscript or other submissions.

*"...if, in its sole and absolute judgment..."* The sample clause bestows upon the publisher alone the right to determine whether or not the book project is still economically viable. Although, as we have already noted, the law of contracts generally imposes an obligation on every contracting party to act in good faith, the publisher reserves almost unfettered discretion in making the crucial determination of whether or not the author's work is worth publishing, and no objective criteria or standards of reasonableness are imposed on the publisher.

*"...whether before or after acceptance of the Work..."* Since the publisher's right to terminate the contract due to changed market conditions is unrelated to the quality of the author's work, the publisher may exercise its right at any time, *"whether before or after acceptance of the Work."* Even if the manuscript has already been accepted, even if the advances have been paid, and even if the book is ready to go to press, the publisher still enjoys the right to cancel the book project and terminate the contract.

*"...Publisher determines that supervening events or circumstances since the date of this Agreement have materially and adversely changed the economic expectations of the Publisher regarding the Work at the time of making this Agreement..."* Technically, the publisher's right to terminate the contract *is* conditioned on a determination that certain events have taken place since the book contract was originally signed: the publisher must determine that *"supervening events or circumstances have materially and adversely changed the economic expectations of the Publisher."* Since the determination may be made by the publisher alone in its *"sole and absolute judgment,"* however, and since the publisher's *"economic expectations"* are largely subjective, the author who disagrees with the publisher's determination will be hard-pressed to argue otherwise.

As a general proposition, I have interpreted the words and phrases of the sample clause to refer primarily to changes in market conditions, but the language permits an even broader application of the publisher's right to terminate. Indeed, the *"events or circumstances"* need not touch directly on the marketability of the book itself. Suppose, for example, the author falls ill and cannot participate in publicity for the book, or the cost of paper goes up, or the publisher merges with another publishing house with an existing title on the same subject as the author's work. All of these and many more *"events or circumstances"* might be cited by a publisher as grounds for a change in its own *"economic expectations."*

*"...Upon making such a determination, Publisher may terminate this Agreement without further obligation by notice in writing to Author..."* As a technical matter, the publisher is required to make a formal determination that a change of

circumstances has resulted in a change in its economic expectations, and the cautious publisher will put such a determination in the formal notice that is required to be given to the author under the sample clause, i.e., *"Having determined that supervening events or circumstances since the date of this Agreement have materially and adversely changed our economic expectations regarding the Work at the time of making this Agreement, we are hereby giving notice of termination of the Agreement as required by Section ___ of the Agreement."* Once these final technicalities have been completed, the contract has been terminated and the publisher has no *"further obligation"* to the author.
(➤ *Chapter 10: Cessation of Publication* )

*"...and Author may retain all payments previously made to Author under this Agreement."* The sample clause allows the author to keep *"all payments previously made to Author,"* which usually consist of the portions of the advance that have already been paid to the author at the time of termination. Thus, the advance is converted into a kind of "kill fee"—a commonplace in magazine publishing but an unusual feature in a book publishing contract—and the author is partially compensated for his efforts even though the contract itself is terminated.

Not every such cancellation clause includes the payment of a "kill fee" to the author, but the clause itself—and arguably the entire contract—may be rendered unenforceable if the publisher enjoys the unfettered right to cancel the contract without any obligation to the author, monetary or otherwise. Under the law of contracts, an agreement that does not impose any binding obligation on one party—here, it would be the publisher that is entitled to cancel the contract without any consequences—may be deemed an "illusory" contract and, under certain circumstances, will not be enforceable at all!

---

📖 **$ Consideration for the Cancellation Clause.** If the advance paid to the author was especially large, of course, the publisher is unlikely to allow the author to keep *all* of it. But, as noted above, the payment of some form of "kill fee" to the author upon exercise of the right to cancel the contract is a prudent legal precaution and arguably an essential one. Even if the publisher is unwilling to forego

---

repayment of the entire advance, the author should be allowed to retain at least some portion of the advance, i.e., "**...and Author may retain ___% of all payments previously made to Author under this Agreement.**" If no advance has been paid, then the publisher ought to pay *something* to the author on termination, i.e., "**...and Publisher shall pay Author a 'kill fee' of $____.**"

# 5

## PUBLICATION

Once the author has delivered the manuscript of her work, the typical book contract reserves to the publisher alone the right to make virtually all decisions about the time and manner of publication, ranging from the selection of the title to the specification of paper stock. The author is required to read "proofs" of the work before it is actually published, and permitted to correct typographical errors, but the legal right of the author to participate in the preparation of her manuscript for publication often begins and ends there. Any greater role must be secured in the course of negotiations and written into the publisher's standard contract, and if no greater role for the author is agreed upon, then the typical contract reserves to the publisher both the right and the responsibility to turn the manuscript into a finished book.

## TIME AND MANNER OF PUBLICATION
### EDITING AND PUBLICATION FORMAT

Publisher shall have the right to edit and revise the Work for any and all uses contemplated under this Agreement, provided that the meaning of the Work is not materially altered, and shall have the right to make any changes in the Work as advised by Publisher's counsel. Publisher shall have the right to manufacture, distribute, advertise, promote, and publish the Work in a style and manner which Publisher deems appropriate, including typesetting, paper, printing, binding, cover and/or jacket design, imprint, title, and price. Notwithstanding any editorial changes or revisions by Publisher,

Author's warranties and indemnities under this Agreement shall remain in full force and effect.

*"Publisher shall have the right to edit and revise the Work for any and all uses contemplated under this Agreement..."* A fundamental legal right of the publisher—and one of the essential functions of a publisher—is the preparation of the author's work for publication, including *"edit[ing] and revis[ing] the Work,"* not only for the initial release of in book form but also for *"any and all uses contemplated under this Agreement."* As we shall see, the publisher's right to make decisions about the details of publication are expansive, ranging from the title of the work to the paper stock on which it is printed, and the author who wishes to participate in such decisions must bargain for the right to do so.

**Author's Rights of Consultation and Approval.** Authors will often demand—and sometimes succeed in obtaining—a greater role in the publishing process than the publisher's standard contract allows. A publisher is more likely to grant the author a right of *consultation*—that is, the right to review and comment upon the publisher's decisions on the details of publication—than a right of *approval*, which arguably bestows upon the author a veto over some or all of the publisher's decisions. And a publisher is more likely to give the author a say in a few specific decisions—title and the cover design are the best examples— than a general right of consultation or approval on *all* particulars of publication. Since few standard contracts afford the author *any* role in such matters, it is important to modify the contract to reflect any agreement the author and publisher may reach in the course of negotiation, i.e., **"Publisher agrees that Author shall have the right to review and approve or disapprove the title of the Work, and Author shall be reasonably consulted on cover design of the Work in book form."**

✍ **Editor Clause.** Some authors, if only a precious few with the greatest clout, are able to secure what is known as an "editor clause," a clause in the book contract that designates a particular individual as the editor of the author's work and permits the author to terminate the contract if the editor leaves the publishing house. Since a loyal and committed editor can be the author's greatest ally and champion in the internal politics of a publishing house, the departure of an editor is sometimes said to leave an author and her work "orphaned." Indeed, a book may be at risk of cancellation if the editor who first acquired it is no longer there to argue for its merits. But an editor's clause is a rare concession, and only the most valued authors will succeed in tying themselves to an editor of choice.

✍ **Specialized Editorial Resources**. Some books require specialized resources that the publisher is unable to provide with its own staff and facilities. One author of my acquaintance, for example, insisted on a copy editor with a specialized background in the subject matter of hers book. None of the editors on staff at the publishing house were suitable, and so the publisher agreed to hire a freelance copy editor with the requisite skills—but only if the author agreed to pay half the cost of the specialist editor! Any such arrangements ought be confirmed in writing, whether in the contract, a rider to the contract, or a side letter signed before or concurrently with the contract.

*"...provided that the meaning of the Work is not materially altered..."* The only stated limitation on the publisher's right to edit and revise the author's work in the sample clause is a vague assurance that the *"meaning of the work"* will not be *"materially altered,"* a standard that imposes very little restraint on the publisher and bestows very little protection on the author. After all, much of the author's *expression* might be cut or changed by an assertive text editor before the *meaning* of the book is *"materially altered."* Although most publishers tend to be deferential to the author in making editorial changes in the author's work— and very few publishers would have the courage or the *chutzpah* to publish a book under the author's name but against the author's will—the fact remains that the contract bestows upon the publisher great discretion in making such decisions.

✍ **Approval of Changes in Text**. Since the choice of words and phrases that appear in a book is the author's most urgent and legitimate concern, the author may wish to bargain for a more restrictive approach to the publisher's right to edit, i.e., **"No changes shall be made in the text of the manuscript except for routine copyediting and correction of grammar and spelling without the author's prior**

**written consent.**" Even if the publisher is unwilling to grant the author any greater role in the making decisions about the author's work (►*Author's Rights of Consultation and Approval, Page 161*), a limited right of approval on changes in the text is more likely to be regarded by the publisher as an acceptable compromise.

---

📖 **Cancellation for Noncooperation of the Author.** If the publisher agrees to grant the author the right to approve the final text of the author's work, and the author refuses to approve a change recommended by the publisher's attorney, then the publisher should reserve the right to terminate the contract rather than publish a book that poses a legal risk. Thus, if the contract is modified to provide for manuscript approval by the author, the following phrase should be used: "**If Author declines to make a change in the Work as advised by Publisher's counsel, then Publisher shall have the right to terminate this Agreement without further obligation to Author according to procedures provided elsewhere in this Agreement for termination by Publisher prior to publication.**" The reference to "*procedures provided elsewhere in this Agreement*" refers to the clause that allows the publisher to terminate the contract and demand repayment of the advance. (►*Chapter 10: Cessation of Publication*)

---

"*...and shall have the right to make any changes in the Work as advised by Publisher's counsel...*" Not every publisher routinely submits the author's work to its attorneys for the process of legal review called "vetting," but if the publisher elects to do so, the sample clause confirms the publisher's right "*to make any changes in the Work as advised by Publisher's counsel.*" Arguably, the publisher already enjoys the right to make such changes under the sample clause, which entitles the publisher to generally "*edit and revise*" the author's work, but the clause can be read to indicate that changes on the advice of counsel may be made whether or not they alter the meaning of the work. (►*Review by Publisher's Counsel, Page 165*)

"*Publisher shall have the right to manufacture, distribute, advertise, promote, and publish the Work in a style and manner which Publisher deems appropriate, including typesetting, paper, printing, binding, cover and/or jacket design, imprint, title, and price...*" All of the particulars of publication are re-served to the discretion of the publisher in a standard book con-tract, ranging from the physical specifications of the book—size and configuration, paper stock and typography, kind and qual-ity of binding—to the title, cover design, imprint, and suggested retail price, to the marketing efforts that may determine whether the book is a success. Marketing decisions reserved to the pub-lisher include the size and placement of the author's book in the publisher's catalog, how many review copies will be sent out, whether or not there will be an author tour, and how much money, if any, will be spent on advertising. Inevitably, some books on the publisher's list will be in greater favor than others at the time of publication, and the decision of where to put the resources will be made by the publisher alone, under the sample clause and most book contracts. Any role for the author in mak-ing such decisions—and any commitment by the publisher to adopt a particular title, format, or marketing effort—must be negotiated and added to the contract.

---

✍️ **Publisher's Commitment to Imprint, Format, and Other Par-ticulars**. A publisher will often give informal assurances or even make promises to the author about the particulars of publication in the course of negotiations. For example, if the book contract is a "hard-soft" deal, the publisher may agree that the first edition of the author's work will be a hardcover book. If the publisher issues books under several different imprints, the publisher may agree that the book will be published under a particular imprint. And the publisher may prom-ise to pay for an author tour or advertisements for the author's book. Any such assurances ought to be put into writing, either as a modifi-cation of the standard contract or, as some publishers prefer, in a side letter that is signed before or concurrently with the contract itself. (➤*Entire Agreement, Page 247*)

---

"*...Notwithstanding any editorial changes or revisions by Publisher, Author's warranties and indemnities under this Agreement shall remain in full force and effect.*" Under the typical book contract, the author gives a series of formal assur-ances to the publisher—"*warranties and indemnities*"—that the author's work will not expose the publisher to a lawsuit for copyright infringement, defamation, invasion of privacy, or other legal claims. (➤*Author's Representations and Warranties, Page 207; Author's Indemnity of Publisher, Page 213*) The sample clause specifies that these assurances apply not only to the author's work as originally submitted in its unedited form but also to the fully edited and revised version of the manuscript. Thus, the clause imposes liability on the author for additions, deletions, and changes that the publisher may make in the author's work during the editing process, and the publisher is entitled to rely on the author for the legal sufficiency of the work in its final version.

---

✍ **Excluding Publisher's Changes from Author's Indemnity.** Since the author may not enjoy the right to determine the final form of her work—and, as a practical matter, some of the publisher's changes may go unnoticed during the hectic process of reading proofs of the author's work—the author might reasonably object to taking legal responsibility for material that the publisher inserts into her work in the process of editing, revising, and illustrating the book. For that reason, many publishers are willing to exclude such additional material from the scope of the warranties and indemnities by adding a phrase to the sample clause: "*Author's warranties and indemnities shall remain in full force and effect* except as to new matter inserted in the Work by Publisher without the Author's prior written approval.*" Under the sample clause as modified, the publisher would not enjoy the benefit of the author's warranties and indemnities as to changes in the original text unless it took the trouble of showing the new material to the author and asking her to "sign off" on the changes.

---

### REVIEW BY PUBLISHER'S COUNSEL

Notwithstanding any other provision of this Agreement, Publisher shall have the right, but not the obligation, to submit the Work for review by counsel of its choice to determine if the Work contains material which is or may be unlawful, violates the rights of third parties, or violates the promises, warranties, and representations of Author set forth in this Agreement.

1. Publisher shall not be obligated to publish the Work if, in the sole opinion of Publisher or its counsel, there appears to be a risk of legal action or liability on account of any aspect of the Work.

2. If, in the sole opinion of Publisher or its counsel, the Work is determined to require additions, deletions, modifications, substantiation of facts, or other changes to avoid the risk of legal action or liability, then Author shall make all such changes at the direction of Publisher or its counsel.

3. If Author declines to make such changes, or if Publisher deems the changes made by Author to be insufficient, or if Publisher or its counsel shall deem that such changes will not eliminate the risk of legal action or liability, then Publisher shall have the right to terminate this Agreement without further obligation, and Author shall be obligated to repay all amounts advanced by Publisher. Upon such repayment by Author, all rights granted to Publisher shall revert to Author.

4. Nothing contained in this Agreement shall be deemed to impose on Publisher any obligation to review or verify the contents of the Work, or to affect in any way the promises, warranties, and representations of Author and/or the duty of indemnification of Author, all of which shall continue to apply to the Work, whether or not the Work is changed at the request of Publisher or Publisher's counsel.

Even though the publisher already enjoys the fundamental right to make changes in the author's work as recommended by its counsel under an earlier clause of the model book contract (➤ *Editing and Publication Format, Page 160*), some contracts also include a more elaborate clause on the same subject of "vetting," a term that refers to the process of reviewing a manuscript to identify and eliminate any potential legal risks. The sample clause goes into considerable detail in describing the rationale and results of a legal review of the manuscript, but some publishers rely on their general right to edit and revise in place of such a clause.

*"...Publisher shall have the right, but not the obligation, to submit the Work for review by counsel of its choice..."* Nothing in a standard publishing contract *prevents* the publisher from submitting the author's work to its attorneys, but the sample clause makes it explicit that the publisher enjoys the right to do so. The purposes of vetting a manuscript, as the clause suggests, is to *"determine if the Work contains material which is or may be unlawful, violates the rights of third parties, or violate the promises, warranties and representations of Author set forth in this Agreement."* The *"warranties and representations,"* which include sweeping assurances by the author that the work is free of legal defects, is the subject of a separate clause in the typical book contract. (▶ *Author's Representations and Warranties, Page 207*) Of course, the sample clause carefully notes that the publisher is not *obliged* to vet the manuscript, and the decision of whether or not to vet is reserved to the publisher alone.

---

✍ **Publisher's Obligation to "Vet" the Manuscript.** Since the author is the ultimate guarantor of her work under the customary warranties, representations, and indemnities that appear in every book contract, it is very much in the author's interest for her manuscript to be properly vetted in advance of publication, especially if the publisher is paying an attorney to do so, if only to find out in advance what changes ought to be made to reduce the risk of a lawsuit. Thus, the author may wish to ask the publisher to commit to vet the manuscript at its expense. But not every publisher is willing to bear the cost, and some publishers or their insurers, when faced with what appears to be a risky or provocative manuscript, may require the author to obtain a legal opinion at her own expense!

---

*"...Publisher shall not be obligated to publish the Work if, in the sole opinion of Publisher or its counsel, there appears to be a risk of legal action or liability..."* Whether or not the manuscript is actually vetted, the sample clause empowers the publisher to cancel the project if *"there appears to be a risk of legal action or liability"*—a standard that bestows a considerable

degree of discretion on the publisher. As we have already noted, however, the broad discretion already enjoyed by the publisher under other clauses of the contract is probably enough to justify the publisher's refusal to publish a legally questionable work.

> ✍ **Limits on Cancellation Due to Legal Concerns**. If the author is concerned that the publisher will rely on feigned legal concerns as an excuse to cancel the book, the author may wish to seek a modification of the sample clause in order to *require* an opinion of the publisher's counsel before the book deal may be canceled.

*"...If...the Work is determined to require additions, deletions...or other changes to avoid the risk of legal action or liability, then Author shall make all such changes at the direction of Publisher or its counsel."* The publisher already enjoys the right to generally edit and revise the manuscript, as noted above, but the sample clause makes explicit the publisher's right to direct the author to do so in order to eliminate a legal risk. Essentially, the sample clause bestows upon the publisher the right to choose between canceling the publication of the book, or directing the author to make changes as a condition to publication.

*"...If Author declines to make such changes...then Publisher shall have the right to terminate this Agreement without further obligation..."* The sample clause addresses a circumstance in which the author *declines* to make the changes recommended by the publisher's counsel. Strictly speaking, such a circumstance would not arise under the sample clause that broadly empowers the publisher to "edit and revise" the author's work, since the author is not given an opportunity to agree or disagree with such editorial changes. (➤ *Editing and Publication Format, Page 160*) But the publisher would probably *not* publish a book against the author's wishes, even if legally entitled to do so, and the sample clause addresses precisely such a predicament. The sample clause also addresses the possibility that the author will attempt to comply with the changes recommended by the publisher or its attorney, but the changes will be deemed *"insufficient...[to]...eliminate the risk of legal action or liability."* Under any of these circumstances, the sample clause permits the publisher to formally *"terminate this Agreement without further obligation,"* and the author is then

obliged to repay the advance, if any. Only then will "*all rights granted to Publisher...revert to Author.*"

"*...Nothing contained in this Agreement shall be deemed to impose on Publisher any obligation to review or verify the contents of the Work, or to affect in any way the promises, warranties, and representations of Author and/or the duty of indemnification...*" The sample clause carefully notes that the publisher is not *obliged* to submit the manuscript to legal review, and even if the manuscript is vetted and all recommended changes are made, the author remains fully liable to the publisher for the legal sufficiency of hers work under the warranties, representations and indemnities set forth elsewhere in the contract. (➤*Author's Representations and Warranties, Page 207; Author's Indemnity of Publisher, Page 213*) The vetting of the manuscript is always in the best interests of the author and publisher alike, if only because it reduces the risk of a lawsuit. However, if such a claim is made, the author is still obligated to indemnify and defend the publisher.

### PROOFS

Publisher shall furnish Author with a proof of the Work. Author agrees to read, correct, and return all pare proofs within seven (7) calendar days after receipt thereof. If any changes in the page proofs or the printing plates (other than corrections of printer's errors) are made at Author's request or with Author's consent, then the cost of such changes in excess of 5% of the cost of typesetting (exclusive of the cost of setting corrections) shall be paid by Author. If Author fails to return the corrected page proofs within the time set forth above, Publisher may publish the Work without Authors approval of the page proofs.

Even if the contract reserves all particulars of publication to the publisher alone, the standard book contract almost invariably allows the author one last look at her work before the book goes to press—the right to read and correct the "galley proofs" or "page proofs" of the book. Not so long ago, galleys and page proofs were imprints of the lead type with which a book was printed; galleys referred to columns of type not yet set in page form, and page proofs referred to the designed pages. Both terms are still found in various contracts, but nowadays proofs usually take the form of computer-generated printouts of the typeset and designed pages of the book. Proofs are used for final editing changes and for corrections of typographical and printer's errors. Then and now, uncorrected proofs are sometimes bound and circulated to book reviewers in advance of publication, but once the final corrections are made, the author will usually not see her work again until she holds a copy of the finished book in her hands.

*"Publisher shall furnish Author with a proof of the Work..."* The publisher is required to provide the author with proofs prior to publication, and unless the contract provides for some greater role in the preparation of the author's work for publication, the reading and correction of proofs may be the *only* opportunity for the author to see what has become of her work in the hands of the publisher, after the revised and edited manuscript is delivered. Thus, the proofreading clause is not merely a logistical matter—proofreading should be regarded as a fundamental right of the author—but as the crucial last step before publication.

*"...Author agrees to read, correct, and return all page proofs within seven (7) calendar days after receipt thereof..."* Since proofreading generally comes late in the production process, the publisher will prefer a short turn-around time for reading, correcting, and returning proofs. Seven days, as set forth in the sample clause, is an especially urgent deadline, but the period allowed for proofreading in the typical contract is rarely much longer. The author, of course, almost always prefers a more leisurely pace for poring over proofs, and some publishers are willing to give the author more time to do so, but a period as long as 30 days would be highly unusual.

*"...If any changes in the page proofs or the printing plates (other than corrections of printer's errors) are made at Author's request or with Author's consent, then the cost of such changes... shall be paid by Author..."* One reason why publishers insist on quick turn-around of proofs is that they are fearful of the universal tendency of authors to polish and fine-tune their work

down to the very last minute, a process known in publishing as "rewriting on proofs." Since it is time-consuming and expensive to make text changes once the book is already set in the form of designed pages, and since any such changes may delay the publication date, the publisher typically discourages the author from rewriting on proofs by charging for the privilege of doing so. That is why the sample clause requires the author to pay for the cost of *"any changes in the page proofs or the printing plates"* which are *"made at Author's request or with Author's consent."* The sample clause sets forth a formula for charging the author for the cost of making such changes: the author need not pay for correction of typographical errors, here called *"printer's errors,"* or for a limited number of purely stylistic changes, but otherwise the author pays for changes in proofs that exceed *"5% of the cost of typesetting."*

*"...If Author fails to return the corrected proof sheets within the time set forth above, Publisher may publish the Work without Author's approval of the page proofs."* A fail-safe mechanism is provided in the sample clause to protect the publisher against the author who is neglectful of her duty to read proofs or simply cannot stop rewriting on proofs: if the author does not return the corrected proofs by the time allowed in the contract, *"Publisher may publish the Work without Author's approval of the page proofs."* Thus, the tardy author takes the risk that her work will appear in print without the changes and corrections that the contract otherwise empowers her to make.

---

✍ **Review of Cover and Other Graphic Elements**. Proofs usually consist of the text of the book. Artwork, if it appears at all on the proof sheets, may be reproduced in the form of blurry photocopies. For that reason, if the book will include illustrations and other graphic material, the author should seek to modify the proofreading clause to make it clear that she is entitled to read and correct not only text but also artwork, maps, charts, and other graphic material. Moreover, the proofs rarely include the *cover* of the book, and if the author has bargained for the right to consult upon or approve the cover design, the proofreading clause should be modified to include these elements, too.

---

## TIME OF PUBLICATION

Publisher agrees that the Work, if published, shall be published within twenty-four (24) months of the Final Delivery Date, except as the date of publication may be extended by forces beyond Publisher's control. The date of publication as designated by Publisher, but not later than the date of first delivery of bound volumes, shall be the "Publication Date" for all purposes under this Agreement.

*"Publisher agrees that the Work...shall be published within twenty-four (24) months of the Final Delivery Date..."* Among the strategic decisions reserved to the publisher in a standard book contract is the fundamental issue of *when* the book will actually be published. Rarely will the publisher commit to a specific publication date; rather, as the sample clause illustrates, the publisher will allow itself a period of time, sometimes quite lengthy, within which to publish the author's work. Few publishers will agree to a period shorter than one year or seek a period longer than two years, but the time of publication is often the subject of vigorous negotiation between an author and publisher. "Final Delivery Date," which starts the clock on the period within which the book is to be published, is a defined term and refers to a specific date that is established elsewhere in the contract. (➤*A Clause Providing for Author's Right to Revise the Manuscript Prior to Rejection, Page 148*)

---

✍ **Fixing the Time of Publication.** Under rare circumstances, it may be in the interest of both author and publisher to fix the time of publication with greater certainty. For example, if the book is intended to coincide with a specific event—the Olympics, a presidential election, the anniversary of the birth or death or a famous figure, and so on—the contract ought to be modified to oblige both author and publisher to meet deadlines that will enable the book to be published on time. However, if such deadlines are written into the contract, the publisher will probably insist on the right to cancel the book deal if the author fails to meet *her* deadlines.

---

*"...if published..."* The time-of-publication clause does not unconditionally obligate the publisher to actually publish the

author's work. For example, the date of publication may be *"extended by forces beyond Publisher's control,"* a phrase which is generally understood to include "acts of God"—earthquakes, floods, hurricanes, etc.—or riots and strikes that make it impossible for the publisher to meet the publication deadline. (➤*Force Majeure, Page 251*) And, as the sample clause notes, if only obliquely, the publisher enjoys the right to cancel the publication of the book under circumstances specified elsewhere in the contract. (➤*The Publisher's Right to Reject the Manuscript, Page 144; Force Majeure, Page 251*),

*"...The date of publication...[shall be]...not later than the date of first delivery of bound volumes..."* The sample clause bestows upon the publisher the right to designate a particular date as the *"Publication Date,"* and thereafter the date will be used *"for all purposes under this Agreement."* For example, if a portion of the advance is payable "on publication," the payment will be due on the designated publication date. (➤*Advances, Page 104*) However, the discretion of the publisher is not unlimited, and the designated publication date may not be *"later than the date of first delivery of bound volumes,"* a functional definition that is often used in the publishing industry to indicate the publication date.

> ✍ **Penalty for Failure to Publish**. The sample clause, and similar clauses in most book contracts, are pointedly silent on what actually happens if the publisher fails to publish within the permitted time. As a technical matter, the publisher will be in breach of the contract—and the author will be entitled to sue for damages—but the cautious and practical author will seek a more specific definition of her rights and remedies, i.e., **"Without limiting any other remedy of Author at law or equity, if Publisher fails to publish the Work within the time allowed, then all rights in and to the Work shall revert to Author, wholly and automatically, and Author shall be entitled to retain any and all advances and other amounts paid to date."** Few publishers, however, will be quick to agree to such a straightforward provision, and some publishers actually prefer the ambiguity of the sample clause when it comes to the consequences of non-publication.

# $

## AUTHOR'S COPIES

Publisher shall provide Author with ten (10) copies, free of charge, of each edition of the Work published by Publisher. Author shall be permitted to purchase additional copies of the Work, at the normal dealer discount, to be paid upon receipt of Publisher's invoice, for Author's personal use and not for resale.

Among the most frequently negotiated clauses in any book deal is the one that allocates a few copies of the book to its author. Authors, of course, want as many as they can get, but publishers tend to be conservative when it comes to handing out free copies. Only a modest amount of money is at stake here, but I have characterized the sample clause as a "deal point" precisely because it attracts such fervent attention from the typical author!

*"Publisher shall provide Author with ten (10) copies, free of charge..."* A standard book contract will almost always provide for at least some free copies of the author's work for the author herself, although the number of copies varies from deal to deal and from publisher to publisher. Five or ten copies are not unusual, and it is rare that a significant number of copies is given to the author free of charge.

---

✍ **Complimentary Copies.** One way for the author to conserve her supply of free copies is to ask the publisher to send out a specified number of complimentary copies to individuals designated by the author. Of course, the publisher will send review copies on its own initiative, but it may be willing to send free copies to "opinion-makers," columnists, celebrities, and other individuals designated by the author. Any such concession should be added to the contract or embodied in a rider or a side letter agreement.

---

*"...of each edition of the Work published by Publisher..."* The sample clause entitles the author to free copies of not only the first edition but *every* edition issued by the publisher, including a paperback edition or a revised edition of the book. Some

contracts are not quite so generous, and limit the free copies to the first edition only. Other contracts are even more generous, and oblige the publisher to require a third-party licensee such as a paperback or audio publisher to give free copes of their editions to the author.

"*...Author shall be permitted to purchase additional copies of the Work...*" The author is almost always permitted to *buy* as many additional copies as she wants from the publisher, usually at some wholesale discount such as the one designated in the sample clause, i.e., "*at the normal dealer discount.*" But, as noted below, the terms on which such copies may be purchased and the purposes for which the copies may be used may vary from contract to contract.

"*...to be paid upon receipt of Publisher's invoice...*" The sample clause requires payment for the purchase of additional copies "*upon receipt of Publisher's invoice,*" which may put an uncomfortable financial burden on some impecunious authors. Other contracts permit payment within a specified number of days after receipt of invoice—30, 60 or even 90 days are not uncommon. The most generous publishers agree to debit the cost of such copies against the author's account and deduct the cost from earned royalties (➤*Accounting, Page 193*), but that's a rare accommodation, especially if no limit is placed on the number of copies that the author may purchase.

---

✍ **Author Sales at Favorable Discounts**. "*Normal dealer discount*" varies from publisher to publisher, but 40% off the suggested retail price is regarded as a standard wholesale discount for trade books. Some wholesale transactions, however, are based on much deeper discounts, and the author may seek "the best available wholesale discount" for her own purchases. Publishers, on the other hand, are likely to insist that the author comply with the standard terms of sale in order to qualify for the deepest discounts, since the most favorable terms are usually offered only to purchasers who buy bulk on a nonreturnable basis.

---

"*...for Author's personal use and not for resale.*" The sample clause allows the author to keep or give away the copies that she purchases from the publisher, but no resale by the author is permitted. The rationale for such restrictions, which are not uncommon in book contracts, is that the publisher does not want go into competition with the author who seeks to sell books to the publisher's wholesale accounts or who diverts retail sales by making direct sales to the consumers.

---

✍ **Author's Right of Resale.** The customary restrictions on resale are especially threatening to those authors who enjoy the opportunity to sell their own books. Consultants, lecturers, and performers can make a significant amount of money by purchasing their books at wholesale and reselling them at the suggested retail price at the venues where they appear. Such authors may wish to negotiate for at least a limited right of resale, and publishers are inclined to agree to allow authors to sell copies in certain specified channels and settings, i.e., "outside the conventional channels of distribution in the book trade," or "at personal appearances of the Author" or "by direct marketing by the Author."

✍ **Royalties on Author's Copies.** Many book contracts provide that no royalties are payable on copies sold to the author, a restriction that makes little sense from an accounting point of view. The publisher, after all, receives precisely the same wholesale income whether a copy is sold to a retail bookstore or the author herself, and there is no sound reason why the author should not receive the agreed-upon royalty on both transactions. The vigilant author may seek to delete such a restriction on royalties if it appears in a book contract, whether on limited categories of sale to the author or on all sales to the author. Still, even if no royalty is paid, the author who buys her own books from the publisher at a 40% wholesale discount and resells them to the public at the cover price makes more money on the spread than even the most generous royalty!

---

## MARKETING AND PROMOTION

### $

### ADVERTISING AND PROMOTION

Publisher shall have the right to determine the time, place, method, and manner of advertising, promotion, and other exploitation of the Work, except as Author and Publisher may set forth in a writing signed by both parties.

Among the most fundamental and crucial decisions that are customarily reserved to the publisher alone in a typical book contract are all aspects of *"advertising, promotion, and other exploitation of the Work,"* including all particulars of *"time, place, method, and manner"* of marketing the book. These are decisive factors that may determine whether the author's work soars, or sinks like a stone, but the typical book contract is either completely silent on the subject or else, as in the sample clause, explicitly excludes the author from any role in advertising and promotion of her book.

Of course, much is often said in the course of negotiations between author and publisher about the marketing resources that the publisher intends to put behind the book, but the typical book contract specifically rules out any promise or understanding that does not actually appear in the contract itself. (➤*Entire Agreement, Page 247*) The sample clause warns the author that none of the marketing plans that may have been mentioned during negotiations are binding on the publisher *"except as Author and Publisher may set forth in a writing signed by both parties."* Thus, if the author has been led to expect any particular marketing efforts—an author tour, an advertising budget, the hiring of a freelance publicist, a specific number of review copies, and so on—the commitments must be put into the contract, a rider to the contract, or a side letter agreement if they are to be binding on the publisher, each of which should be *"signed by both parties."*

> 📖 **Author Availability for Promotion.** Most publishers are reluctant to specify what marketing efforts they are willing to undertake in support of a newly published book, but a publisher may ask the author to guarantee her availability at the publisher's request, i.e., **"In publisher's sole discretion and upon publisher's request, Author shall make herself available and participate in a publicity tour of no less than two weeks in duration at such time(s), date(s) and place(s) as Publisher may designate."** Unless the contract otherwise specifies, the expense of the author tour is chargeable to the publisher, but the contract should reflect whether some other arrangement has been agreed upon.

## USE OF AUTHOR'S NAME AND LIKENESS

**Publisher shall have the right to use, and to license others to use, Author's name, image, likeness, and biographical material for advertising, promotion, and other exploitation of the Work and the other rights granted under this Agreement.**

The publisher's right to use the author's name to market the author's work is so fundamental that it goes unspoken in many book contracts, but the sample clause expressly grants to the publisher *"Author's name, image, likeness, and biographical material,"* not only *"for advertising, promotion, and other exploitation of the Work,"* but also for exploitation of *"the other rights granted under this Agreement,"* whether by the publisher itself or by third parties to whom the publisher may license rights under the contract. The sample clause is increasingly popular among publishers and their attorneys because of the heightened awareness of the so-called "right of publicity"—that is, the right of an individual to control how her name, image and likeness are used in advertising and merchandising. (See *Kirsch's Handbook, Chapter 5: Preparing the Manuscript*)

---

✍ **Approvals of Name, Image, and Likeness**. The author, of course, cannot reasonably object to the use of her name and likeness, although many authors seek to the right to approve the materials to be used by the publisher, i.e., *"...Author's* approved *name, image, likeness, and biographical material..."* Approval rights are especially crucial if the author is using a pseudonym, and the contract should be modified to specify exactly what byline and biographical information should be used in connection with the author's work. (➤ *Title and Series Rights, Page 231*) The cautious publisher, however, will wish to confirm that photographs, biographical data, and other material actually provided by the author is deemed to have been approved for use!

---

## REVISED EDITIONS

The obligation of the author does not always end on publication of the book itself. Under many book contracts, especially those for nonfiction books, the author is required to keep the book up to date so that the publisher may issue new and revised editions. A novel, of course, or a work of topical nonfiction, is unlikely to be revised even if it is reissued in a different format at some point in the future. However, self-help books, reference works, textbooks, professional, and scientific manuals, and a wide range of general nonfiction, are routinely kept in print indefinitely—and are sold more than once to the same book buyer—as new and revised editions are issued.

## REVISIONS

Author agrees to revise the Work as Publisher may deem appropriate during the effective term of this Agreement. The provisions of this Agreement shall apply to each revision of the Work by Author, which shall be considered a separate work, except that the manuscript of each such revision shall be delivered to Publisher within a reasonable time after Publisher's request for such revision.

1. If Author fails to provide the manuscript of a revision of the Work which is acceptable to Publisher, or should the Author be deceased, then Publisher shall have the right, but not the obligation, to make such revisions, or engage a skilled person to make such revisions, and Author shall reimburse Publisher for all its actual costs of making such revisions.

2. If Publisher engages one or more persons to make such revisions, then Publisher, in its sole discretion, may afford appropriate credit (including authorship or co-authorship credit) to such person(s).

*"Author agrees to revise the Work as Publisher may deem appropriate during the effective term of this Agreement..."* The basic obligation of the author to revise her work under the sample contract remains in effect *"during the effective term of this Agreement,"* a period that might, under certain circumstances, extend past the death of the author. And, since the work must be revised *"as Publisher may deem appropriate,"* it is the publisher that determines how often and how many times the work is to be revised.

*"...The provisions of this Agreement shall apply to each revision of the Work by Author..."* No new contract is required for the publisher to issue a revised edition of the author's work, and the same basic provisions of the original contract will apply to each new edition—the grant of rights, the royalties rates, the territory, and so on. The only provision of the original contract that is deemed to have changed is the manuscript delivery date, which is vaguely defined as *"a reasonable time after Publisher's request for such revision."* Thus, as a practical matter, the actual delivery date is left to the mutual agreement of the author and publisher. And, since each revision *"shall be considered a separate work,"* a new term of copyright protection will begin on publication of the revised work, any escalating royalty rate will be reset to the starting rate, and the rate will escalate according to the sales of the latest edition. (➤*A Clause for Escalating Royalties Based on Retail Price, Page 115*)

> ✍ **Number and Frequency of Revisions.** The revision clause is often left intentionally open-ended because the publisher does not want to limit how many times and how frequently the work will be revised and reissued. The author, however, may wish to confirm the particulars of the future revisions of her book, either because the author wants to know how much more work will be required of her over the life of the contract, or because the author wants the publisher's commitment to revise and republish the book at specified intervals. Any terms regarding revision of the book which may be agreed upon during negotiations should be added to the standard contract before it is signed.

*"...If Author fails to provide the manuscript of a revision of the Work which is acceptable to Publisher...then Publisher shall have the right...to make such revisions..."* The author is under a contractual duty to complete the revisions of her work as requested by the publisher. But the publisher enjoys the right to revise the author's work with its own resources or to *"engage a skilled person to make such revisions"* under several circumstances: if the author fails to complete the revisions, if the author revises the book but the publisher finds the revisions to be

unacceptable, or if the author is dead and gone. In these cases, the author is required to *"reimburse Publisher for all of its actual costs of making such revisions,"* a reimbursement that may take the form of a demand for immediate payment or a debit against the author's account, at the publisher's option.

*"...Publisher, in its sole discretion, may afford appropriate credit (including authorship or co-authorship credit) to such person(s)."* If the publisher elects to engage a writer or editor to complete the revision of an existing book, whether because the author is unwilling or unable to do so or because the publisher is unhappy with the author's revisions, the publisher may find it convenient to offer authorship credit to the person who actually completes the revisions. The sample clause leaves it to the publisher's discretion to afford what it regards as *"appropriate credit"* to the person(s) responsible for the revisions. By implication, if the revisions are sufficiently extensive, the publisher is even entitled to remove the original author's name from the book, although *"co-authorship credit"* is the more common and legally defensible approach to crediting the author of a revised edition.

📖 **Shared Royalties**. Some book contracts permit the publisher to afford not only co-authorship credit to the person(s) who revise the work but also a share of the original author's royalties to the person(s) who revise the work, i.e., **"...in proportion to the percentage of the revised work as published which is directly attributable to the person(s) who actually complete the revision."** Under such a clause, the share of the original author might diminish and even disappear as the book is more and more extensively revised. (➤*Author's Reservation of Credit and Royalties in Revised Editions,* See below) As a practical matter, the risk of losing authorship credit and royalty participation may be enough to motivate the otherwise reluctant author to complete future revisions of the book.

✍ **Author's Reservation of Credit and Royalties in Revised Editions**. The author will be understandably reluctant to sign a contract that permits a publisher to delete her name and deny her royalties on future editions of her own book, even if she is not inclined to participate in revisions or is unable to do so due to illness or disability. If the publisher seeks to include such a clause in the book contract, the author may seek a guarantee that her name will always be credited as a co-author and that she will always participate in some guaranteed minimum percentage of the royalties no matter how extensively her book may be revised in subsequent editions, i.e., **"Author shall always be credited as the first-named author, and shall always be entitled to no less than ___% of the base royalties under this Agreement, on any and all revised editions of the Work, whether or not Author participates in any such revisions."**

# 6

## COPYRIGHT

The rights that are conveyed by an author to a publisher in a book contract are governed largely, if not entirely, by the body of law known as copyright. Some fundamental concepts of copyright law—for example, the various "sticks" in the "bundle of rights" that make up the copyright in a work of authorship—are used to define and allocate the rights in a book between the author and the publisher; and, in many contracts, the duration of copyright is used to define the term of the contract itself. (➤ *Chapter 2: Transfer of Rights*)

Under the typical book contract, the publisher is obligated to publish a proper copyright notice and register the author's work in the U.S. Copyright Office, and is empowered to sue for copyright infringement. Both the author and publisher are required to observe other "formalities" of copyright. All of these copyright-related clauses are discussed below.

A summary of the substantive principles of copyright law that apply to book publishing are discussed in greater detail in *Kirsch's Handbook of Publishing Law*, Chapters 2 and 6.

### COPYRIGHT FORMALITIES

#### COPYRIGHT NOTICE AND REGISTRATION

Publisher shall, in all versions of the Work published by Publisher under this Agreement, place a notice of copyright in the name of Author in a form and place that Publisher reasonably believes to comply with the requirements of the United States copyright law, and shall apply for registration of such copyright(s) in the name of Author in the United States Copyright Office. Publisher shall have the right, but not the obligation, to apply for registration of copyright(s) in the Work as published by Publisher elsewhere in the world. Nothing contained in this section shall be construed as limiting, modifying, or otherwise affecting any of the rights granted to Publisher under this Agreement.

*"Publisher shall...place a notice of copyright...that Publisher reasonably believes to comply with the requirements of the United States copyright law..."* The responsibility for formulating a proper copyright notice and making sure that it appears in the right place is generally allocated to the publisher, and thus it is the publisher that must understand and satisfy the technical requirements of copyright law. But the publisher need only act according to its "reasonable belief" as to "the requirements of the United States copyright law." Since it is no longer mandatory to publish a copyright notice at all—and the consequences of an improper notice are no longer catastrophic—a publisher enjoys a good deal of latitude in fulfilling such obligations. Indeed, a publisher might conclude that *no* copyright notice is required. But it is almost always advantageous to both the author and publisher to include a copyright notice, and thus, a proper notice should be included in every copyrighted work unless there is some compelling legal reason to omit it.

*"...in the name of the Author..."* Strictly speaking, the author's name ought to be used in a copyright notice if *any* rights in the work have been reserved by the author, and the publisher's name ought to appear in the notice if *all* rights in the author's work have been transferred to the publisher. By long and gracious tradition in publishing, the copyright notice is usually given in the name of the author even if the author has retained *no* rights in the work, a practice that is not technically correct but rarely presents any adverse consequences. The conventional practice is a matter of courtesy rather than strict compliance with copyright law, however, and there are circumstances in which the author's name ought not appear in the copyright notice or registration. For example, if the work is a work made for hire, then the publisher is the "author" for all purposes, and only the publisher's name should be used in both the notice and the registration.

✍ **Identity of Copyright Owner**. Some authors transfer ownership of their copyrighted work to a corporation, a trust, or some other legal entity, generally for tax and estate-planning purposes. If so, the legal entity that owns the rights in the author's work (and *not* the author himself) ought to be named in the contract as "grantor" and in the copyright notice as "owner" of the copyright. The identification and description of the proper contracting party is often a highly technical matter and should be made in consultation with an attorney.

*"...in all versions of the Work published by Publisher under this Agreement..."* The publisher's duty to include an appropriate copyright notice applies only to the editions actually issued by the publisher itself, according to the sample clause, and *not* to editions that may be published by third parties under a license from the publisher. For example, the sample clause does not oblige the book publisher to make sure that a licensee—the publisher of an audio version of the book, for example, or the publisher of a foreign-language edition—publishes a proper copyright notice in its editions. However, virtually all publishers require their licensees to include a copyright notice in their editions of the author's work, and the cautious author may wish to modify the book contract to confirm the duty of the publisher to do so. (➤*Copyright Duties of Licensees, Page 186*)

*"...and shall apply for registration of such copyright(s) in the name of Author in the United States Copyright Office..."* Formal registration of copyright in a newly published or newly revised work is a standard practice in publishing and provides important benefits to both author and publisher. (See *Kirsch's Handbook, Chapter 6: Copyright Formalities*) The sample clause obligates the publisher to complete the registration of the author's work in the United States Copyright Office *"in the name of Author,"* but no further details or deadlines are prescribed, and the publisher is not required to complete the registration within any stated time limit. Prompt and accurate registration, however, is always in the best interests of both the author and publisher.

✍ **Advantages of Prompt Registration**. Prompt registration of copyright bestows crucial legal protection on the copyright owner, especially when completed within 90 days of publication, and every published work of authorship ought to be promptly registered unless there is some compelling legal reason not to do so. For that reason, the author may wish to seek a modification of the sample clause that obliges the publisher to complete the registration of each edition of the Author's work "**...promptly upon publication of each edition...**" or, even better, "**...within 90 days of publication of each edition...**" To confirm that the publisher has complied with its obligation, the modified clause might include an assurance that: "**Publisher will provide Author with written evidence of the timely filing of all required applications for registration and copies of Certificates of Registration when issued.**" An especially vigilant author may wish to check the records of the Copyright Office to make sure the registration has been filed—and some authors go ahead and file for registration of their published work on their own initiative.

*"...Publisher shall have the right, but not the obligation, to apply for registration of copyright(s) in the Work published by Publisher elsewhere in the world..."* Similarly, the publisher is empowered but not obligated to register the author's work in foreign countries. As a practical matter, U.S. publishers generally rely on their licensees to comply with copyright formalities in foreign countries, and the contracts between a book publisher and a licensee will often oblige the licensee to publish a specified notice and complete the appropriate copyright registration, if available, in the place where the work is published. But the sample clause does not *require* the publisher to make sure that copyright formalities are observed in foreign countries where the book is published. Publishers are rarely willing to take on the legal obligation to do so, especially because the formalities of copyright law vary from country to country around the world.

✍ **Copyright Duties of Licensees**. The author may wish to negotiate for more far-reaching obligations on the part of the publisher by straightforwardly requiring the publisher *and* its licensees to publish a proper copyright notice and apply for registration of copyright wherever the book is published, i.e., "**Publisher shall secure and**

> confirm in writing from each of its licensees the obligation to publish a proper copyright notice and to register the copyright in any and all licensed editions in strict conformity with the terms and conditions of this Agreement."

*"...Nothing...shall be construed as limiting...the rights granted to Publisher under this Agreement."* Although the *author's* name will, under most circumstances, appear in the copyright notice and the application for copyright registration, the sample clause makes it clear that the *publisher's* substantive rights are not limited by the formalities of notice and registration. In other words, the publisher's rights of ownership and use of the author's work as defined elsewhere in the contract remain in full effect (➤*Chapter 2: Transfer of Rights*); and the use of the author's name in the notice and registration—or, for that matter, the failure of the publisher to observe the formalities described here—will not result in the forfeiture or limitation of those rights.

### ADDITIONAL DOCUMENTS

Author shall execute and deliver to Publisher any and all documents which Publisher deems necessary or appropriate to evidence or effectuate the rights granted in this Agreement, including but not limited to the Instrument of Recordation attached hereto as an Exhibit to this Agreement.

Although a book contract is generally intended to define all aspects of the legal relationship between an author and publisher—and most contracts expressly say so (➤*Entire Agreement, Page 247*)—the publisher usually reserves the right to ask for *additional* documents to be signed by the author in order to confirm the rights of the publisher in the author's work.

*"Author shall execute...any and all documents which Publisher deems necessary or appropriate..."* The author is contractually obliged to sign additional documents at the request of the publisher in order to *"evidence or effectuate the rights granted in this Agreement."* The clause is rarely invoked, but

it reflects a lawyerly concern that there may come a time when a third party—a licensee of subsidiary rights, for example, or the Copyright Office—will demand confirmation from the author that rights have been granted to the publisher. Under the sample clause, the author will be in breach of contract if he refuses to sign and deliver the documents that the publisher *"deems necessary or appropriate."* The author may take some comfort, however, in the notion that any such additional documents must be consistent with the original grant of rights in the contract itself. (➤*Restrictions on Additional Documents, See below*)

---

📖 **Power of Attorney.** Some book contracts go one step beyond the sample clause and require the author to grant the publisher a power of attorney that empowers the *publisher* to sign documents on behalf of the *author*, i.e., **"Author hereby appoints Publisher as its attorney-in-fact and hereby grants Publisher a Power of Attorney to execute documents in the name of Author in order to evidence and effectuate the rights granted to Publisher."** A power of attorney solves the problem of the author who cannot be located or who balks at signing such "additional documents." Some authors, however, are uncomfortable with giving the publisher such a sweeping authority to sign documents and may insist on deleting the power-of-attorney clause.

---

✍ **Restrictions on Additional Documents.** Although the sample clause implies but does not straightforwardly say that the "additional documents" will be consistent with the terms of the contract itself, a cautious author may wish to ask for written confirmation by adding the following words: **"...*any and all documents*, strictly consistent with and subject to the terms and provisions of this Agreement, *which Publisher deems necessary...*"**

---

*"...including but not limited to the Instrument of Recordation attached hereto..."* The sample clause does not limit the number or kind of documents that the publisher may ask the author to sign, but one document in particular is identified—an "Instrument of Recordation," which is a "short-form" version of the book contract that confirms the transfer of rights

by author to publisher but generally leaves out the other deal points. (See *Kirsch's Handbook, Chapter 6: Copyright Formalities* and *Forms Library, Form 6*) The short form is especially designed for recordation in the Copyright Office, where it serves to perfect and protect the legal rights of both the author and publisher. Ideally, the Instrument of Recordation will be signed at the same time as the contract itself, and then the publisher will record the document when the book has been published and registered.

## COPYRIGHT ENFORCEMENT

Once the publisher has acquired some or all of the rights to the author's work, it is generally the publisher that will monitor the marketplace for infringement of the author's work and bring lawsuits to stop any such infringement. Indeed, as a practical matter, the publisher is usually better able to afford the cost of hiring attorneys and prosecuting lawsuits against infringers. However, the typical book contract affords the author an opportunity to participate in lawsuits for the enforcement of copyright. And the author is also invited to share the burdens as well as the benefits of litigation.

### COPYRIGHT INFRINGEMENT.

If, at any time during the term of this Agreement, a claim shall arise for infringement or unfair competition as to any of the rights which are the subject of this Agreement, the parties may proceed jointly or separately to prosecute an action based on such claims. If the parties proceed jointly, the expenses (including attorneys' fees) and recovery, if any, shall be shared equally by the parties. If the parties do not proceed jointly, either or both parties shall have the right to proceed separately, and if so, such party shall bear the costs of litigation and shall own and retain any and all recovery resulting from such litigation. If the party proceeding separately does not hold the record title of the copyright at issue, the other party hereby consents that the action be brought in his, her, or its name. Notwithstanding the foregoing, Publisher has no obligation to initiate litigation on such claims, and shall not be liable for any failure to do so.

"*...If...a claim shall arise for infringement or unfair competition as to any of the rights which are the subject of this Agreement...*" The sample clause addresses not only copyright litigation but also claims for what is called "unfair competition," a related body of law that includes the right to protect titles, trademarks, and even the appearance or "trade dress" of the book as published. ("Trade dress" is a legal term that refers to the cover design and the overall appearance of the book itself.) Indeed, the clause refers to "*any of the rights which are the subject of this Agreement*," and thus extends to the author's so-called "right of publicity" and other collateral rights in the author's work. (➤ *Use of Author's Name and Likeness, Page 178; Title and Series Rights, Page 231*) The sample clause covers any claim for infringement of these rights that arises "*at any time during the term of this Agreement.*"

"*...the parties may proceed jointly or separately to prosecute an action based on such claims...*" Since both the author and publisher have a stake in an infringement of the author's work, the sample clause empowers either party to undertake such a lawsuit without the consent or participation of the other. The parties, though, are offered an opportunity to proceed jointly and share the expenses and proceeds of the litigation against an infringer, as described below.

"*...If the parties proceed jointly, the expenses (including attorneys' fees) and recovery, if any, shall be shared equally by the parties...*" The sample clause states what is ostensibly a fair and evenhanded principle—if the parties jointly prosecute an action, the costs and expenses of litigation "*shall be shared equally by the parties,*" and so will "*the recovery, if any,*" whether by way of settlement or judgment. Since the publisher is probably better able to afford such costs, however, the burden falls more heavily on the author.

✍ **Costs of Litigation**. The sample clause obliges the author to pay half the costs of litigation if the author and publisher jointly sue an infringer. As a practical matter, however, the author is often unable to bear the running costs of litigation, which can be considerable. So the author is better protected if the sample clause is modified to provide that **"Publisher shall advance the costs and expenses of litigation jointly undertaken by author and publisher, and shall be entitled to recoup such costs and expenses out of first monies received, if any, from any settlement or judgment."**

*"...If the parties do not proceed jointly, either or both parties shall have the right to proceed separately..."* Again, the sample clause appears to be evenhanded, allowing either author or publisher to proceed separately against an infringer on its own initiative, bearing its own costs of litigation, and keeping whatever recovery may be obtained in the lawsuit. As a practical matter, however, it is unlikely that *both* the author and publisher will choose to maintain separate lawsuits of their own, and under some circumstances, the courts would not permit them to do so. Since the publisher is better positioned and thus more likely to file an infringement action, the author may wish to seek a share of the recovery even if the publisher proceeds on its own resources.

✍ **Sharing the Recovery**. A certain intuitive sense of fair play seems to underlie the sample clause: whoever bears the financial burdens of a lawsuit is entitled to enjoy its benefits. But an argument can be made that the author ought to share in a recovery obtained by the publisher even if the publisher finances the lawsuit. After all, the publisher has acquired the right to put the author's work into the marketplace, and whatever financial gain the publisher realizes—whether by selling copies of the book to a consumer or extracting a measure of damages from an infringer—ought to be shared with the author. Thus, the author may seek a modification of the sample clause that obliges the publisher to share the recovery, i.e., **"Publisher shall pay Author a share of any actual recovery, net of Publisher's actual costs and expenses of litigation (including attorneys' fees), in a like proportion to the author's right to royalties under this Agreement."** Thus, for example, if an infringer issues a pirated paperback edition of the author's work, the author would be entitled to the same percentage of the publisher's net recovery in litigation that would have been paid on a paperback edition actually issued by the publisher.

*"...If the party proceeding separately does not hold the record title of the copyright at issue, the other party hereby consents that the action be brought in his, her, or its name..."* To make it possible for either the author or the publisher to file a lawsuit of its own against an infringer, the sample clause addresses a narrow legal technicality: What happens if, for example, the publisher has acquired only domestic rights in the author's book, the author has reserved foreign rights, and an infringer issues a pirated edition in a foreign country? Since the author rather than the publisher actually owns the rights that have been infringed, the sample clause permits the publisher to file a lawsuit in the name of the author. Under other provisions of the sample clause, even if the publisher files a lawsuit in the author's name, the publisher will keep the recovery if the author declines to join the lawsuit and share the expenses.

# 7

## ACCOUNTING

All financial dealings between the author and publisher are generally channeled through a formal system of accounting. On signing the book contract, the publisher opens an account in the name of the author, and the account remains in effect throughout the life of the contract. Based on various other clauses of the contract, the publisher will *credit* the author's account with the amounts that the publisher owes the author, such as royalties, a percentage of income from licensing the author's work to third parties, grants and expense advances, and other payments. (➤*Chapter 4: Author Compensation*) The publisher will *debit* the author's account for the amounts that the author owes the publisher, such as the advance (➤*Advances, Page 104*), a reserve against returns (➤*Reserve Against Returns, Page 199*), and other costs and charges. (➤*Artwork, Permissions, Index, and Other Materials, Page 137; Author's Copies, Page 174*)

As a general rule, the publisher actually writes a check and sends it to the author only when a formal statement of account is rendered. So the accounting provisions of a book contract, however tedious they may appear, are a crucial mechanism; often enough, the statement of account may represent the *only* communication between author and publisher after the fanfare of first publication has faded away.

### ACCOUNTING

**Publisher shall render to Author a statement of Net Units sold and Net Revenues from sale of Publisher's editions and other exploitation and disposition of rights to the Work, and other credits and debits relating to the Work and the rights**

granted in this Agreement, and pay Author any amount(s) then owing, for each six-month accounting period, not later than thirty (30) days following the close of each such period.

1. As used herein, "Net Units" shall refer to copies of the Work in any Publisher's edition actually sold and delivered, net of returns, damaged or spoiled copies, and promotional and Author's copies.

2. Publisher shall have the right to debit the account of Author for any overpayment of royalties, and any and all costs, charges, or expenses which Author is required to pay or reimburse Publisher under this Agreement, and any amounts owing Publisher under any other agreement between Publisher and Author.

*"Publisher shall render to Author a statement..."* The basic obligation of the publisher—and the method by which the author is informed of what is actually owed by one party to the other party under a book contract—is the rendering of formal statements of account at specified intervals. The accounting format varies significantly from publisher to publisher—some are praised for their lucidity, others are famously impenetrable. Only rarely, however, will a publisher agree to modify its accounting clause or tinker with the time and manner of rendering accounts, since the accounting system of a publishing house is so deeply embedded in both tradition and technology. (➤*How to Read a Royalty Statement, Page 195*)

*"...of Net Units sold and Net Revenues from sale of Publisher's editions..."* Exactly what goes into a statement of account is rarely specified in the contract itself except in the most general terms. According to the sample clause, the publisher promises to disclose two basic items of information: "*Net Units,*" a defined term that means the number of "*copies of the Work in any Publisher's edition actually sold and delivered, net of returns, damaged or spoiled copies, and promotional and Author's copies;*" and "*Net Revenues from sale of Publisher's editions and other exploitation and disposition of rights to the*

*Work.*" "Net Revenues" is a term defined elsewhere in the contract to mean the amount of "*money actually received by Publisher from the sale of copies of the Work, net of returns, after deduction of shipping, customs, insurance, fees and commissions, currency exchange discounts, and costs of collection.*" (➤*A Clause for a Fixed Royalty Based on Publisher's Net Income, Page 119*) Some book contracts in common use specify more particulars, some even less, and some mention only that the publisher will render statements at a specified interval and are otherwise silent on what will appear on the statements.

The basic accounting information identified in the sample clause contemplates the sales of the author's work in "*in any Publisher's edition*" that is, an edition actually released and distributed by the publisher itself. The publisher is allowed to deduct certain items from the total number of copies reported on the statement; the phrase "*net of*" as used in the sample clause means not counting "*returns, damaged or spoiled copies, and promotional and Author's copies.*" "Returns" are copies of the author's work that a retail bookseller has been unable to sell and has returned to the publisher for a refund or credit, and thus do not constitute a sale. (➤*Returns, Page 113*) The same is true of copies returned for credit or refund because they are "*damaged or spoiled,*" or copies given away free of charge to the author or to others for promotional and publicity purposes. And the publisher is entitled to deduct certain items from the total amount of income reported on the statement—"*shipping, customs, insurance, fees and commissions, currency exchange discounts, and costs of collection*" are defined deductions from gross revenues in the sample clause. Other contract forms may provide for additional or different deductions.

---

✍ **How to Read a Royalty Statement**. Perhaps nothing in the business of publishing is quite so challenging as the task of reading a royalty statement. The problem is made even more daunting because the publishing industry does not rely on a standard form for rendering accounts. And if the contract provides for multi-tiered royalty rates (➤*Royalties, Page 109*), then the statement may tax the skills of even an experienced accountant. And yet more than one author has discovered that her royalties were undercalculated and underpaid only after scrutinizing the publisher's statements. At a minimum, then, the publisher should include—and the author should look for—the following categories of information in the statement: actual number of units sold for each title and edition; applicable royalty rate for each sale (i.e., escalated royalty based on actual sales, sales at ordinary discount, sales at deep discount, other special categories of sale, etc.); itemized adjustments (such as returns, promotional copies, author's copies, etc.); reserves against returns; income from third-party transactions; recoupment of advances; and other authorized debits on the author's account. Often, an error in accounting can be detected only by double-checking the calculations of the publisher or by comparing the current statement with earlier statements and looking for sudden changes and anomalies.

✍ $ **Royalties on Author Purchases.** The sample clause excludes *all* author copies from the calculation of royalties, and thus can be interpreted to deny the author a royalty on copies purchased and paid for by the author. If the publisher agrees to pay a royalty on author purchases, then the sample clause should be modified accordingly. (➤*Author's Copies, Page 174*)

*"...and other exploitation and disposition of rights to the Work..."* The typical book contract allocates to the author not only a royalty on sales of the publisher's editions but also a share of the money that the publisher collects from the licensing of rights in the author's work to third parties. For that reason, the sample clause goes on to specify that the publisher's statements of account will also disclose the revenues from *"...other exploitation and disposition of rights to the Work,"* a catch-all category that includes royalties and other revenues from third-party licensing and any other income generated by the publisher in exploiting any of the rights in the author's work. Thus, for example, if the publisher licenses another publisher to issue a book club edition of the author's work, or a foreign edition, or an audio version, then the money actually received from each of these transactions will be disclosed on the author's statement of account.

*"...and other credits and debits relating to the Work and the rights granted in this Agreement..."* Depending on the deal that

has been struck by the author and the publisher, a great many other credits and debits may appear in the author's statement of account, and the sample clause obliges the publisher to include them all. For example, if the publisher has agreed to pay the author a share of the revenues from an electronic edition of the author's work (➤ *Sharing of Revenues From Subsidiary Rights, Page 125*), the income actually received from the electronic publisher should appear as a credit on the author's statement. If, on the other hand, the author is obliged to reimburse the publisher for the purchase of author's copies or payments for artwork and permissions (➤ *Artwork, Permissions, Index, and Other Materials, Page 137*), such items will appear as debits on the author's account. And the statement will include certain amounts held in reserve by the publisher, most commonly and most importantly a "reserve against returns." (➤ *Reserve Against Returns, Page 199*)

"*...and pay Author any amount(s) then owing...*" The sample clause provides that the publisher's obligation to actually pay money to the author coincides with the obligation to render statements of account. Thus, the publisher is entitled to retain and hold *all* of the revenues from exploitation of the author's work throughout the accounting period, and the author is entitled to payment of the amounts owed by the publisher only at the stated intervals. Of course, the publisher is not obliged to make *any* payments to the author unless and until the book has "earned out"—that is, when the publisher has recouped the advance and other amounts owed by the author and the credits on the author's account actually exceed the debits.

---

✍ $ **Flow-Through and Other Accelerated Payments**. Some authors enjoy enough clout to demand a "flow-through" clause, which obligates the publisher to pay the author her share of revenues from third-party transactions promptly upon receipt of money by the publisher. (➤ *Flow-Through, Page 126*) Other non-standard clauses, such as a "bestseller clause," may oblige the publisher to pay additional advances or bonuses without waiting for a formal accounting period. (➤ *Bonuses, Page 107*)

---

&#x1F4D5; **Payments to Multiple Authors**. If the publisher enters into a deal for a book with several co-authors, the contract should include a clause that confirms how the publisher is to divide up and issue the payments owing under the contract. (➤*Co-Authors, Page 130*) If the contract includes an agency clause, and the agent represents all of the co-authors, then it is up to the agent to make the appropriate disbursements. The agency clause should confirm that payment by the publisher to the agent is a full discharge of the publisher's monetary obligations to *all* of the co-authors. (➤*Agency, Page 203; Multiple Authors, Page 250*)

*"...for each six-month accounting period, not later than thirty (30) days following the close of each such period..."* The sample clause requires the publisher to render statements on a semiannual basis, and the formal statement of account must be issued *"not later than thirty (30) days following the close of each such period."* Six months is a common interval for the rendering of accounts in the publishing industry, but some publishers report quarterly and others only once a year. Thirty days is a relatively short period in which to collect, organize, and report the information from the previous accounting period, especially one as long as six months, and some book contracts allow for 45 or even 90 days before the publisher is required to render a statement and pay what is owed to the author.

&#x1F4D5; **Suspension of Statements**. The accounting clauses used by many publishers include a provision that relieves them of the obligation to render statements when the sales of a particular book fall off, i.e., **"No statement need be rendered by publisher for any accounting period in which author's earned royalties are $500 or less."**

*"...Publisher shall have the right to debit the account of Author for any overpayment of royalties, and any and all costs, charges, or expenses which Author is required to pay or reimburse Publisher under this Agreement..."* As noted above, the author's account may reflect both credits and debits, and the sample clause goes on to specify some of the items that will be debited. For example, if the publisher has paid an advance against royalties, or if the publisher has paid a royalty on books

that were sold and later returned for a credit or refund, then the author's account will be debited for "*overpayment of royalties.*" If the contract provides for any other "*costs, charges or expenses*" that are to be paid or reimbursed by the author—for example, the cost of preparing an index—then such items will also appear as debits on the author's account.

"*...and any amounts owing Publisher under any other agreement between Publisher and Author.*" The sample clause provides for a mechanism that is variously known as "joint accounting," "cross-collateralization," or "bundling"—that is, if the publisher has contracted for more than one title by the same author, then the publisher is entitled to apply the debits from one book against the credits from another book by the same author. Publishers, of course, regard such clauses as inherently fair; as far as the publisher is concerned, all the money comes out of one pot and goes to one person. However, a joint accounting clause may mean that the author will not be entitled to earned royalties on a successful book if an unrecouped advance remains outstanding on another book from the same publisher, and that is why joint accounting is often a hot issue in negotiations between an author and a publisher. (➤*Joint Accounting,* See below)

---

✍ $ **Joint Accounting.** The author's best interests are served if the book contract does *not* allow for joint accounting. Under a joint accounting clause, as discussed above, the royalties otherwise payable to the author on sales of a successful book will be applied by the publisher to recoup the advance and other charges on less successful books. Of course, the issue of joint accounting only arises if and when the publisher has contracted for more than one book by the same author. But if the contract includes an option clause (➤*Option on Author's Next Work, Page 222*), then the joint accounting clause will automatically come into play when the publisher picks up the author's next book.

---

## RESERVE AGAINST RETURNS

Publisher shall have the right to allow for a reasonable reserve against returns. If royalties have been paid on copies that are thereafter returned, then Publisher shall have the right to deduct the amount of such royalties on such returned copies from any future payments under this or any other Agreement.

According to fundamental principles of accounting in the publishing industry, the sale of a book is recorded—and a royalty is posted to the author's account—when an order is placed and filled at the wholesale level. However, the reality is that a book that has been sold to a retail bookstore may be returned to the publisher for a credit or refund if it sits too long on the shelf. Once returned, of course, the original transaction is not considered a sale and the royalty is no longer owed. To protect itself against paying royalties on the sale of books that may end up as returns, the publisher typically establishes a "reserve against returns"— that is, a hold-back of royalties otherwise payable to the author.

*"Publisher shall have the right to allow for a reasonable reserve against returns..."* According to a long-established custom and practice of the publishing industry—and, almost invariably, a standard provision in book contracts—the publisher is entitled to hold back money otherwise payable to avoid payment of royalties on books that may be returned. Typically, the sample clause authorizes the publisher alone to decide what percentage of the author's royalties will be held back, and for how long. Twenty-five percent is not uncommon, although there is no standard percentage used to determine the amount of the reserve. Similarly, some publishers maintain the reserve for one accounting period, other publishers hold back the reserve for a year, and not a few carry the reserve for even longer periods. As a practical matter, the reserve exists only on paper, and the publisher is expected to release the reserve as time passes and the actual returns are calculated. (➤ *Limits on Reserves, Page 201*)

Let us suppose, by way of example, that the author has earned $4,000 in royalties on the sale of 1,000 books in a particular accounting period—a royalty of $4.00 per book. The publisher elects to hold back a 25% reserve for two semiannual accounting periods, a total of one year. The publisher assumes that 250 of the 1,000 books will eventually be returned, and thus holds back $1,000 of the royalties otherwise payable to the author. After a year passes, the publisher confirms the actual sales and returns during the intervening one-year period, and the royalties earned on actual "sales less returns" during the initial accounting period will now be paid. Hence, if only 150 books are actually returned, then an additional royalty on the sale of 100 books, or $400, is now owed.

By then, of course, the actual reserve has *increased* because additional amounts are held back against possible returns on the sales reported in each accounting period. As a practical matter, the reserve against returns is fully liquidated only when the book goes out of print and the publisher sets a deadline for returns.

---

📖 **Limits on Reserves.** Since the sample clause allows the publisher to decide how much the reserve against returns will be and how long it will be maintained, some authors negotiate for specific limits, i.e., **"The reserve against returns may not exceed 15% of earned royalties in any accounting period, and the reserve may be held for one accounting period only."**

---

📖 **Reserve Against Legal Claims.** Most book contracts bestow upon the publisher the right to maintain a separate and additional reserve if a lawsuit or other claim is brought against the publisher on the basis of the author's work, a reserve that is covered elsewhere in the typical contract. (➤*Author's Indemnity of Publisher, Page 213*)

---

## AUDIT RIGHTS

Author shall have the right, upon reasonable notice and during usual business hours but not more than once each year, to engage a certified public accountant to examine the books and records of Publisher relating to the Work at the place where such records are regularly maintained. Any such examination shall be at the sole cost of the Author, and may not be made by any person acting on a contingent fee basis. Statements rendered under this Agreement shall be final and binding upon Author unless Author sets forth the specific objections in writing and the basis for such objections within six (6) months after the date the statement was rendered.

*"Author shall have the right...to examine the books and records of Publisher relating to the Work..."* The sample clause establishes the right of the author to verify the competence and good faith of the publisher in rendering statements of account by conducting an audit of *"the books and records...relating to the Work."* But the typical book contract goes on to discourage such audits by imposing a series of restrictions on when, where, and how often an audit may be conducted, i.e., the audit must take place at the location *"where such records are regularly maintained,"* whether it is the publisher's office or elsewhere, and only *"during usual business hours."* The author must give the publisher *"reasonable notice"* of the audit, and she may conduct no more than one audit in any year. The actual inspection of books and records must be conducted by *"a certified public accountant"* who is not acting *"on a contingent fee basis."* Since the audit is to be conducted *"at the sole cost of the Author,"* the fact that she is contractually obliged to use a CPA on a fee basis is a strong disincentive.

---

✍ **Enhanced Audit Rights.** Authors often seek—and some book contracts already include—a clause that obliges the *publisher* to pay for the audit if errors are discovered, i.e., **"If errors in favor of Author are detected, then Publisher shall pay all amounts found to be owing and the actual costs of the audit."** And, similarly, some authors negotiate for enhanced audit rights, i.e., the audit may be conducted **"...by the Author's literary agent during the course of the agent's regular and customary representation of Author,"** a formulation that sidesteps the restriction against auditors acting on a contingency basis.

---

📖 **Author as Auditor.** The sample clause does not permit the author herself to show up at the publisher's office and start rummaging through the files, a prospect that most publishers regard with horror. Thus, even if the publisher is inclined to soften the language of its audit clause to permit audits by someone other than a CPA, or by someone acting on a contingency fee basis, most publishers will prefer that the audits be conducted by a qualified third party rather than the author.

---

*"...Statements rendered under this Agreement shall be final and binding...unless Author sets forth the specific objections...within six (6) months after the date the statement was rendered."* As a further limitation on the exercise of audit rights, the sample clause establishes a six-month cut-off date for any objections to the accuracy or completeness of a particular statement of account, and each objection must be presented in writing along with the factual basis for the alleged error. If the clause is strictly enforced, errors in statements more than six months old are deemed to be waived, which raises the risk that some vigilant authors will be more likely to demand an audit— and will be tempted to do so more with greater frequency— than they would have been otherwise.

---

✍ **Remedies for Accounting Irregularities.** The sample clause establishes a kind of private statute of limitations on accounting claims, but the clause probably would not preclude a lawsuit against the publisher for breach of contract or fraud based on accounting errors more than six months old. Still, the author is better protected if the time limitation on presenting errors is removed or, at least, if the time period during which objections may be raised is considerably lengthened.

---

## AGENCY

Author hereby authorizes and appoints [ *Name and address of Author's literary agent or agency*] ("Agent") to act as Author's agent in connection with this Agreement, including but not limited to the disposition of any and all rights in the Work, any sequels to the Work, and any options to future work of the Author under this Agreement. Accordingly, Agent is hereby fully empowered by Author to act on behalf of Author, to collect and receive all sums of money payable to Author, and to receive any and all statements, notices, or other communications to Author in connection with this Agreement. Receipt by Agent of any such payments, statements, notices, and other matter shall be a valid discharge of

Publisher's obligations to Author for such matters under this Agreement. This clause creates an agency coupled with an interest as between Author and Agent.

Even if the publisher's standard contract does not include an agency clause, any author who is represented by an agent will probably find that her agent has taken the initiative to request one. Indeed, many agents provide the text of the agency clause directly to the publisher, and their agency agreements authorize them to do so. But the author should bear in mind that an agency clause is mostly for the protection of the agent, not the author, and thus the author must raise objections to the agency clause with the agent rather than the publisher.

*"Author hereby authorizes and appoints...Agent...to act as Author's agent in connection with this Agreement..."* The sample clause generally confirms the authority of the designated literary agent to act on behalf of the author *"in connection with this Agreement,"* and then goes on to specify the scope of the agent's authority and some specific responsibilities.

*"...including but not limited to the disposition of any and all rights in the Work granted to Publisher under this Agreement..."* The sample clause illustrates how an agent uses the agency clause to confirm the authority to represent the author, not only in connection with the author's work as published in book form by the publisher, but also in *"the disposition of any and all rights in the Work"* under the agreement. Of course, the crucial subtext of the sample clause is that the agent is entitled to a *commission* on any of the subsidiary rights acquired by the publisher in the book contract, including *"any sequels to the Work"* and any *"future work of the Author"* that is under option to the publisher.

---

✍ **Scope of Agency.** The author must carefully evaluate the agency clause in a book contract to make sure that the scope of the agency is defined to her satisfaction. For example, the author may not wish to tie herself to the agent for sequels and optioned works, especially if there is no formal agency agreement that entitles the agent to represent the author for such future works.

---

*"...Accordingly, Agent is hereby fully empowered by Author...to collect and receive all sums of money payable to Author..."* As far as the agent is concerned, the single most important component of an agency clause—and the *only* component in some agency clauses in common use—is the one that instructs the publisher to pay advances, royalties, and other payments under the book contract to the agent, rather than the author. Under the custom and practice of the publishing industry—and the typical agency agreement, if the author has signed one—the agent is entitled to deduct the agreed-upon commission and expenses, and then disburse the balance of the publisher's payments to the author.

*"...and to receive any and all statements, notices, or other communications to Author in connection with this Agreement..."* Not only royalty checks, but *"statements, notices, or other communications to Author"* are to be sent to the agent rather than the author under the sample clause.

*"...Receipt by Agent of any such payments, statements, notices, and other matter shall be a valid discharge of Publisher's obligations to Author for such matters under this Agreement..."* Here is what the publisher is likely to regard as the single most crucial sentence in the agency clause. Once the publisher has issued a check to the author's designated agent in payment of its monetary obligations under the book contract, or sent a formal notice to the author in care of the agent, the receipt of such payments or notices by the agent is *"a valid discharge of Publisher's obligations to Author."* If the agent fails to honor any obligations to the author—that is, if the agent fails to disburse a royalty payment or pass along a notice—the publisher will not be liable for the agent's misconduct.

> 📖 **Duplicate Notices to Author and Agent**. As long as the author and her agent are on good terms, the author generally regards the agency clause as a convenience, but if the agency relationship comes to an end, the author may request that royalties, statements, and notices be sent directly to the author alone. However, since the agency clause makes the agent a "third-party beneficiary" of the book contract and the publisher may face a lawsuit for breach of contract if the agency

clause is disregarded, most publishers insist on formal written consent from the agent before it will send checks and communications directly to the author. Moreover, the cautious publisher will be sure to send duplicate copies of crucial communications to both the author and agent, especially if there is a question about whether the agent is still authorized to act on behalf of the author.

*"...This clause creates an agency coupled with an interest as between Author and Agent."* The sample clause includes a sentence that many agents write into their standard agency clauses on the strength of a hoary old principle of law that *"an agency coupled with an interest"* is irrevocable. In reality, an agent's right to receive a commission is *not* "an interest" as the phrase is interpreted under the law of agency, and so the effort is probably in vain. However, the presence or absence of the sentence does not directly affect the publisher, and most publishers sensibly leave it up to the author to negotiate the fine points of the agency clause with the agent.

✍ **Agency Agreement.** The agency clause in a book contract sometimes takes the place of a formal agreement between an author and an agent, but it is a better practice for the author and agent to negotiate and sign a separate agreement that defines their respective rights and duties. If a separate agency agreement is signed, the agency clause in the book contract may be much more concise and focused, and the publisher need not be concerned with the details of the agency agreement. (See *Kirsch's Handbook, Chapter 3: Agents and Packagers*)

✍ **Termination of Agent.** Only rarely does the agency clause address what happens if the author terminates her agent at some later date, although the contract form used by one major publisher does provide: **"The Publisher may pay all sums hereunder to Agent until the Publisher shall have received written notice from the Author of the termination of such agency. Upon receipt of such notice, the Publisher shall pay all further sums directly to the Author or to such other persons as the Author shall direct in writing."** But it is the rare agent who will consent to such a clause. From an agent's point of view, a more acceptable approach is one that obliges the publisher, in the event of the future termination of an agent, to **"...pay all further sums as follows: ___% to Author and ___ % to Agent,"** since it ensures that the agent will continue to receive the agreed-upon commission.

# 8

## WARRANTIES, REPRESENTATIONS, AND INDEMNITIES

Nothing in a standard book contract is quite so shocking to a new author as the indigestible lump of boilerplate known as warranties, representations, and indemnities. Essentially, the author is asked to guarantee that his work will not result in a lawsuit against the publisher—and to agree that, if a claim is made against the publisher, the author will bear all costs and expenses of defending and paying the claim.

"You mean *I'm* supposed to indemnify *them?*" more than one incredulous author has asked me over the years.

Indeed, the notion of the author indemnifying the publisher strikes many authors as counterintuitive, if not downright bizarre. Publishers, after all, are generally perceived by authors as much wealthier and, therefore, better able to pay lawyers to defend a claim and to pay settlements and judgments if the lawyers fail at their task. But publishers take a very different view of the matter: the author, they like to point out, is the one who conducted the research for the book, interviewed the sources, chose the words and phrases that go down on paper, and so it is the author who is responsible if the work draws a claim. If such a claim is brought, the publisher wants the author to cooperate in the defense of the claim, and nothing frightens an author more than the risk of a sizable judgment that he is liable to pay. For all of these reasons, the warranties, representations, and indemnities are perhaps the least negotiable of all clauses in a typical book contract.

### AUTHOR'S REPRESENTATIONS AND WARRANTIES

Author represents and warrants to Publisher that: (i) the Work is not in the public domain; (ii) Author is the sole proprietor of the Work and has full power and authority, free of any rights of any nature whatsoever by any other person, to enter into this Agreement and to grant the rights which are granted to Publisher in this Agreement; (iii) the Work has not heretofore been published, in whole or in part, in any form; (iv) the Work does not, and if published will not, infringe upon any copyright, trademark, or any other intellectual property rights or other proprietary rights of any third party; (v) the Work contains no matter whatsoever that is obscene, libelous, violative of any third party's right of privacy or publicity, or otherwise in contravention of law or the right of any third party; (vi) all statements of fact in the Work are true and are based on diligent research; (vii) all advice and instruction in the Work is safe and sound, and is not negligent or defective in any manner; (viii) the Work, if biographical or "as told to" Author, is authentic and accurate; and (ix) Author will not hereafter enter into any agreement or understanding with any person or entity which might conflict with the rights granted to Publisher under this Agreement.

*"Author represents and warrants to Publisher..."* The author is asked to make a series of statements of fact (*"representations"*) on which the publisher will rely in entering into the book contract, and to guarantee (*"warrant"*) that the statements are true and correct. The scope and detail of these representations and warranties may vary from one contract to another, but they generally reassure the publisher that the author is free to enter into the contract and that the author's work is free from legal defects of any kind.

*"...the Work is not in the public domain..."* Simply put, *"public domain"* is a phrase that means "not protected by copyright." If a work is *"in the public domain,"* then anyone may freely publish it, and—as a general proposition—the publisher need not bother to acquire rights from the author in the first place. The phrase is used here to reassure the publisher that the author's

work *is* protected under copyright law, and thus the publisher will be entitled to make exclusive use of the rights granted under the contract.

---

✍ **Public Domain Material in Works of Authorship.** Virtually every book includes at least some material that is in the public domain, and not a few books consist of an author's selection, arrangement and presentation of ideas or information that are not otherwise protected under copyright. If the author's work consists largely of such material, the cautious author might ask for a modification of the warranties and representations to acknowledge such circumstances, i.e., "...the Work in its entirety is not in the public domain..." or "...the Work in its present form is not in the public domain."

---

*"...Author is the sole proprietor of the Work and has full power and authority...to enter into this Agreement and to grant the rights which are granted to Publisher..."* The sample clause assures the publisher that the author is the owner (*"proprietor"*) of all rights in his work, and thus possesses the *"full power and authority"* to enter into the book contract and grant the rights that the publisher seeks to acquire. Since the author is reassuring the publisher that his work is *"free of any rights of any nature whatsoever by any other person,"* no one else's signature is required to confirm the transfer of rights to the publisher.

---

📖 **Multiple Authors and Owners of Copyright.** If a work has been co-authored by more than one person and all of the authors sign the book contract, then the warranties and representations are correct and sufficient. However, if the author's work includes material that has been acquired from third parties—a preface contributed by another writer, for example, or artwork created by an illustrator—then care should be taken to modify the warranties clause to make it clear exactly what rights the author is transferring to the publisher and what rights have been or must be obtained from third parties, i.e., *"Author is the sole proprietor of the Work* as defined in this Agreement, consisting of the principal text but excluding the artwork to be provided by an illustrator to be selected jointly by Author and Publisher."

---

*"...the Work has not heretofore been published, in whole or in part, in any form..."* The standard book contract assumes that the author's work is original and unpublished, *"in whole or in part,"* and the author is asked to assure the publisher of these facts. If, in fact, the work—or, for that matter, any portion of the work—has been previously published, then the clause should be modified to reflect its actual publishing history before the contract is signed.

---

✍ **Prior Publication.** Under many circumstances, the representation that the author's work *"has not heretofore been published"* is simply inapplicable, as when the work includes a chapter that has been published as a magazine article or when the author grants paperback rights in a book that has already appeared in hardcover. The clause should be revised to reflect the publishing history of the author's work, whether by interlineating (inserting new material in the margins or between the lines of the printed text) the clause itself, i.e., **"other than the hardcover edition of the Work published in 1998 by Alfred A. Knopf"**, or by cross-referencing a separate document that summarizes the publishing history of the author's work, i.e., **"...except as set forth in the attached Rider 'A,' which is incorporated by reference in this Agreement..."**

---

*"...the Work does not...infringe upon any copyright, trademark, or any other intellectual property rights or other proprietary rights of any third party..."* A fundamental assumption of the publisher in any book deal is that the author's work does not infringe upon any other work that is protected under the laws of copyright or trademark. Here, the sample clause goes even further by asking the author to guarantee that his work does not violate any *"intellectual property rights or other proprietary rights of any third party."* For example, the author reassures the publisher that he has not copied anything from a copyrighted work (even if done innocently or inadvertently); he has not used confidential information or trade secrets belonging to another person; and he has not used a name, word, or symbol that suggests sponsorship by or affiliation with a third party. The clause is intentionally all-inclusive and asks the author to rule out virtually any claim against the publisher by

someone who might claim a property right in the contents of the author's book, whether before or after the book is actually published.

*"...the Work contains no matter whatsoever that is obscene, libelous, violative of any third party's right of privacy or publicity, or otherwise in contravention of law or the right of any third party..."* The sample clause obliges the author to assure the publisher that his work is not so sexually explicit as to violate the criminal law that governs obscenity, does not include defamatory statements about the people who are described or depicted in the work, and does not infringe upon the personal rights of third parties. Such rights include the right of privacy, sometimes defined as the "right to be left alone," and the so-called "right of publicity," which is the right to control how one's name and likeness is used in advertising and merchandising. Typically, the sample clause expands upon the specified categories of liability by asking the author to broadly promise that his work is not *"otherwise in contravention of law or the right of any third party."* (See *Kirsch's Handbook, Chapter 5: Preparing the Manuscript*)

*"...all statements of fact in the Work are true and are based on diligent research..."* The author is asked to guarantee that his work is accurate and complete—that is, all factual assertions are true and all research has been *"diligent."* These are the underpinnings of a defense against several potential claims, including a lawsuit for libel, which may result from the publication of statements that are false and defamatory, and the claim of "negligent publication," which may be based on some error in the author's work that causes injury to one who relies on the flawed information or instruction. Whether or not the book is fact-checked or "vetted" by the publisher, the author is giving his assurance that his work has been competently researched and is factually sound. (➤*Review by Publisher's Counsel, Page 165*)

---

✍ **Fiction and Nonfiction**. Even though the sample clause refers frequently to the *factual* content of the author's work, the warranties and representations also apply to works of *fiction*. As a general rule, a novel or other work of fiction may draw a claim for defamation or invasion of privacy (even though it purports to be strictly fictional) whenever a

---

real person is identifiable despite the author's effort to fictionalize him or her. (See *Kirsch's Handbook, Chapter 5: Preparing the Manuscript*)

*"...all advice and instruction in the Work is safe and sound, and is not negligent or defective in any manner..."* The sample clause extracts further assurances from the author that relate specifically to the claim of negligent publication, an issue of special concern to authors and publishers whose readers rely on the author's *"advice and instruction."* The clause applies broadly to books that offer medical, psychological, legal, or financial advice; "how-to" and "self-help" books; and even travel books that encourage the reader to visit particular destinations where dangers may be present.

*"...the Work, if biographical or 'as told to' Author, is authentic and accurate..."* The narrowest of the customary warranties and representations focuses on a genre that raises the acute risk of a claim based on libel, invasion of privacy, or right of publicity: a biography of a living person or a book written by the author on behalf of another person. Essentially, these assurances repeat and reinforce several of the warranties and representations that have already appeared in the sample clause, but care is taken to apply them to a specific kind of book. One additional nuance is the confirmation that an "as-told-to" book is not only *"accurate"* but also *"authentic"*—that is, the author has actually interviewed the person in whose name he is purporting to write.

---

📖 **Consents and Permissions**. The prudent publisher ought to secure a signed written consent from any person who is the subject of an "as-told-to" book. Indeed, the principal author of an "as-told-to" book—that is, the person in whose name the book is written—or the subject of any ghostwritten memoir or autobiography is usually a party to the publishing contract itself. Even more cautious publishers will require the author to seek written consents and permissions from any person whose interviews with the author or whose depiction by the author form a substantial basis for the author's work. And since it is the author who is impliedly guaranteeing that all necessary consents and permissions have been obtained, it is in the author's best interest to do so. (➤*Artwork, Permissions, Index, and Other Materials, Page 137*)

---

*"...Author will not hereafter enter into any agreement or understanding with any person or entity which might conflict with the rights granted to Publisher under this Agreement."* The final assurance by the author is so fundamental that it might go without saying. Still, virtually all publishers say it anyway: once the book contract is signed, the author promises not to grant the same rights in his work to someone else! The sample clause carefully rules out not only formal contracts but also *"understanding*[s]" and any *"agreement*[s]" that *"might"* raise a conflict between the publisher and someone else with whom the author later makes a deal. (➤*Reservation of Rights, Pages 56, 228*)

---

✍ **Selling the Same Book Twice.** No sensible author would actually sell the same book twice, but sometimes the issue of copyright ownership in the author's work is not so straightforward. If the book contract does not carefully distinguish among the various subsidiary rights in the author's work, then it is entirely possible that the author may unwittingly enter into a deal for the sale or license of rights that are actually owned and controlled by the book publisher. Suppose, for example, that the book publisher has acquired audio rights in the author's work, and the author later sells "motion picture, television, and allied and ancillary rights" to a movie producer. If the movie deal includes the incidental right to create an audio product, then the book publisher may claim that its audio rights have been infringed. As a general rule, the second deal is probably invalid, at least as far as the audio rights are concerned, and the author may face lawsuits from both the book publisher and the movie producer. That is why the book contract should be carefully reviewed *before* the author enters into any deal for subsidiary rights in his work. (➤*Chapter 2: Transfer of Rights*)

---

### AUTHOR'S INDEMNITY OF PUBLISHER

Author shall indemnify, defend, and hold harmless Publisher, its subsidiaries and affiliates, and their respective shareholders, officers, directors, employees, partners, associates, affiliates, joint venturers, agents, and representatives, from any and all claims, debts, demands, suits, actions, proceedings, and/or prosecutions ("Claims") based on allegations which, if true, would constitute a breach of any of the foregoing warranties and representations or any other obligation of Author under this Agreement, and any and all liabilities, losses, expenses (including attorneys' fees and costs) and damages in consequence thereof.

1.    Each party to this Agreement shall give prompt notice in writing to the other party of any Claims.

2.    In the event of any Claims, Publisher shall have the right to suspend payments otherwise due to Author under the terms of this Agreement as security for Author's obligations under this section.

3.    Author's warranties, representations, and indemnities as set forth in this Agreement shall extend to any person or entity against whom any Claims are asserted by reason of the exploitation of the rights granted by Author in this Agreement, as if such warranties, representations, and indemnities were originally made to such third parties.

4.    All such warranties, representations, and indemnities shall survive the termination or expiration of this Agreement.

The warranties and representations in a standard book contract set forth the assurances on which the publisher is entitled to rely, but they are not merely soothing words. The author's promises are backed up with "indemnities"—that is, the legal obligation of the author to pay the attorneys who will defend the publisher if a lawsuit is brought; to put up the money for a settlement of the claim; and, if no settlement is possible, to satisfy any judgment that may be entered against the publisher if the publisher loses at trial. Although the indemnity clause that is buried in the boilerplate of every book contract is rarely invoked, it is perhaps the single most ominous—and potentially catastrophic—of all.

*"Author shall indemnify, defend, and hold harmless Publisher..."* The ritualistic words and phrases of the indemnity clause are intended to invoke an elaborate body of law that

defines the duties of one who indemnifies another against legal risks. Essentially, the author is promising to pay *all* costs that may result from a legal claim against the publisher, including attorneys' fees and any other legal expenses; any money that might be paid to settle a claim; the cost of defending a claim in court; and the final judgment that may be entered against the publisher if a claim goes to trial. The author's obligation to "*hold* [the publisher] *harmless*" is meant quite literally: the publisher is entitled to look to the author to bear all costs and expenses of defending, settling and/or satisfying a claim.

"*...its subsidiaries and affiliates, and their respective shareholders, officers, directors, employees, partners, associates, affiliates, joint venturers, agents, and representatives...*" The author's obligations are not limited to the individual, corporation, or other legal entity that owns the publishing company. Any person linked to the publisher, ranging from "*subsidiaries and affiliates*" to "*agents and representatives*," is also entitled to be held harmless by the author if drawn into a lawsuit. Thus, for example, if someone who claims to have been defamed in the author's book names not only the publishing company itself but also the majority shareholder of the corporation, the editor who acquired the book, and the sales representative who called on bookstores and encouraged them to stock the book, then all of them would fall within the scope of the author's indemnity obligations.

"*...from any and all claims, debts, demands, suits, actions, proceedings, and/or prosecutions ('Claims')...*" The author's indemnity is not limited to claims that ultimately go to court. Rather, the scope of the indemnity is broad enough to include not only "*actions, proceedings and/or prosecutions*" but also "*claims, debts* [and] *demands,*" even if they are informally presented and resolved without litigation of any kind. So expansive and all-inclusive are the author's indemnity obligations that the defined term "*Claims*" is introduced in the sample clause as a convenient shorthand reference to the full range of such obligations.

The sample clause goes on to specify that the author's obligation is not limited solely to amounts paid directly to a claimant in settlement or to satisfy a judgment. Rather, the author must pay or reimburse the publisher for "*any and all liabilities* [and] *losses*"—another all-embracing definition that puts the author at risk for the costs of defense and any other damages incurred "*in consequence*" [of] the claims.

"*...based on allegations which, if true, would constitute a breach of any of the foregoing warranties and representations...*" Here is the cutting edge of the author's indemnity: A claim is covered under the indemnity clause so long as the claimant's allegations, "*if true,*" would amount to a breach of any of the assurances given by the author to the publisher in the long list of warranties and representations. The allegations need not be proven true in order to invoke the author's indemnity, and even if the charges are ultimately proven to be utterly false, the publisher is still entitled to indemnity for the costs and expenses of defending the claims.

---

✍ **Limits on the Author's Indemnity**. Authors tend to regard the obligation to indemnify the publisher against meritless claims to be unjust and even insulting, and some authors seek a modification in the indemnity clause to limit their obligation to claims which are ultimately proven true. The more moderate author might ask for the financial burden to be reduced if it is shown that the author was not at fault, i.e., "**Author's obligations under the indemnity provisions of this Agreement shall be limited to 50% of Publisher's reasonable costs of defense and settlement unless Author is found to be at fault in a trial on the merits.**" Few publishers, however, are likely to soften the indemnity clause even if the author is faultless, if only because the defense of even an utterly spurious claim is a significant expense and raises the risk of an adverse judgment.

---

"*...or any other obligation of Author under this Agreement..*" The sample clause extends the author's indemnity to circumstances where no breach of warranty or representation is at issue, but the author is in default under some other obligation of the book contract. Suppose, for example, that the publication of the author's work is linked to an important event—the Olympics, for example, or a presidential election—and the publisher is unable to publish on time because of the author's late delivery of the manuscript. Under such circumstances, the publisher might seek an indemnity from the author for the additional costs of rushing the book to press or the lost sales resulting from late publication—on the theory that such damages resulted from the author's breach of his obligation to deliver the manuscript by a specified date.

"*...Each party to this Agreement shall give prompt notice in writing to the other party of any Claims...*" As a practical matter, the author or the publisher may learn of a potential legal problem long before the claim is formally presented or a lawsuit is filed. Since it is in the best interest of both the author *and* publisher to evaluate and respond to potential legal problems at the earliest possible moment, the sample clause requires each to let the other know of any such problems, "*prompt*[ly]" and "*in writing*."

✍ **Prompt Notice of Claims**. Although the author may be tempted to ignore a potential problem in the hopes that it will just go away, the fact is that an early warning may permit the publisher to take preventive measures that will avoid a formal claim or reduce the cost of settling one. Suppose, for example, that a legal defect in the first printing of the author's book could be corrected in the next printing. The sooner the publisher finds out about it, the better will be the position of both the author and publisher in mitigating damages and reducing the risks of a claim. Failure to give prompt notice, of course, is itself a breach of the book contract.

✍ **Approval of Settlements**. Some book contracts include a provision that obliges the publisher to seek the approval of the author before settling a claim at the author's expense. This is a fair and decent approach that restrains the publisher against rushing to pay off a meritless claim and then charging the settlement to the author's royalty account. If the contract does not include such a clause, the author ought to ask for one to be added, i.e., "**No compromise or settlement of any Claims at the Author's expense shall be made or entered into without the prior written approval of Author.**" The publisher, however, may insist on a further qualification to prevent the author from vetoing a settlement and compelling the publisher to litigate the claim: "**...such approval not to be unreasonably withheld.**" Some publishers will go even further and reserve the right to settle a claim without the author's consent unless the author agrees—and is able—to pay the continuing costs of defense out of his own pocket.

*"...In the event of any Claims, Publisher shall have the right to suspend payments...as security for Author's obligations under this section..."* The publisher generally enjoys the right to debit the author's royalty account for costs and expenses owed by the author (➤*Accounting, Page 193*), and the right to hold back some portion of the author's royalties and other payments as a reserve against returns. (➤*Reserve Against Returns, Page 199*) Here, the same principle is applied in the indemnity clause: The publisher need not pay the author *anything* while a claim is pending in order to provide a fund from which to satisfy the author's obligation to pay the costs of defense, settlement, and judgment. As a practical matter, the suspension of royalty payments may be the only way for the publisher to actually extract money from an author without going to the trouble and expense of filing a lawsuit against the author to enforce the indemnity obligations.

*"...Author's warranties, representations, and indemnities... shall extend to any person or entity against whom any Claims are asserted by reason of the exploitation of the rights granted by Author in this Agreement..."* The sample clause assumes that the book contract entitles the publisher to transfer various rights in the author's work to third parties, i.e., the publisher may have assigned its rights to publish the author's work in book form to another publisher, or licensed one or more of the subsidiary rights to another *"person or entity"* such as a foreign publisher, an audio publisher, a motion picture producer, and so on. If so, all of the author's *"warranties, representations, and indemnities"* are deemed to apply to all of the publisher's licensees as if they were *"originally made to such third parties."* Thus, for example, if someone depicted in the author's novel chooses to sue for libel only when the book is made into a movie, then the author is obliged to indemnify the movie producer on the same terms and to the same extent as he would have been obliged to indemnify the publisher if the claim had been brought on the basis of the book rather than the movie.

✍ **Limits on Third-Party Indemnity**. The extension of the author's indemnity obligations to third parties applies only to the extent that the publisher is entitled to transfer rights in the author's

> work. If the contract limits the publisher's right to do so, then the indemnity clause should be modified by eliminating or limiting the third-party indemnity provisions.

*"...All such warranties, representations, and indemnities shall survive the termination or expiration of this Agreement."* At least in theory, a lawsuit or other claim might arise *after* the publisher has taken the author's work out of print, the rights have reverted to the author, and the book contract has expired or otherwise terminated. (➤*Chapter 10: Cessation of Publication*) The sample clause, however, provides that the *"warranties, representations, and indemnities"* of the author *"survive the termination or expiration,"* and thus the publisher is entitled to look to the author to honor his indemnity obligations even though the contract itself is no longer in full effect.

### INSURANCE

Publisher, at its own expense, shall name Author as an additional insured on any policies of insurance that Publisher, in its sole and absolute discretion, may maintain during the term of this Agreement.

The single best way for the author to lighten the burdens and soften the risks of his indemnity obligations is to ask for a so-called insurance clause—that is, a promise by the publisher to include the author on its policies of insurance. Not every publisher is insured, and the publishers that carry insurance are reluctant to promise that they will always do so. Many publishers, though, are willing to include an insurance clause in the book contract itself or as a rider to the contract.

*"Publisher...shall name Author as an additional insured..."* The sample clause does not require the publisher to acquire insurance coverage especially for the author but only to add the author *"as an additional insured"* on its own policies, and to do so *"at its own expense."* As a practical matter, the inclusion of additional insureds on a policy is not likely to trigger an increase in the premium, but it confers an important benefit upon the author: he will be entitled to a notice from the

insurance company if the policy is canceled or not renewed, which will enable him to secure replacement insurance if he chooses to do so.

*"...any policies of insurance that Publisher, in its sole and absolute discretion, may maintain..."* Significantly, the sample clause does not actually obligate the publisher to maintain *any* insurance; the decision is left to the publisher in its *"sole and absolute discretion."* However, if the publisher elects to obtain coverage, then the author is entitled to be named on any and all such policies.

*"...during the term of this Agreement."* The sample clause applies only to insurance policies that the publisher may choose to maintain during the term of the agreement. Once the agreement has expired or otherwise terminated, the obligation to name the author as an insured comes to an end.

---

✍ **Effect of Insurance on Author's Indemnity**. The fact that the author is named on the publisher's insurance policy does *not* relieve the author of his obligations under the indemnity provision of the book contract. (➤ *Author's Indemnity of Publisher, Page 213*) Some publishers, however, may agree to limit the author's indemnity obligation to the costs that are *not* covered by insurance, i.e., "**Author shall be responsible for 50% of any applicable insurance deductible and all amounts in excess of policy limits in connection with the Claims.**" Other publishers may demand that the author pay the entire deductible "...**in the event that an adverse judgment is entered on a claim for copyright infringement.**" And here is an important caveat: since the publisher's insurance is primarily intended to cover the *publisher*'s conduct, any insurance clause, and any policy of insurance to which it relates, should be carefully reviewed to make sure that it extends to the risks undertaken by the *author*—a task that is best performed by an experienced attorney. Even if the author's indemnity obligation remains fully intact, however, insurance coverage is a significant benefit because the insurance company will generally provide attorneys to defend the claim—an expense that may be sizable even if the claim itself is settled for a modest amount of money.

✍ **Certificate of Insurance**. To verify that the publisher has provided insurance coverage for the author, the insurance clause may be modified to provide that "**Publisher shall provide Author with a certificate of insurance or other proof of coverage for each policy on which Author is an additional insured, and shall notify Author in writing of the expiration, termination, cancellation, or nonrenewal of any such coverage.**"

✍ **Coverage After the Contract Ends.** According to a clause found in many book contracts, including the model contract in *Kirsch's Guide*, the author's indemnity obligations "survive" the expiration or termination of the contract. (➤*Rights Surviving Termination, Page 243*) For that reason, the watchful author may ask that the insurance clause be modified to apply to any policy that the publisher maintains in effect "*during the term of this Agreement* **or so long as the Author remains obligated to Publisher under any warranties, representations, or indemnities.**"

# 9
## OPTIONS, NONCOMPETITION, AND OTHER RIGHTS AND RESTRICTIONS

The allocation of rights between author and publisher is generally described in the grant-of-right clauses that appear at the outset of a standard book contract. (➤ *Chapter 2: Transfer of Rights*) But the ownership and control of certain crucial rights in the author's work—the publisher's option to acquire rights in future works of the author, for example, and the author's reservation of rights—are found elsewhere in the book contract, sometimes buried away in the tedious boilerplate that eager authors seldom read with much care or attention. Each of these clauses, however, can be regarded as a fundamental deal point that will have long-lasting effects on the author's career and the future dealings between the author and publisher.

### $

#### OPTION ON AUTHOR'S NEXT WORK

Publisher shall have the right to acquire Author's next book-length work on the same terms and conditions set forth in this Agreement. Author shall submit a detailed outline and sample chapter of such work to Publisher before submitting the work to any other publisher, and Publisher shall have a period of thirty (30) days in which to review the submission and determine whether or not to exercise the option. The thirty (30)-day period described above shall not begin to run earlier than sixty (60) days after the publication of the Work. If Publisher declines to exercise its option, then Author may submit the work to other publishers or otherwise dispose of the work.

An option entitles the publisher to acquire future works by the author under specified circumstances. The publisher regards its option rights as a fair return on its investment in the author's career. If publication of a book by the author creates a demand for more of her work, the publisher reasons, then the publisher is entitled to participate in her success by publishing her next book, too. The author, on the other hand, tends to regard such an option as a kind of indentured servitude, tying her to the publisher and denying her the opportunity to put her next book up for auction to the highest bidder. The sample clause embodies the kind of option that a publisher regards as ideal—the unconditional right to publish the author's next book on the same terms as the first book. But there are other, more evenhanded ways to address the publisher's option rights.

*"Publisher shall have the right to acquire Author's next book-length work..."* The sample clause bestows upon the publisher the unconditional right to acquire the rights to the next book written by the author *"on the same terms and conditions set forth in this Agreement."* If the publisher exercises its option, no negotiations are necessary: the advance, the grant of rights, the royalty rates, and all the other particulars of a deal for the author's next book will be exactly the same as those set forth

**Other Approaches to the Option.** The option described in the sample clause is known as a *right of first refusal*—the author must submit her next work to the original publisher before offering it to any other publisher, and the original publisher is entitled to acquire the new work on the same terms as those set forth in the current agreement. Another approach is called a *right of first negotiation*, which guarantees the original publisher a period of exclusive negotiation—if no agreement on terms is reached, the author is free to submit the book to other publishers. A *right of last refusal* is yet another approach that allows the author to solicit offers from various publishers. But the original publisher enjoys the right to acquire the book by matching the best deal offered by any other publisher. Some publishers seek both the right of first negotiation *and* the right of last refusal, which means that the author must negotiate with the original publisher before shopping the book to other publishing houses—and the author must go back to the original publisher before closing a deal with anyone else.

in the original book contract. Some option clauses, however, leave some or all of the deal points and other contract terms open for future negotiation between the author and publisher—an approach that strongly favors the author and renders the option clause far more evenhanded.

The sample clause applies only to the next "*book-length*" work that the author undertakes, and thus the publisher is not entitled to articles, short stories, or other shorter works. Still, the clause does not define what constitutes a "book-length" work, and even works of rather modest length—a novella, for example, or a long essay—arguably fall under the option clause.

Since the sample clause applies only to the author's "*next*" work, the author satisfies her obligations under the option by submitting the next book she proposes to write to the publisher. If the publisher declines to exercise its option, the author is then free to offer the same book or any other book to other publishers. But the law imposes an implied obligation of good faith on the author, and it is *not* legally sufficient to offer the publisher a book that the author does not really intend to write (and hopes the publisher will not want to publish) just to extricate herself from the option. (➤*Complete Manuscript Submissions, Page 225*)

"*...Author shall submit a detailed outline and sample chapter of such work to Publisher...*" The sample option clause does not require the author to actually *write* her next book and submit the manuscript to the publisher. Rather, the author need only submit "*a detailed outline and sample chapter*," and the publisher is required to decide whether or not to exercise its option on the basis of these limited materials. Many contracts in common use, however, require the submission of a complete manuscript—a vastly greater burden on the author and a significant benefit to the publisher, who is able to judge the merits of the book itself before exercising its option rights. The precise requirements for submission of the author's next work under an option clause—complete manuscript, outline and sample chapter, or something in between—is often the subject of vigorous negotiation in a book deal.

📖 **Complete Manuscript Submissions.** The requirement that the author submit a complete manuscript, rather than an outline and sample chapter or other proposal materials, bestows some significant advantages on the publisher. Aside from the most obvious one—the publisher may exercise its option on the book itself and not merely the author's proposal for a book—the requirement for complete manuscript submission discourages the author from intentionally submitting a bad idea for a book in an effort to defeat the rights of the publisher under the option clause.

*"...before submitting the work to any other publisher..."* Strictly speaking, the author may not make any submission of her next work to a rival publisher until the original publisher has seen the author's next work and decides whether or not to exercise its option. Thus, the author who informally shops around a manuscript or book proposal, whether or not she discloses the fact that another publisher enjoys an option to acquire it, is in breach of the sample clause.

*"...Publisher shall have a period of thirty (30) days in which to review the submission and determine whether or not to exercise the option..."* The sample clause establishes a clear deadline by which the publisher must exercise its option or else forfeit the right to acquire the author's next work. The option period itself is subject to negotiation, and 30 days is probably the shortest period to which a publisher will agree; some publishers, in fact, ask for 45, 60, or even 90 days, and longer periods are not unheard of. Other option clauses in common use refer only to a "reasonable" period of time, an approach that invites a future dispute over exactly what is reasonable. As a general rule, a firm deadline is always best because it permits both parties to know exactly when their rights begin and end.

*"...The thirty (30)-day period described above shall not begin to run earlier than sixty (60) days after the publication of the Work..."* Publishers are reluctant to exercise their option rights on the author's *next* work until they know how well her *current* book is doing. For that reason, the option period is almost always linked to the publication date of the current work, and the publisher is not obliged to consider and act upon a

submission under the option clause until the current book is actually published and the early sales figures are known.

The author, by contrast, is put in an awkward position by any option clause that is linked to the publication date. On the day that the book contract is signed, the publication date lies in the distant future. The author must finish the manuscript and complete any necessary revisions, and even then, the publisher usually enjoys a long period before it is required to actually publish the work. As a practical matter, many months and sometimes even years will pass before the current book is actually published, and, until then, the option clause keeps any new project of the author off the market.

---

✍ **Limits on the Option Clause.** A few authors possess sufficient clout to negotiate an option clause out of the contract, but most authors find it necessary to submit themselves to *some* form of option. The worst features of an option may be softened, however, by putting certain limits on the publisher's rights. The time within which the option must be exercised or forfeited might be shortened. The option clause may be modified so that it applies only to a certain category of work by the author, i.e., "**...the Author's next work of nonfiction only...**" or "**...the Author's next work featuring the main character of the Work.**"

---

"*...If Publisher declines to exercise its option, then Author may submit the work to other publishers or otherwise dispose of the work.*" The sample clause explicitly confirms that the author is restrained from selling or even submitting the next work to other publishers unless and until the original publisher actually "*declines to exercise its option.*" Thus, if the deadline established in the contract passes and the publisher has not acted, the author is free to submit her work elsewhere. However, if the option clause does not specify a deadline—and refers only to a "reasonable" period—then the author takes a certain risk in submitting her work to other publishers until the original publisher actually notifies the author that her next work has been declined. Also, if the option clause includes a "right of last refusal" (➤*Other Approaches to the Option, Page 223*), then the author may be obliged to come back to the original publisher after submitting the book to other publishers.

---

✍ **Breaking the Chain of Options.** Since the sample clause entitles the publisher to acquire the rights in the author's next work *"on the same terms and conditions set forth in this Agreement,"* the publisher automatically acquires a new option on the author's third book when it exercises its option to acquire the second book! Thus, the sample clause raises the distinct risk that the author will remain under an endless chain of options that will be broken only if and when the publisher does *not* exercise its option on a future work. To avoid the dilemma, some authors ask for one slight modification to the clause, i.e., "*...on the same terms and conditions set forth in this Agreement* **except that the contract for publication of Author's next work shall not include an option of any kind in favor of Publisher, and Publisher shall not acquire the right to publish Author's subsequent work.**"

---

### AUTHOR'S NEXT WORK

Author acknowledges and agrees that the Work shall be Author's next published work in book form, and Author shall not publish or permit the publication of any other work in book form prior to publication of the Work by Publisher under this Agreement.

A few book contracts include a clause that restrains the author from publishing *any* other book before the publisher issues the book under contract, whether or not the next work is subject to an option. Indeed, such a clause is all the more important to the publisher if the contract does not include an option on the author's next work. The publisher seeks a certain period of exclusivity as the publisher of the author's work and wants to avoid competition from another book by the same author that reaches the market before its book. Thus, the sample clause requires the author to promise that "*the Work shall be Author's next work published in book form,*" and specifically prevents the author from "*publish*[ing] or *permit*[ting] *the publication of any other work in book* form" unless and until the book under contract to the publisher is actually released.

Like an option clause, however, the sample clause imposes an uncomfortable burden on the author by keeping her out of the book market until the publisher finally releases its first edition of the work under contract. Months, and more likely years, will pass between the date of signing a book contract and the publication date, and the author is restrained from publishing any other of her work until then.

## RESERVATION OF RIGHTS

**All rights in the Work not expressly granted to Publisher under this Agreement are wholly and exclusively reserved to Author.**

The sample clause expressly confirms something that is implicit in any book contract: any particular right in the bundle of rights that makes up the copyright in the author's work that is *not* granted to the publisher still belongs to the author. (➤ *The "Bundle of Rights" in a Copyrighted Work, Page 50*) Strictly speaking, the sample clause ought not be necessary (especially if the contract has been carefully and expertly drafted), but some watchful authors and their attorneys will ask for a reservation of rights clause as a matter of caution, and some book contracts already include one. Indeed, if the author asks for such a clause and the publisher refuses, then the publisher must be confronted with a probing question *before* the contract is signed—namely, what rights does the publisher regard as not "*wholly and exclusively reserved by Author*" even though such rights are not "*expressly granted to Publisher*"?

Some book contracts, however, include a reservation of rights clause with one additional phrase that presents far more problems than it solves: **"Author shall not exploit any of the reserved rights in a manner that injures or interferes with Publisher's exploitation of rights under this Agreement."** In other words, the publisher is willing to confirm that all rights not granted to the publisher are reserved by the author, but then seeks to impose some limits on how the reserved rights may be exploited by the author. Essentially, the additional sentence is a kind of noncompetition clause—that is, a promise by the author not to go into competition with the publisher by releasing any works that might injure the sales of the publisher's editions of the author's work, even if the competing works are based on rights that the author has expressly reserved. (➤*Author's Noncompetition,* See below)

The restriction on the use of the author's reserved rights serves the best interests of the publisher by reducing the number and kind of competitive products in the marketplace. And the author may reasonably conclude that her reserved rights will be rendered valueless. Suppose, for example, that the author has granted hardcover rights in her work to the publisher and reserved softcover rights for herself. The reservation-of -rights clause arguably prevents her from actually making a softcover deal with another publisher, since the availability of a less expensive paperback edition would surely reduce the sales of the hardback edition. Above all, the additional sentence is so blurry in its restrictions that it raises the risk of future conflicts between author and publisher. Both parties are better served if the reservation-of-rights clause makes it clear exactly what the author can and cannot do with the reserved rights in her work.

---

✍ **Hold-Backs on Reserved Rights**. A fairer and more realistic approach to restricting the use of reserved rights is a "hold-back"—that is, an agreement by the author that certain reserved rights will not be exploited for a specified period of time, i.e., "**Notwithstanding her reservation of rights in the Work, Author acknowledges and agrees that no softcover edition of the Work shall be published earlier than one year after publication of Publisher's first edition of the Work.**"

---

## AUTHOR'S NONCOMPETITION

**During the duration of this Agreement, Author shall not prepare, publish, or participate in the preparation or publication of, any competing work that is substantially similar to the Work, or which is likely to injure the sales of the Work.**

As a general rule, the book contract bestows upon the publisher the exclusive right to publish or exploit the author's work in one or more specified medium. (➤*Chapter 2: Transfer of Rights*) By definition, the author may not authorize anyone else to make use of rights that have been granted exclusively to the publisher. (➤*Author's Warranties and Representations, Page 207; Author's Indemnity of Publisher, Page 213*) But many publishers go one step further by asking the author to refrain from competing with the publisher's editions of the author's work in what is commonly known as a "noncompete" clause.

*"During the duration of this Agreement..."* According to the sample clause, the author's duty of noncompetition remains in effect only so long as the contract itself is in effect. Once the contract has expired or terminated for some other reason (➤*Chapter 10: Cessation of Publication*), the author need no longer heed the restrictions in the noncompetition clause.

*"...Author shall not prepare, publish, or participate in the preparation or publication of..."* The sample clause reflects a lawyerly effort to comprehensively rule out competition with the publisher's edition of the author's work by the author herself or by anyone with whom the author may work. Thus, the clause prevents the author both from preparing or publishing a competitive work on her own initiative, or *"participat*[ing]*"* in any competitive publication.

*"...any competing work that is substantially similar to the Work or which is likely to injure the sales of the Work."* The fundamental purpose of a noncompete clause is, of course, to rule out the publication of a *"competing work."* But the sample clause qualifies the restriction in two rather subtle ways. First, the author may not publish a work that is *"substantially similar"* to the work acquired by the publisher, a phrase that echoes the legal definition of infringement under copyright law. Thus, the author is essentially promising to do nothing more than refrain from infringing those rights in her work that she has already conveyed to the publisher, a duty that is already imposed on the author by law. Then the sample clause goes on to impose a much more expansive restriction: The author may not publish a competing work that *"is likely to injure the sales of the Work,"* whether or not the competing work is substantially similar to the work acquired by the publisher.

✍ **Reducing the Scope and Effect of a Noncompetition Clause.** Rarely, if ever, will a publisher agree to delete a noncompetition clause that already appears in its standard book contract; indeed, the request to do so is likely to raise some troubling anxieties in the publisher about the commitment of the author to the book project under negotiation. Some agents and attorneys, however, will ask the publisher to reduce the scope and effect of a noncompete by inserting words that intentionally blur the lines, i.e., a restriction upon a **"directly *competing work"*** or one that *"substantially and materially injures the sale[s] of the Work."* Sometimes the best approach is to define the specific books that the author is actually seeking permission to publish and to exempt them from the noncompete, i.e., **"The foregoing noncompetition clause shall not apply to any works by the Author on the subject of publishing law."**

## TITLE AND SERIES RIGHTS

**Publisher reserves all rights in and to the title (including series title, if any), logotype, trademark, trade dress, format, and other features of the Work as published and promoted by Publisher. Publisher shall have the sole right to develop sequels or "prequels," new or additional titles in a series, or related works using any and all such elements, and shall be free to commission or contract with any other person(s) for the preparation of such sequels, series, or related works.**

Some of the most enduring successes in publishing begin as a single book and then proliferate into a series of related titles. Among the many examples to be found in any bookstore are the "*Dummies*" and "*Idiot*" how-to books and the "*Frommer*" and "*Fodor*" travel guides, each one written by a different author and addressing a different subject but expertly designed and marketed as a series. A vigilant publisher will make sure that the right to establish a series and spin off new titles is secured in every book contract.

*"Publisher reserves all rights..."* The sample clause permits the publisher to acquire the right to publish a single work by a specific author, create a distinctive format for publication, and then publish a series of related works using the same format but

**Ownership of Title, Character, and Pseudonyms.** A book title, a distinctive fictional character, or an author's pseudonym are all potentially valuable property rights that can and should be allocated between an author and a publisher in a book contract. A freelance travel writer who works on a travel book for Fodor would hardly expect an ownership interest in the series itself, for example, but Samuel Clemens was surely entitled to regard himself as the exclusive owner of the pen name "Mark Twain," and Raymond Chandler would not have given up the right to produce the further adventures of Philip Marlowe. Thus, the author may reasonably seek to reserve such rights, i.e., **"Publisher acknowledges and agrees that all rights in and to the author's pseudonym, the title of the Work, and the characters and settings in the Work are solely and exclusively owned by Author and may be used only with Author's prior written consent."** Some publishers, especially in the field of romance and juvenile fiction, seek to acquire ownership of these elements so that they can use several different writers on the same series, and such publishers will almost always refuse to acknowledge the ownership of a pseudonym or other features of the author's work.

without using or crediting the original author.

*"...in and to the title (including series title, if any), logotype, trademark, trade dress, format, and other features of the Work as published and promoted by Publisher..."* The sample clause specifies that the publisher owns and controls not only the title of the author's work, but also the *"other features of the Work as published and promoted by Publisher,"* including the *"logotype, trademark, [and] trade dress."*

*"...Publisher shall have the sole right to develop sequels or 'prequels,' new or additional titles in a series, or related works using any and all such elements..."* The publisher's reservation of rights in title, trademark, and trade dress is intended to enable the publisher to use all such elements in *"prequels"* or *"sequels"*—that is, works that lead up to or follow from another work set at an earlier or later point time—and any other *"new or additional titles,"* whether *"in a series"* or in any other *"related works."* The author need not be credited, compensated, or even consulted in the development and publication of such new works, and the publisher is perfectly free to *"commission or contract with any other person(s)"* to do so.

✍ **Author's Right to Participate in a Series**. The author, of course, may seek a much greater role in the preparation of future titles in a series. The most aggressive approach is to seek outright ownership of the right to develop new and additional titles using the same title or character. (➤ *Ownership of Title, Characters, and Pseudonyms, Page 232*) A more moderate stance is to seek an option that entitles the author to participate in future titles, i.e., **"Author shall enjoy the right of first negotiation and last refusal to participate as author in any such new or additional titles."** Some authors are able to secure a modest royalty on the sales of new titles in a series even if they do not choose to participate in the writing of the new works, i.e., **"Whether or not Author participates in the preparation of any such new or additional titles, Publisher shall pay Author a royalty of ___% of Net Revenues from the sale of copies or other exploitation of rights in any sequels, series, or other new and additional products or services related to the Work."**

# 10

## CESSATION OF PUBLICATION

At some point in the life span of the standard book contract, whether early or late, the contract will expire and the rights to the author's book will either revert to the author or pass into the public domain. Some of the circumstances that result in the termination of a book contract may arise even before the manuscript is delivered and accepted for publication. If the author fails to finish and submit the manuscript, for example, or if the publisher deems the manuscript unacceptable, the contract may end then and there. More commonly, however, the contract comes to an end when the demand for the book drops off, sometimes only weeks or months after publication, sometimes after a few years. All but the most enduring books—what publishers call "evergreens"—eventually go out of print, and when they do, the typical book contract reaches its final chapter.

### REMAINDERS

If Publisher determines that there is not sufficient demand for the Work to enable it to continue its publication and sale profitably, the Publisher may dispose of the copies remaining on hand as it deems best. In such event, Author shall have the right, within two (2) weeks of the giving of written notice by Publisher, to a single purchase of some or all of such copies at the best available price, and the purchase of film and plates at Publisher's actual cost of manufacture. If Author declines to purchase such copies or other materials, Publisher may dispose of them and shall pay Author, in lieu of royalties or any other amounts otherwise payable under this Agreement, a sum equal to 5% of the amounts actually received by Publisher in excess of the cost of manufacture.

When the publisher decides that it is no longer profitable to keep the author's work in print, whether in a particular edition or *all* editions, the publisher is generally entitled to stop printing and publishing the book and to sell off the remaining inventory. The leftover books are known in the publishing industry as "remainders," and the process of selling them off is called "remaindering." Sometimes remainders are sold off in bulk to be shredded and recycled; more often, remainders are sold at a drastically reduced price, sometimes no greater than the cost of manufacture and sometimes even less, to "remainder houses"—that is, distributors, catalog publishers, and other marketers that specialize in remainders.

Remaindering is often, but not always, the first step toward taking the author's work out of print, an event that will generally result in the termination of the book contract and the reversion of rights to the author. (➤*Reversion of Rights, Page 238*) If, for example, the publisher first releases a book in a hardcover edition and later publishes a softcover edition, it

---

**Termination of Transfers.** One of the best-kept secrets of copyright law is the fact that *all* book contracts are subject to termination at the author's option after a certain number of years, generally between 35 and 40 years after signing of the contract or publication of the book. The framers of the U.S. Copyright Act bestowed the right on authors—a right that cannot be waived or modified by contract—in order to protect the author who signs a highly disadvantageous contract at the outset of a literary career and then produces an enduring bestseller. Precisely when and how a book contract or other copyright agreement may be terminated is a highly technical matter and requires careful analysis of the underlying book contract and publishing history of the book itself. In any event, the right does not become available until several decades after the contract is signed. As a result, few authors are aware of their right to terminate a book contract, and fewer still actually exercise the right to do so. (See *Kirsch's Handbook, Chapter 8: Remaindering, Reversion and Copyright Termination*)

is not unusual for the hardback edition to be remaindered—but the book is not out of print and the contract remains in effect. Remaindering and reversion are so often linked, however, that the two issues may be covered in the same clause in a book contract, although they are treated separately in the model contract in *Kirsch's Guide.*

*"If Publisher determines that there is not sufficient demand for the Work to enable it to continue its publication and sale profitably..."* The decision to remainder a book is almost always based on the bottom line. The publisher will not continue to print, stock, and sell a book that is losing money. Of course, what constitutes a profitable book depends on the publisher, and the sales that a major corporate publisher might regard as pathetic or even catastrophic might seem very attractive to a smaller publisher with more modest overhead. But the decision is always a subjective one, and it is always left to the publisher's discretion. As a practical matter, the author cannot compel the publisher to keep a book in print once the decision has been made to remainder it. His only remedy is a reversion of rights, which permits him to resell the book to another publisher that sees a way to make money on it. (➤*Reversion of Rights, Page 238*)

📖 **Remaindering for Noneconomic Reasons.** Sometimes, if only rarely, a publisher may decide to take a book out of print because it has prompted a lawsuit or the threat of one. Strictly speaking, the sample clause, like the remainder clauses in most book contracts, applies only to market demand and thus may not apply to such circumstances. However, the model contract in *Kirsch's Guide* includes several other clauses upon which the publisher might rely in taking a book out of print for noneconomic reasons. (➤*A Clause Providing for Publisher's Right to Terminate Due to Changed Conditions, Page 156; Review by Publisher's Counsel, Page 165*)

*"...the Publisher may dispose of the copies remaining on hand as it deems best..."* The publisher enjoys the right to decide how to remainder a book, whether by destroying the existing copies by sending them to a recycler or by selling them off at distress prices to a distributor that specializes in remainders, or sometimes by both methods. The only restraint on the publisher's decision to dump the author's work is the right of the author to buy some

or all of the remainders before they end up on the sale table at the local bookstore or in the shredder at some recycling plant.

*"...In such event, Author shall have the right...to a single purchase of some or all of such copies..."* The sample clause allows the author an opportunity to make a *"single purchase"* of the remainders before the publisher disposes of them, and the right must be exercised within a two-week period following *"the giving of written notice by Publisher."* By definition, of course, the right to buy remainders is afforded only once, and whatever the author does not buy will be sold or destroyed. For that reason, many authors avail themselves of the right to buy their remaindered books, and, as I can attest from personal knowledge, boxes of them can be found in garages and basements across America!

*"...at the best available price..."* The sample clause presumes that the publisher will solicit offers to purchase the remainders from a remainder house or a recycler or both, and then offer the remainders to the author at the highest price offered by a third party. Technically, the author is entitled to pay only the market price of the remainders—that is, the best offer from a bona fide third party purchaser. As a practical matter, however, the publisher may simply state a price at which remainders are offered to the author, often the original cost of manufacture or a specified discount from the cost of manufacture, i.e., **"Publisher's actual cost of manufacture less 10%."**

*"...and the purchase of film and plates..."* The sample clause also allows the author to purchase *"film and plates"*—that is, the materials that a printer uses to actually manufacture copies of the book. The right to purchase printing materials is increasingly attractive to authors who either seek to resell their work to another publisher or who decide to publish their own books. The price is set in the sample clause at *"Publisher's actual cost of manufacture,"* although the market value of these production materials is probably much less than it cost the publisher to acquire them in the first place.

*"...If Author declines to purchase such copies or other materials, Publisher may dispose of them..."* Once the author has availed himself of the right to purchase remainders or printing materials—or declined to so, whether by giving notice to the

publisher or by failing to act within the two-week window of opportunity—the publisher is free to *"dispose of them"* by selling or destroying the remainders.

*"...and shall pay Author, in lieu of royalties or any other amount otherwise payable under this Agreement, a sum equal to 5% of the amounts actually received by Publisher in excess of the cost of manufacture."* Some share of the proceeds from remainders is usually allocated to the author. The sample clause, for instance, entitles the publisher to deduct *"the cost of manufacture"* and then obliges the publisher to pay 5% of the *"amounts actually received"* to the author. Such payments are modest at best, often negligible, and sometimes nothing at all is owed if the publisher sells remainders *below* the cost of manufacture. Since such payments, if any, are *"in lieu of royalties...otherwise payable,"* the publisher owes the author no other financial compensation in connection with the sale of remainders.

## REVERSION OF RIGHTS

If the Work goes out of print in all Publisher's editions, Author shall have the right to request that Publisher reprint or cause a licensee to reprint the Work. Publisher shall have twelve (12) months after receipt of any such written request from Author to comply, unless prevented from doing so by circumstances beyond Publisher's control. If Publisher declines to reprint the Work as described above, or if Publisher agrees to reprint the Work but fails to do so within the time allowed, then Author may terminate this Agreement upon sixty (60) days' notice in writing. Upon such termination, all rights granted under this Agreement, except the rights to dispose of existing stock, shall revert to Author, subject to all rights which may have been granted by Publisher to third parties under this Agreement, and Publisher shall have no further obligations or liabilities to Author except that Author's earned royalties shall be paid when and as due. The Work shall not be deemed out of print within the meaning of this section so long as the Work is available for sale either from stock in Publisher's, distributor's, or licensee's warehouse, or in regular sales channels.

If the author's work is taken out of print in all editions, the author is generally entitled to reclaim the rights in his work and terminate the book contract—that is, the rights *revert* to the author, and thus the clause is often called a "reversionary clause." Remaindering of a single edition, of course, is not enough, and even after the author's work is out of print in all editions, the author is required to follow a rather elaborate procedure, as described below, before the publisher finally relinquishes its rights to the author's work.

*"If the Work goes out of print in all Publisher's editions..."* The triggering event in the sample clause—and virtually all reversionary clauses—is the publisher's decision to take the author's work "out of print," a concept that generally means the work is no longer being published and distributed. As noted below, exactly what constitutes "out of print" is *not* a matter of common usage in the publishing industry and is often the subject of heated negotiation. According to the sample clause, *all* of the publisher's editions must be out of print before the author enjoys the right of reversion.

*"...Author shall have the right to request that Publisher reprint or cause a licensee to reprint the Work..."* The fact that the author's work is out of print, however, does not result in an immediate reversion of rights. Rather, the sample clause prescribes an elaborate series of requests that the author is obliged to direct to the publisher, all of which are intended to afford the publisher an opportunity to put the book back into print. The first of these requests, which must be conveyed in writing, asks the publisher (or a third party acting under license from the publisher) to put the book back into print. Only if the publisher fails to do so—and only after the passage of a considerable period of time—is the author actually entitled to reclaim the rights to his work.

*"...Publisher shall have twelve (12) months after receipt of any such written request from Author to comply, unless prevented from doing so by circumstances beyond Publisher's*

*control..."* The period within which the publisher must respond to the author's request to put his book back into print varies considerably in book contracts. It is seldom less than six months, and the sample clause affords the publisher a full year *"after receipt of such written request."* What's more, the period is automatically extended if the publisher is *"prevented from doing so by circumstances beyond Publisher's control"* such as strikes, riots, or natural disasters. (➤*Force Majeure, Page 251*)

*"...If Publisher declines to reprint the Work as described above..."* Some publishers will promptly and straightforwardly confirm that they have no intention of putting the author's book back into print, a gracious gesture that greatly accelerates the date on which the rights revert to the author. More often, however, the publisher will use the time allowed in the reversionary clause to decide whether or not to issue its own new edition or to look for another publisher to do so.

*"...or if Publisher agrees to reprint the Work but fails to do so within the time allowed..."* The sample clause obliges the publisher to respond to the author's initial request by indicating whether or not it *"agrees to reprint the Work."* As noted above, many publishers will give such an indication, if only to preserve their right to put the author's work back into print and to delay the actual reversion of rights while they consider whether and how to do so. But the sample clause establishes a firm deadline; if the publisher *"fails to do so within the time allowed,"* then the author is entitled to reclaim the rights in his work.

*"...then Author may terminate this Agreement upon sixty (60) days' notice in writing..."* Even if the publisher readily concedes that it does not intend to reprint the author's work, or if the period allowed in the reversionary clause passes without the reissue of the author's work by the publisher or a licensee, the rights will not actually revert the author under the sample clause unless and until the author gives formal notice in writing to the publisher. And, even then, the reversion does not take effect for another 60 days. The 60-day notice period, however, does not allow enough time for the publisher to rush a new edition into print. So once the notice is given, it is only a matter of time before the rights are restored to the author.

> 📖 **Restrictions on Reversionary Clauses.** Some publishers are unwilling to allow the rights to revert to an author whose book has not yet earned out or who is otherwise indebted to the publisher. For this reason, the reversionary clause in some book contracts provides that the author is not entitled to reclaim the rights to his work **"so long as Author is indebted to Publisher for any unrecouped advance or other amount owing by Author to Publisher under this Agreement or any other agreement between Author and Publisher."**

*"...Upon such termination, all rights granted under this Agreement shall revert to Author..."* Once the author has complied with the various notice provisions and waiting periods prescribed in the reversionary clause—according to the sample clause, a process that may take 14 months or even longer—the rights to the author's work finally revert to the author. Even then, however, the sample clause continues to reserve a few rights to the publisher. For example, the reversion of rights does not prevent the publisher from *"dispos*[ing] *of existing stock"*—that is, remaindering any copies still on hand. More significantly, the reversion of rights is *"subject to all rights which may have been granted by Publisher to third parties under this Agreement."*

Suppose, for example, the publisher has licensed the right to publish a foreign edition or an audio version of the author's work to another publisher, but the publisher's own editions have gone out of print. Under the sample clause, the fact that the *publisher* is no longer publishing the book permits the author to reclaim his rights from the publisher, but the publisher's *licensees* are still entitled to exploit the rights licensed to them. Thus, the agreements between the publisher and various third parties will remain in effect even though the rest of the rights to the author's work have reverted, and the author may not exploit the licensed rights until the third-party licenses have expired or otherwise terminated.

*"...Publisher shall have no further obligations or liabilities to Author except that Author's earned royalties shall be paid when and as due..."* Once the reversion of rights is effective, the publisher generally owes *"no further obligations or liabilities to Author."* But there is one important exception: If the publisher owes royalties to the author under the agreement,

whether on past sales of the publisher's editions or as a share of future income from third-party licenses, then the publisher must continue to account for these revenues and pay them to the author *"when and as due"*—that is, according to the accounting provisions of the contract itself. (➤*Accounting, Page 193*)

**"Out of Print" in the Computer Age.** The definition of "out of print" has taken on new and only dimly understood meanings in today's book industry, where publishers are only beginning to explore new technologies and methods of distribution. Suppose, for example, that a book is longer published in the conventional sense, but the book can be ordered and printed out for single-copy sales through "publish-on-demand" technologies. (➤*Electronic Rights, Page 76*) The customary definition of "out of print" no longer applies, and the publisher that relies on a traditional definition may lose the rights to the author's work if the book is available only through a publish-on-demand distribution system. The author, of course, is justified in arguing that the availability of his book for the occasional single-copy sale is not sufficient to prevent him from reclaiming his rights under a more traditional out-of-print clause.

*"...The Work shall not be deemed out of print...so long as the Work is available for sale either from stock in Publisher's, distributor's, or licensee's warehouse, or in regular sales channels.* Here is the crucial definition of what the sample clause means by the phrase "out of print." The book is *not* considered to be out of print— and the author is *not* entitled to initiate the process by which the rights will ultimately revert to him—if copies of the work are available from one of two sources. The first of these sources is the stock maintained *"in Publisher's, distributor's, or licensee's warehouse,"* which means that the book is still in print as long as a copy can be ordered from the publisher or its distributor or licensee, whether by a retail bookseller or by a consumer. The second of these sources is *"regular sales channels,"* which generally designates the whole distribution system used by publishers to make their book available to the book trade but might also apply to catalog sales or direct marketing. The definition is broad and loose enough to preserve the rights of the publisher even though the book itself no longer appears on the shelves of a retail bookstore. Other definitions of "out of

print" can be found in various book contracts, and authors often negotiate for a more favorable one.

---

✍ **Other Definitions of "Out of Print"**. The author is entitled to be concerned if the book contract deems his work to be in print when, in fact, the consumer must take extraordinary steps to find and buy a copy. Thus, the author may negotiate for a more realistic definition of what it means to be "out of print." For example, the sample clause might be marked up as follows: "*The Work shall not be deemed out of print within the meaning of this section so long as* an English-language edition of *the Work* in book form is listed in the current catalog of Publisher or its licensee and *is available for sale* in ordinary channels of distribution in the book trade in the United States ~~either from stock in Publisher's, distributor's, or licensee's warehouse, or in regular sales channels.~~" (➤ *"Out of Print" in the Computer Age, Page 242*)

---

## RIGHTS SURVIVING TERMINATION

Upon the expiration or termination of this Agreement, any rights reverting to Author shall be subject to all licenses and other grants of rights made by Publisher to third parties pursuant to this Agreement. Any and all rights of Publisher under such licenses and grants of rights, and all warranties, representations, and indemnities of Author, shall survive the expiration or termination of this Agreement.

*"Upon the expiration or termination of this Agreement..."* Even when the book contract has expired or terminated, and the book itself is out of print, some lingering rights and duties will *"survive,"* as the sample clause puts it, and remain in effect. The sample clause specifies two in particular, both of which are continuing obligations of the *author*.

*"...any rights reverting to Author shall be subject to all licenses and other grants of rights made by Publisher to third parties..."* As discussed above, the sample clause confirms that the reversion of rights to the author upon termination of the book is *"subject to all licenses and other grants of rights...to third*

*parties.*" So the author must continue to honor the rights of third-party licensees. (➤*Reversion of Rights, Page 238*)

"*...and all warranties, representations, and indemnities of Author, shall survive the expiration or termination of this Agreement.*" Another lingering effect of the book contract is the survival of the author's obligations to guarantee that his work is free of legal defects and to protect the publisher against any lawsuit or other claim that may be brought against the publisher based on the book. If, for example, a lawsuit for copyright infringement or invasion or privacy is filed *after* the book goes out of print and the contract is terminated, the author is still obligated to "*indemnify, defend and hold* [the publisher] *harmless.*" (➤*Author's Indemnity of Publisher, Page 213*) As a practical matter, it is unlikely that a lawsuit would be filed long after first publication of the author's work, and some such claims would be barred by the statute of limitations. But the author's obligation to defend even a belated claim remains in effect long after the contract itself is a dead letter.

# 11

## GENERAL PROVISIONS

The last several pages of a typical book contract are devoted to the legal miscellany that appears in legal agreements of all kinds. Only rarely do such clauses turn out to be crucial to either author or publisher, but even so, most publishers are reluctant to tamper with the boilerplate. Indeed, few authors actually read these clauses and even fewer agents bother to negotiate them. But the presence or absence of certain provisions—an arbitration clause, for example, or an attorneys' fees clause, or the precise phrasing of such a clause—may make a difference at some unknowable point in the long life of a book contract. For that reason, even these sometimes tedious clauses are worth reading and considering in the course of negotiating a book deal.

### RIGHT TO WITHDRAW OFFER

**Publisher shall have the right to withdraw its offer of agreement at any time prior to delivery of this Agreement to and execution of this Agreement by Publisher.**

Negotiations over a book deal may turn out to be so prolonged that the publisher changes its mind before the contract is actually signed, and the sample clause formally reserves the publisher's right to do so. Even if the contract has been fully revised to reflect the agreement of the parties and sent to the author for signing, the publisher may "*withdraw its offer of agreement*" at any time up to the point when an authorized representative of the publisher puts its own signature on the contract.

> **The Publisher Signs Last.** As a general rule, a written contract goes into effect when the *last* party signs the document—a rule of law that determines both when and where the contract is deemed to have been made. For that reason, a prudent publisher will send the author an *unsigned* contract and countersign it only after the author has signed and returned the document. By doing so, the publisher preserves its right to withdraw from the book deal until the last possible moment.

## COUNTERPARTS

This Agreement may be signed in counterparts, and if so, the counterparts bearing the signatures of all parties shall be deemed to constitute one binding agreement.

When a contract requires the signature of several parties in far-flung locations, attorneys will sometimes use "counterparts,"—that is, identical copies of the contract which are sent to each party, signed by that party alone, and then gathered together and treated as "*one binding agreement.*" The drawback of counterparts is that no single document includes the signatures of all parties, and if one counterpart is separate and misplaced, then it may be difficult or impossible to prove at a later date that the contract was actually signed by all parties. Thus, most publishers will patiently circulate the contract for signing so that the final document will bear the original signatures of all parties.

> **Duplicate Originals.** Some publishers circulate multiple copies of a contract and ask the author to sign and return all of them for countersignature by the publisher. At the end of the process, the publisher ends up with multiple copies of the same contract, each one signed by all parties. Then the publisher countersigns all of the multiple originals and returns a fully signed copy to the author. Essentially, each such copy may be treated as a fully signed original.

## ADVICE OF COUNSEL

Author acknowledges that Publisher has explained that he or she is entitled to seek the advice and counsel of an attorney or other counselor of Author's choice before agreeing to the terms set forth in this Agreement, and Publisher has encouraged Author to do so. Author acknowledges that, in the event Author signs this Agreement without seeking the advice of an attorney or other counselor, it is because Author has decided to forego such advice and counsel.

The fact that one party to a contract is unrepresented does not affect the enforceability of the contract. Still, the publisher may feel reassured by extracting an acknowledgment from the author that she knew of her right *"to seek the advice and counsel of an attorney or other counselor,"* but *"decided to forego such advice and counsel."* Other publishers are reluctant to raise the point at all, since they fear it will only prompt the author to seek legal advice.

### ENTIRE AGREEMENT

Publisher and Author acknowledge that they have communicated with each other by letter, telephone and/or in person in negotiating this Agreement. However, Author acknowledges and agrees that this Agreement supersedes and replaces all other communications between Author and Publisher, and represents the complete and entire agreement of Author and Publisher regarding the Work.

Much is said in the course of negotiating a book deal that never finds its way into the contract that the parties actually sign. The sample clause confirms that nothing uttered by one party to the other, whether in person or by telephone, and none of the letters, E-mail, memoranda, or faxes exchanged between them, is legally enforceable. According to the sample clause, which is known as an "integration" or "merger" clause, the contract itself *"supersedes and replaces all other communications,"* and *"represents the complete and entire agreement"* of the parties. The sample clause is a caution to both parties—but especially the author—against relying on "handshake" deals, informal assurances, and the other "winks and nods" that may have been given by one party to the other party. If it isn't in the contract, then it isn't a legal obligation.

## MODIFICATION AND WAIVER

**This Agreement may not be modified or altered except by a written instrument signed by the party to be charged. No waiver of any term or condition of this Agreement, or of any breach of this Agreement or any portion thereof, shall be deemed a waiver of any other term, condition, or breach of this Agreement or any portion thereof.**

Once it has been negotiated, drafted, marked up, revised, and then signed by the author and the publisher, a book contract should not be subject to informal or inadvertent changes. Thus, the sample clause establishes a formal procedure for any amendment or modification of the contract. No changes in the terms or conditions of the signed contract will be effective unless they are set forth in "*a written instrument*" (a rider, an amendment, a letter agreement, or some other written document) and then "*signed by the party to be charged*"—that is, the party to the contract who bears the burden of the new or modified clause.

Suppose, for example, the author secures an informal agreement from an editor at the publishing house to extend the manuscript delivery date set forth in the contract. (➤ *Preparation and Delivery of Manuscript, Page 134*) The publisher may still argue that the original deadline remains in effect unless the author can show a written acknowledgment of the new delivery date signed by an authorized representative of the publisher, who is "*the party to be charged*" with the obligation to accept the belated manuscript.

Similarly, the sample clause warns that the fact that one party did not stand on its rights under the contract on one occasion does not mean that the right is waived for all time and all purposes. If, for example, the publisher accepts the manuscript of the author's work even though the author has missed the deadline established in the contract—the fact that the publisher overlooked the late delivery, which amounts to a breach of contract by the author—does not mean that the publisher has waived its right to enforce other deadlines in the contract.

> ✍ **The Importance of a Signed Writing**. The sample clause offers a warning to the author who is tempted to treat any contractual obligation in a casual manner. If the author has asked to be excused from a deadline or any other duty under the contract, it is prudent to ask for a formal confirmation in writing signed by the publisher. The cautious publisher, on the other hand, will formally reserve its rights under the contract even if it agrees to waive a deadline or excuse a breach of contract.

## No Employment or Other Relationship

The parties acknowledge and agree that this Agreement is an arm's length transaction between independently contracting parties, and no partnership, joint venture, trust, employer-employee relationship, or other legal relationship is created between them.

The legal, financial, and business relationship between an author and a publisher is complicated enough, but there are other relationships that raise even greater complexities and impose even greater burdens. For that reason, the sample clause rules out any relationship other than "*an arm's length transaction between independently contracting parties.*" Thus, for example, the author is asked to confirm that she is not an employee of the publisher, which means that she is not entitled to employee benefits of any kind; she is not a partner or joint venturer, which means that she is not entitled to participate in the publisher's profits; and she has not entered into a relationship of "trust," a legal concept that imposes a heightened duty of candor, good faith, and selflessness in the dealings between, for example, an attorney and client or a trustee of a family trust and the beneficiaries of the trust.

> 📖 **Authors as Employees**. If the author *is* an ordinary employee of the publisher, then a standard book contract is probably not necessary or appropriate. Copyright in work created by an employee within the course and scope of employment, as a general proposition, is "work made for hire" and is owned by the employer even without a written agreement. (➤ *Work-for-Hire, Pages 51, 97*) But some kind of written

agreement might be appropriate, and the publisher that employs an author ought to consult with an attorney familiar with both publishing and labor law to determine what, if any, written agreement ought to be used in place of the book contract.

## MULTIPLE AUTHORS

**Whenever the term "Author" refers to more than one person, such persons will be jointly and severally responsible for all duties, obligations, and covenants under this Agreement, and shall share equally in all royalties and other amounts to be paid under this Agreement, unless otherwise specified in a writing signed by all parties.**

Most book contracts refer to the author in the singular as a defined term, but the same clause permits the publisher to use the same contract form for a project with more than one author. Significantly, the multiple authors are *"jointly and severally responsible for all duties, obligations, and covenants,"* which means that the publisher is entitled to enforce all contractual obligations against any or all of the co-authors.

Suppose, for example, that the publisher pays an advance, which is shared equally by the co-authors, but later demands repayment of the advance because the manuscript is rejected. (➤ *Termination for Nondelivery or Unsatisfactory Delivery, Page 151*) Under the sample clause, the publisher is not limited to recovering the share of the advance actually received by each co-author; rather, if one co-author is wealthier or closer at hand than the others, the publisher is entitled to recover the entire advance from a single co-author. Similarly, even if the authors have agreed among themselves to divide up the responsibility for completing the manuscript, each one may be held responsible by the publisher for the completion of the entire manuscript.

The sample clause confirms the publisher's right to assume that the co-authors *"shall share equally in all royalties and other amounts to be paid under this Agreement,"* and thus payments will be issued in equal amounts *"unless otherwise specified in a writing signed by all parties."* If, in fact, the co-authors have reached some other arrangement, the contract should be revised to reflect the actual split of revenues, whether by adding a new clause to the contract to specify how money is to be allocated (➤*Co-Authors, Page 130*), attaching a formal collaboration agreement among the authors as an exhibit to the contract, or simply delegating the responsibility for disbursing money to the designated agent. (➤*Agency, Page 203*)

---

✍ **Restrictions on Joint and Several Liability**. Co-authors may wish to negotiate for restrictions on the joint and several liability clause, especially when it comes to repayment of money, i.e., **"If Publisher is entitled to demand the return of the advance under this Agreement, Publisher agrees that each co-author shall be liable only for that portion of the advance allocated to and actually received by him or her."**

---

## FORCE MAJEURE

Publisher's obligations under this Agreement shall be extended by a period equal to any period of force majeure that prevents Publisher from performing such obligations.

"Force majeure" refers to circumstances beyond the control of a party to a contract, such as strike, riot, fire, flood, earthquake, or other natural disaster or "acts of God," which extend or excuse some obligation of the party. The sample clause applies only to the *publisher's* time-related obligations—for example, the time within which the publisher must actually publish the author's work (➤*Time of Publication, Page 172*) is extended if the publisher's printing plant is shut down by a strike, and such extension of time would be equal to the duration of the strike. Authors, of course, may reasonably seek the same benefit in negotiations, and publishers that are unwilling to grant such a concession tend to leave out any mention of force majeure from their contracts in the hope that the issue will not come up.

## NOTICES

Any written notice or delivery under any of the provisions of this Agreement shall be deemed to have been properly made by delivery in person to Author, or by mailing via traceable mail to the address(es) set forth in the Recitals and General Provisions above, except as the address(es) may be changed by notice in writing. Author and Publisher agree to accept service of process by mail at such addresses.

Formal written notices are required under various provisions of the typical book contract, and the *failure* to give proper notice may have crucial legal consequences. Examples of when formal notice by one party to the other is important include: the publisher's right to reject an unsatisfactory manuscript (➤*A Clause Providing for Author's Right to Revise the Manuscript Prior to Rejection, Page 148*), the author's right to audit the books and records of the publisher (➤*Audit Rights, Page 201*), and the author's right to demand a reversion of rights when her work goes out of print. (➤*Reversion of Rights, Page 238*) Thus, the sample clause goes into considerable detail in defining exactly when, where, and how notice is to be given or the manuscript and other materials are to be delivered.

A notice that is delivered "*in person to* [the] *Author*" is always proper under the sample clause. Either party may give notice to the other party "*by mailing via traceable mail*," i.e., Federal Express, Express Mail, or a comparable service that permits the sender to confirm delivery to the recipient. The "*address(es) set forth in the Recitals and General Provisions*" of the contract are deemed to be correct and sufficient unless the addresses that originally appeared in the contract have been "*changed by notice in writing*." Some contracts place the addresses in the notice clause itself. In either case, formal changes of address should be given promptly to the other party, and in writing, whenever necessary over the term of the contract.

The sample clause obliges each party to "*accept service of process by mail at such addresses*," which means that either party may initiate a lawsuit and serve legal papers on the other party by simply mailing legal papers to the address given in the contract.

BINDING ON SUCCESSORS

This Agreement shall be binding on the heirs, executors, administrators, successors, and assigns of Author, and the successors, assigns, and licensees of Publisher, but no assignment by Author shall be made without prior written consent of Publisher.

The sample clause confirms that anyone who legally succeeds to the interests of either author or publisher will be bound by the terms and provisions of the book contract. At the same time, the clause prevents the *author* from voluntarily assigning the book contract to a third party "*without prior written consent of Publisher*"—a restriction that is not imposed on the publisher.

The clause addresses two very different circumstances that may arise in the near or distant future. One circumstance is an *involuntary* transfer of the contract to a third party. On the death of the author, for example, the contract will pass by will—or, if the author dies without a will, by "operation of law"—from the deceased author to her "*heirs, executors, administrators* [and] *successors,*" each of whom will acquire no greater rights or bear no greater duties under the contract than the author herself.

The other circumstance is the *voluntary* assignment of the contract to a third party. Suppose, for example, that the publisher licenses the subsidiary rights under the book contract to an audio publisher, or the publisher merges with another publishing house, or the publisher is acquired by a conglomerate. In each of these situations, the book contract will bind and benefit the "*successors, assigns, and licensees*" of the publisher with the same force and effect as it originally bound the publisher.

As noted, however, the sample clause restricts the author from assigning the contract to a third party without the consent of the publisher, and for obvious reasons: the publisher is seeking to acquire a particular work of authorship by a particular writer and does not want a new author to take over the book project unless the publisher consents to the replacement.

✍ **Assignment of Royalties.** Many publishers are willing to modify the assignment clause to provide that the author **"may assign the benefits but may not delegate the burdens of this Agreement."** That is, the author can designate someone else to receive royalties and other revenues under the contract, but the author herself remains responsible for actually writing, revising, and promoting the book. Some publishers, however, are not entirely comfortable with an assignment of royalties, since they fret that the author will be less motivated to perform her obligations under the contract if she knows in advance that the money will go to someone else.

✍ **Restrictions on Assignment by Publisher.** The rationale for the rule against assignment by an author applies with equal force to an assignment by the publisher. After all, the author may be comfortable with the stature and resources of the publisher that offers the book contract, but what if the contract is assigned to a less capable or less prestigious house? Still, publishers rightfully regard their book contracts as an important asset and are not willing to restrict themselves by agreeing not to sell it off.

📖 **Sole Proprietors in Publishing.** Independent publishing houses may start out as businesses owned by an individual or a group of individuals who have not yet bothered to incorporate or organize as limited liability companies. For such entrepreneurial publishers, I recommend a specific clause that reserves the right to transfer both the rights and the duties of the book contract to a new entity that may be organized in the future, i.e., **"Publisher is free to assign all rights and delegate all duties under this Agreement to a corporation, limited liability company, or other legal entity to be formed by Publisher. If and when assigned to such corporation or other legal entity, Author agrees to look to such legal entity alone and not to** [*Insert name of individual(s) who own and operate the publishing house*] **as an individual for performance of all obligations of Publisher under this Agreement."** The author, on the other hand, may prefer to keep the individual publisher "on the hook" for the obligations of the publishing house, even if it is reorganized as a corporation or other business entity.

## APPLICABLE LAW

**Regardless of the place of its physical execution, this Agreement shall be interpreted, construed, and governed in all respects by the laws of the state of** [*Insert name of applicable state*].

The basic law that applies to ownership and use of rights under copyright is federal law that applies with equal force throughout the United States. But the law of contract is state law, and it may vary in small but sometimes significant ways from state to state. As in the sample clause, the book contract will almost invariably designate the law of the state where the publisher maintain its business office as the "applicable law," and any dispute relating to the contract itself will be decided under the designated state law. The sample clause carefully notes that the choice of state law applies no matter where the contract was actually signed (or, as lawyers put it, "*executed*").

### ARBITRATION

**If any dispute shall arise between Author and Publisher regarding this Agreement, such dispute shall be referred to binding private arbitration in [*Insert city and state where arbitration will take place*] in accordance with the Rules of the American Arbitration Association, and any arbitration award shall be fully enforceable as a judgment in any court of competent jurisdiction. Notwithstanding the foregoing, the parties shall have the right to conduct reasonable discovery as permitted by the arbitrator(s) and the right to seek temporary, preliminary, and permanent injunctive relief in any court of competent jurisdiction during the pendency of the arbitration or to enforce the terms of an arbitration award.**

Litigation in a state or federal court is always ponderous, open to public scrutiny, and ruinously expensive—all of which makes arbitration an attractive mechanism for resolving any disputes that may arise between author and publisher. Arbitration, whether conducted by the American Arbitration Association or some other "alternative dispute resolution" service, is almost always faster, cheaper, and more discreet than litigation in court.

The sample clause confirms that the arbitration is to be "*private*," the decision of the arbitrator is fully "*binding*" on both parties, and the arbitration award is "*enforceable as a judgment in any court of competent jurisdiction*." At the same time, however, the sample clause preserves some important rights and remedies that are not routinely available in an arbitration. "[R]*easonable discovery*"—that is, formal requests for the exchange of evidence before the hearing—may be conducted "*as permitted by the arbitrator.*" The parties are entitled to apply to a judge in a formal court proceeding for "*injunctive relief*"—that is, a court order that compels the other party to do a particular act or, more commonly, restrains the other party from doing a particular act.

---

📖 **Making Litigation Too Easy.** Not every publisher is willing to submit itself to arbitration, and such clauses are a rarity in the contracts used by major publishers. As a general rule, the party who can best afford the high cost of litigation is the least likely to agree to arbitration. And precisely because arbitration is so much cheaper, the more affluent party does not want to make it too easy for the poorer party to file a formal claim. Indeed, the high cost of court litigation is regarded by some publishers as a useful disincentive that will keep a disgruntled author from filing a legal claim. But the publisher that is no richer than the author—and no more eager to spend money on lawyers—will find an arbitration clause to be an advantage to both sides in a dispute.

📖 **Mandatory Mediation.** Arbitration is a form of dispute resolution in which the parties voluntarily submit their dispute to a third party who conducts a hearing and then issues a *binding* decision. Mediation, by contrast, is a kind of counseling session in which a third party tries to bring the parties to a *voluntary* settlement. Some publishers are willing to agree in advance to participate in mediation before either party is permitted to proceed to either arbitration or litigation, i.e., "**All disputes under this Agreement shall be submitted to mediation before a neutral third party to be jointly selected by the parties in [***Insert city and state where mediation will take place***], and no action may be filed by either party unless and until the parties are unable to resolve the dispute within 60 days after the first written demand for mediation.**"

---

## ATTORNEYS' FEES

**In any action on this Agreement, including litigation and arbitration, the losing party shall pay all attorneys' fees and costs incurred by the prevailing party.**

As a general rule, attorneys' fees are awarded to the successful litigant in a breach of contract case only if the contract at issue so provides; otherwise, both the winning party and the losing party bear their own fees and costs. Many publishers disfavor an attorneys' fees clause on the ground that it only encourages litigation. The author who cannot afford to hire and pay an attorney by the hour will have a hard time finding a lawyer to take her case on a contingency fee basis, but the prospect of recovering attorneys' fees in addition to damages might encourage an otherwise reluctant lawyer to take the case. Of course, the attorneys' fees clause works both ways. Arguably, the fact that the losing party will pay the winning party's lawyer is a disincentive to litigation and a caution to any party who is tempted to file a meritless lawsuit. But the fact remains that attorneys' fees clauses are rarely found in the standard book contracts used by major publishers.

---

✍ **Costs of Travel for Litigation**. When a publisher insists on specifying the location of its business office as the place where arbitration or litigation must take place, the author may ask for a clause that allows the prevailing party to recover "**actual costs of transportation, food and lodging in connection with litigation or arbitration**," a mechanism that compensates the author who is forced to travel in order to litigate and then wins the case.

---

## HEADINGS

**Headings and footers are for convenience only and are not to be deemed part of this Agreement.**

Not once in my 20-plus years of practice have I ever encountered a case where the legal effect of the headings and footers was at issue, but hyper-vigilant attorneys prefer to use a bit of boilerplate like the sample clause to announce that such incidental words and phrases are "*for convenience only*" and do not affect the meaning or effect of the text of the contract itself.

## BANKRUPTCY

**If a petition in bankruptcy or a petition for reorganization is filed by or against Publisher, or if Publisher makes an**

assignment for the benefit of creditors, or if Publisher liquidates its business for any cause whatsoever, Author may terminate this Agreement by written notice within sixty (60)
days after any of the foregoing events, and all rights granted
to Author by Publisher shall thereupon revert to Author.

One of the great perils of publishing, and especially from the
author's perspective, is the publisher that files for bankruptcy or
seeks some other form of legal protection from insolvency, thereby
consigning the author's work and the royalties owed on sales of
the work into a kind of limbo. Once a publisher has filed for protection under the bankruptcy law, the assets and liabilities of the
publisher come under the control of a court-appointed trustee,
and the publisher's creditors file claims for payment of their un-
satisfied obligations. The money in the publisher's bank accounts,
if any, as well as the rights to the author's book and even the copies
on hand are all considered assets of the publisher, and the trustee
will not lightly release any of them. Thus, even if the author enjoys the right to *"terminate this Agreement by written notice,"* as
the sample clause provides, and the rights to the author's work
are supposed to *"revert to Author,"* it may still take the efforts of
an attorney to wrest these assets out of the bankruptcy proceedings. Indeed, the process may take months and even years despite the clear language of the sample clause.

### RIDERS AND EXHIBITS

This Agreement consists of Paragraphs 1 through [*Insert
number of last numbered paragraph*], and the following
Exhibit(s) and Rider(s), if any:

---

[*Insert identifying name, number and/or letter of all attached
exhibits and riders, or strike out if not applicable*]

As a "housekeeping" detail, it is useful to summarize exactly
what elements are to be found in the book contract, if only to
avoid any later dispute over what was and was not meant to be

incorporated in the final version of the contract as signed. The sample clause calls for two insertions. First, the last numbered paragraph or section should be inserted where indicated, and, second, any attached exhibits or riders should be identified on the blank line. These insertions, like *all* insertions, deletions, or other changes made by hand or typed into the document, should be initialed in the margins of the page where they appear, to confirm that the author and the publisher have agreed on their inclusion. (➤*Initialing and Signing, Page 260*)

## SIGNATURE BLOCK

**IN WITNESS WHEREOF, Author and Publisher have executed this Agreement as of the Effective Date.**

**"AUTHOR"**
[*Insert full name of Author*]

**"PUBLISHER"**
[*Insert full name and legal description of Publisher*]

_____
(Signature of AUTHOR)

By: _____

Title: _____

The signature block of a contract is the crucial mechanism by which the parties confirm their willingness to enter into a legally binding agreement with each other and be bound by the terms and provisions of the contract itself. Care should be taken to ensure that the names of the author and publisher are complete, correct, and consistent with the usage given in the introductory clauses. (➤*An Example of an Introductory Clause in a Book Publishing Contract, Page 45*)

**Safe Storage of Signed Contracts.** Once properly signed, the original contract and any photocopies provided to the parties should be maintained in safe storage, preferably in more than one location. The contract is a crucial legal document that will continue to govern the rights and duties of the parties long into the future, and the unavailability of the contract in its complete and final form may pose awkward and even catastrophic problems if a dispute arises. Ideally, both parties will maintain a copy, and it is not merely obsessive to make a few extra copies and salt them away in a safety deposit box or an attorney's office.

If, for example, the publisher is described as "POSTCARD PRESS, a California limited liability company" at the outset of the contract, then the same name and legal description should appear in the signature block. A contract signed by an individual need not (and should not) have the word "By" on the signature line; but the word ought to be used if the contract is signed on behalf of a corporation, a partnership, a limited liability company, or some other legal entity—and the proper legal title of the person signing on behalf of the legal entity (i.e., "President," "General Partner," "Member," etc.) should be inserted on the blank line.

No date is required in the sample signature block because the contract is dated *"as of the Effective Date,"* a defined term whose precise meaning is set forth in the introductory clause. (➤*Effective Date, Page 45*) If no such defined term is used, then the contract form should be modified to provide a blank line for the actual date when each person signs the document. As a general rule, unless the contract provides otherwise, the contract will be deemed to be effective on the date when the last person signs the contract.

---

📖 **Initialing and Signing**. As a rule, a contract must be properly signed by all parties, and any handwritten or typewritten changes must be initialed by all parties before the document goes into effect. Indeed, if a change is made in a contract that has been signed by both parties but the change is initialed by only one, it is unlikely to be treated as a binding contract at all, because there is no way to determine whether the uninitialed change was added before or after the contract was signed. To eliminate any doubt, it is good practice for *all* parties to initial *every* page, including riders and exhibits, and then put their signatures where indicated in the signature block.

---

# GLOSSARY

*Advance*. A sum of money paid by the publisher to the author as a prepayment of royalties and other amounts that may be due to the author on sales of a book or the exploitation of other rights in a book.

*Agency clause*. The clause in a book publishing contract that identifies the author's agent and describes the rights and duties of the agent.

*Agent* or *literary agent*. An individual or entity that represents the author in negotiating for the exploitation of rights in a work of authorship, usually in exchange for a commission calculated as a percentage of the money received by the author.

*Agent's boilerplate*. Contract terms that a particular literary agent is able to secure from a publishing house on most or all book deals on the basis of earlier deals with the same house.

*Ancillary* or *allied rights*. One or more subsidiary rights in a work of authorship that is closely related to another right in the same work.

*Arbitration*. A form of binding dispute resolution in which a legal dispute is voluntarily submitted by the parties to a neutral third party, who conducts a hearing and issues a binding award that may be entered and enforced as a judgment in court.

*As told to*. An autobiographical book written by an author in the name of the person whose life experiences are the subject of the book. See *Ghostwriter*.

*Audio rights*. The right to use the contents of an author's work in the preparation and exploitation of a sound recording, i.e., an audiocassette, a compact disc, or other audio product.

*Audit*. As used in the publishing industry, a formal inspection of the books and records of the publisher to verify the accuracy and completeness of the statements of account. See *Statement*.

*Author*. Under the law of copyright, the person who creates a work of authorship by "fixing" it in a "tangible medium of expression," whether it takes the form of a book or some other work eligible for copyright protection, e.g., a poem, a song, a software program, a motion picture, etc.

*Author changes*. Changes and corrections in the proofs of a book by the author after it has been set into type and page form, but usually excluding corrections of printer's errors. See *Page proofs, Printer's errors*.

*Backmatter.* A term that generally refers to the contents of a book that appear after the main text, i.e., an afterword, epilogue, index, etc. See *Frontmatter.*

*Bestseller clause.* The clause in a book publishing contract that establishes a bonus, usually an additional advance against royalties, if the book appears on a bestseller list.

*Boilerplate.* As used in reference to contracts, an informal term for the standardized legal provisions that are routinely used in legal documents. See *Deal points.*

*Book club rights.* The right to sell copies of a book through a book club such as the Book of the Month Club or to authorize a book club to print and sell its own edition of the book.

*Breakpoint.* A specified measure of performance that triggers an increase in the royalty rate or some other change in the terms of the contract. For example, if the author is entitled to a royalty of 10 percent on sales up to 5,000 copies, 12½ percent on sales of 5,001 to 10,000, and 15 percent on sales above 10,000 copies, then the "breakpoints" in the contract are 5,000 and 10,000 copies.

*Bulk sales.* The sale of books in a large quantity to a purchaser as a single transaction, i.e., the sale of a quantity of books to a discount store or some other purchaser for resale, often at a reduced wholesale price and on a nonreturnable basis. See *Special sales, Returns.*

*Bundling.* An informal term that is variously and loosely used to describe several unrelated concepts and practices in publishing, i.e., the packaging and sale of a book with another item of merchandise; and the joint accounting of two or more books by the same author. See *Joint accounting.*

*Clause.* A sentence, paragraph, or section of a contract that addresses a specific and limited subject. The "agency clause" in a book contract, for example, identifies the author's agent and describes the rights and duties of the agent.

*Co-Author.* One of several persons who contribute copyrightable matter to a single work of authorship and who owns and controls a share of the copyright in the work.

*Collaborator.* An informal term that is used to refer to a co-author, a ghostwriter, or some other person who renders assistance to an author in the preparation of a work of authorship. See *Co-Author, Ghostwriter.*

*Commercial rights.* The right to adapt and use some element of a work of authorship in connection with other goods and services, i.e., the right to make and sell a doll based on a character from a bestseller; sometimes also called "merchandising rights."

*Copyright.* The body of law that defines and protects the rights in a work of authorship such as a book, a sound recording, a motion picture, a television program, and the like.

*Corporate sales.* See *Special sales.*

*Cost of manufacture.* The actual costs incurred by the publisher in manufacturing a book, generally understood to include "paper, printing, and binding" (sometimes abbreviated as "PPB") but excluding design, development, and general overhead; sometimes also called "plant, paper, printing, and binding."

*Counterparts.* Two or more identical copies of a contract, each of which is signed by one party, and when assembled, the signed counterparts are deemed to constitute one complete contract.

*Cover price.* The suggested retail price of a book as recommended by the publisher and printed on the cover or dust jacket of the book itself. The cover price of a book may include an additional amount, known as a *Freight Pass Through* (FPT), which is added to the suggested retail price to cover the costs of shipping but is generally excluded from calculation of the author's royalties. See *Invoice price, Freight Pass Through.*

*Cross-collateralization.* See *Joint accounting.*

*Deal memo.* An informal term that identifies a preliminary or summary agreement, often in the form of a letter or memo, in which some but not all "deal points" are identified and agreed upon by the parties to a transaction. See *Long form, Short form.*

*Deal points.* An informal term that identifies the points regarded as essential by the parties to a book deal or other transaction, which are often understood to include rights, territory, term, advance, and royalty rates. See *Boilerplate.*

*Defined terms.* Words and phrases that are given specific definitions in a contract and used consistently throughout the contract. Defined terms are often capitalized, i.e., "Author," "Publisher," "the Work."

*Direct-response marketing rights.* The right to sell copies of a book directly to the consumer through various direct-response marketing channels, including direct-mail advertising, mail-order catalogs, and home shopping programs. The transaction between the publisher and the consumer is generally known as a "direct sale."

*Direct sales.* See *Direct-response marketing rights.*

*Earn out.* The point at which the publisher has recouped the advance previously paid to the author out of income from a particular book. When a book has "earned out," the publisher is obliged to start paying royalties and the author's share of other revenue from the sale of books or exploitation of other rights in the work.

*Edition.* A work of authorship as published in any particular content, length, and format by a particular publisher, i.e., the hardcover version of a book, the softcover version, the abridged version, and the French-language version are all considered to be separate editions of the same work. If a work is materially revised or redesigned in any manner, or changed in length or content, then the revised version is generally considered a new edition.

*Editor clause*. The clause in a book publishing contract that permits an author to terminate the contract if a specific editor, usually the acquiring editor, leaves the publishing house.

*Effective date*. The date on which the contract is deemed to go into effect according to the agreement of the parties.

*Electronic books* or *electronic versions*. See *Electronic rights*.

*Electronic rights*. The right to adapt and use the contents of the author's work in the form of one or more computer-based media and technologies. Among the principal electronic rights now recognized in publishing contracts are: the right to reproduce the literal and verbatim contents of a book in the form that permits the user to read the text of the book on a computer screen ("electronic books"); the right to make some or all of the contents of a book available to users of a database, a network, or other computer service; the right to retrieve the contents of a book from an electronic file or database, print out the book on paper, and then sell a single printed copy to a consumer ("publishing-on-demand"); and the right to combine some or all of the contents of a book with other text, images, and sounds to create an "interactive" or "multimedia" product or service, sometimes called an "electronic version," which is generally accessed and used on a computer ("interactive rights" or "multimedia rights").

*Execution*. As used in contracts, the signing of a written contract by one or more of the parties to the contract. Strictly speaking, a contract is said to have been "executed" when it has been signed, delivered, and accepted by the parties.

*Exhibit*. A document that is attached to and "incorporated by reference" in a contract such that the exhibit is considered to be a part of the contract itself. The terms "amendment," "addendum," "exhibit," "rider," and "schedule" are often used loosely and interchangeably to identify a document that has been attached and added to a contract, although each term has a slightly different technical meaning when used by attorneys. See *Side letter agreement*.

*"Favored nation" clause*. See *"Most favored nation" clause*.

*First serial rights* or *second serial rights*. See *Periodical rights*.

*Flow-through*. The payment of the author's share of third-party revenue immediately upon receipt by the publisher rather than upon the rendering of a formal statement of account.

*Force majeure*. A circumstance beyond the control of a party to a contract that extends or excuses an obligation of the party, i.e., strike, riot, fire, flood, earthquake, or other natural disaster or "acts of God."

*Foreign rights*. The right to publish a work of authorship in one or more specified foreign countries or territories. See *Translation rights*.

*Freight Pass Through (FPT)*. An amount of money that is added to the cover price of a book to cover the costs of shipping. The cover price less the FPT is often used as the basis for calculating the author's royalty. See *Invoice price, Cover price*.

*Frontmatter.* A term that generally refers to the contents of a book that appear before the main text, i.e., a preface or a foreword. See *Backmatter.*

*Galleys* or *galley proofs.* Once common in publishing but now mostly obsolete, galley proofs were long strips of paper on which the text of a book that had been set into type was printed for proofreading. Advance copies of books that are inexpensively printed and bound for use by book reviewers are still called "bound galleys." See *Page proofs.*

*Ghostwriter.* A professional writer who writes books and other materials on behalf of and in the name of another person, sometimes anonymously and sometimes with a secondary form of credit, i.e., "as told to" or "with."

*Grant.* A sum of money provided by the publisher to the author to pay for specified categories of costs and expenses in connection with a book project, usually on a nonrecoupable basis; sometimes also called a "subvention."

*Grant of rights.* A legal mechanism by which ownership of some or all of the author's right in a work of authorship is transferred to a publisher or other person or entity. See *License of rights.*

*Hardcover rights.* The right to publish a work of authorship in the form of a book with a hard cover.

*Hard-soft deals.* A book contract in which the publisher acquires the right to publish the author's work in both hardcover and softcover editions, although the softcover rights may be licensed to another publisher that specializes in softcover books.

*Hold-back.* As used in the publishing industry, an agreement by one party to a book contract to refrain from exploiting a given right in the author's work for a specified period of time.

*Imprint.* The name and/or logo under which a publishing house or one of its divisions publishes its line of books. For example, Ballantine, Del Rey, Fawcett, Ivy, House of Collectibles and One World are all separate imprints of the Ballantine Publishing Group, which is itself a division of Random House, Inc.

*Indemnities.* See *Warranties, representations, and indemnities.*

*Institutional sales.* See *Special sales.*

*Instrument of recordation.* A summary version of a book contract or other legal document, especially designed for recordation in the U.S. Copyright Office, which confirms the transfer of rights in a work of authorship but does not disclose financial details or other confidential terms.

*Insurance clause.* The clause in a book contract by which the publisher promises to provide insurance coverage to the author.

*Integration clause.* The clause in a contract by which the parties confirm that the contract is their entire agreement and supersedes previous agreements, understandings, negotiations, and communications; sometimes also called a "merger clause."

*Interactive rights.* See *Electronic rights.*

*Institutional sales.* See *Special sales.*

*Invasion of privacy.* An action for damages and other legal remedies based on the publication of statements that intrude upon the privacy of a living person.

*Invoice price.* The price printed on a publisher's invoice to indicate the suggested retail price of a book and used by the publisher to calculate the wholesale discount, i.e., the discount is subtracted from the invoice price to yield the actual wholesale price. The invoice price of a book may differ from the cover price. See *Cover price, Freight Pass Through, Wholesale discount.*

*Joint accounting.* The right of a publisher to apply debits arising in connection with one of the author's books against any other books under contract with the same author. By way of example, if two books by the same author are subject to joint accounting, the publisher is entitled to recoup the advance paid on one book against the royalties earned on sales of another book by the same author.

*Joint and several liability.* A legal doctrine by which the liabilities of several persons, such as the co-authors of a book, may be fully enforced against each of them or all of them.

*Kill fee.* A payment owed by a publisher to an author when the publisher declines to publish the author's work after it has been timely submitted in satisfactory form.

*Libel.* An action for damages and other legal remedies based on the publication of false and defamatory statements about a living person.

*License of rights.* A legal mechanism by which the right to *use* certain specified rights in a work of authorship is conveyed to a publisher or other party, usually in specified media and territories and/or for a limited period of time. See *Grant of rights.*

*Long form.* An informal term used to identify a formal legal document, often a contract, which is intended by the parties as a detailed and comprehensive statement of their respective rights and duties. See *Short form.*

*Manuscript.* The work product of an author in its original form. Technically, a manuscript is handwritten, but the term is used in book contracts to refer to the typewritten or word-processed document that embodies the author's work.

*Mark up.* The process of indicating additions, deletions, or other changes in the terms and conditions of a contract by writing or marking the changes on the contract itself.

*Mass-market* or *"rack" paperback.* A paperback book, usually printed on lower-quality paper and with a page (or "trim") size smaller than a hardcover book and distributed through bookstores as well as retail outlets outside the book trade, including racks in airports, drugstores, and so on.

*Mediation.* A form of non-binding dispute resolution in which the parties voluntarily submit a legal dispute to a neutral third party who attempts to bring the parties to settlement on mutually agreeable terms.

*Merchandising rights.* See *Commercial rights.*

*Merger clause.* See *Integration clause.*

*Microfilm* or *microfiche rights.* The right to use the content of an author's work in the form of microfilm, microfiche, or similar photography-based media. See *Transcription rights.*

*"Most favored nation" clause.* A term borrowed from the language of diplomacy to describe a clause that assures the author that he or she is receiving (and will continue to receive) terms at least as favorable as those offered by the publisher to any other author.

*Motion picture rights.* The right to use the contents of an author's work in the preparation and exploitation of a motion picture. See *Video rights.*

*Multimedia rights.* See *Electronic rights.*

*Name, image, and likeness.* See *Right of publicity.*

*Negligent publication.* A legal theory that may be used in seeking to hold an author or publisher liable for damages and other legal remedies for injuries suffered in reliance on the advice, instruction, or information contained in a book.

*Net income* or *net revenue.* The money actually received by a publisher or other copyright owner from the sale of books or exploitation of other rights in the author's work after deduction of specified costs, expenses, and charges.

*Net revenue.* See *Net income.*

*Net royalty.* A royalty calculated on publisher's net income rather than on the retail price of a book. See *Net income.*

*Noncompete.* See *Noncompetition clause.*

*Noncompetition clause.* As used in a book contract, the clause that prevents one party, usually the author, from competing with the other party by publishing works that might injure the sales of the works under contract; sometimes informally known as a "noncompete."

*Option.* A transaction by which a prospective buyer of rights in a copyrighted work is entitled to buy specified rights in the author's work for a stated price at a future date. For example, a publishing contract will typically grant the publisher an option to acquire the author's next book on specified terms. Options are customarily used in the entertainment industry to tie up motion picture and television rights in a book for a specified period of time, and the option-holder will use the option period to "pitch" the project to a studio, a network, a financing entity, etc., before actually deciding whether or not to exercise the option and buy the rights to the author's work.

*"Orphaned" book*. A book whose acquiring editor has left the publishing house that acquired the right to publish it, thus leaving both book and author book without an advocate within the decision-making apparatus of the publishing house.

*Out of print* or *out-of-print clause*. A book is considered out of print in the book industry when it is no longer being actively published and distributed, although the definition of when a book goes out of print varies greatly from one contract to another and is often the subject of negotiation. An out-of-print clause defines the circumstances in which a book is deemed out of print, the right and duty of the publisher to put the book back in print, and the rights of the author if the publisher does not put the book back in print.

*Page proofs* or *proofs*. Designed and typeset pages of a book that are prepared and used during the early stages of production for final editing changes and corrections of typographical and other errors. "Proofreading" refers to the process of reading and correcting the page proofs. Sometimes also called "galleys," although the terms are not fully interchangeable. See *Galleys*.

*Paperback rights*. The right to publish a work of authorship in the form of a book with paper or "soft" covers; also called "softcover rights."

*Paper, printing, and binding (PPB)*. See *Cost of manufacture*.

*Periodical rights* or *serial rights*. The right to publish some or all of a book in a periodical such as a magazine or a newspaper. "First serial rights" refers to the right to publish the author's work in a periodical *before* it is first published in book form, and "second serial rights" refers to the right to publish *after* first publication in book form.

*Permissions*. The granting of permission by a copyright owner to make limited use of the contents of a published work, usually applied to the use of short quotations from a published work in a book. The right to decide whether or not to grant permission for such uses is a subsidiary right sometimes identified as "selection rights" or "quotation rights."

*Photocopying and facsimile rights*. The right to prepare and sell photocopies and faxed copies of excerpts from a book.

*Power of attorney*. The authority bestowed by one person upon another person to act on behalf of and sign legal documents in the name of the first person.

*PPB*. See *Cost of manufacture*.

*Premium rights*. The right to use the author's work as a premium, i.e., a free item given away by a merchandiser, a corporation, or an institution.

*Premium sales*. See *Special sales*.

*Prequel*. See *Sequel*.

*Primary rights*. The rights in a work of authorship that the publisher actually intends to exploit. For example, in a contract between an author and a book publisher that publishes only English-language hardcover books in the United States, then the right to publish the author's book in hardcover is the "primary" right and all other rights in the author's work—softcover rights, movie rights, foreign rights, etc.—are "secondary" or "subsidiary". See *Secondary or subsidiary rights.*

*Principal Author.* An informal term sometimes used to identify the first-named author of a book with multiple authors or the person whose life experiences are the subject matter of a book written on his or her behalf by a ghostwriter or collaborator. See *Ghostwriter, Collaborator.*

*Printer's errors.* Typographical errors or other flaws in the work of compositor, designer, or printer in preparation of a manuscript for publication.

*Promotional sales.* See *Special sales.*

*Proofs* and *proofreading.* See *Page proofs.*

*Proprietor.* As used in copyright law, the owner of rights in a work of authorship that is protected under copyright, whether it is the author of the work or a person or entity to whom the author has transferred the rights.

*Pseudonym.* A fictional or adopted "pen name" used by an author to identify his or her work in place of his or her given name.

*Public domain.* A legal concept that refers generally to matter that is not protected under the laws of copyright or other intellectual property laws.

*Publication date.* The date of first publication of a book, generally understood to be the date of the first release of copies for sale through the book trade but sometimes a specially designated or defined date in a book contract.

*Publishing-on-demand.* See *Electronic rights.*

*Quotation rights.* See *Permissions.*

*Reading rights.* The right to read all or a portion of a work of authorship before a live audience.

*Recitals.* The introductory clauses in which the assumptions and purposes of the contract are recited to confirm the facts on which the parties are relying in entering into the contract.

*Recordation.* The deposit of a private document as a public record, i.e., the deposit of a book contract as a public record in the U. S. Copyright Office in order to confirm the transfer of rights by author to publisher. See *Instrument of recordation.*

*Recoupment.* The right of the publisher to pay itself back for an advance previously paid to an author out of amounts otherwise due to the author under a book contract. See *Advance, Earn out.*

*Redline.* As used in the context of book contracts, the process of highlighting a contract to indicate additions, deletions, and other changes in the text.

*Registration.* As used in the context of copyright, the formal confirmation of a claim of rights in a copyrighted work as initiated by the filing of an application by the author or owner of rights in the work in the U. S. Copyright Office.

*Remainder house.* See *Remainders.*

*Remainders.* Copies of a book that remain in the publisher's control when the publisher decides to take the book out of print, and "remaindering" refers to how the publisher disposes of them. Sometimes remainders are sent to a recycling or shredding facility and destroyed. More often, the remainders are sold at a drastically reduced price, sometimes no greater than the cost of manufacture and sometimes even less, to "remainder houses," that is, distributors, catalog publishers, and other marketers that specialize in remainders.

*Representations.* See *Warranties, representations, and indemnities.*

*Reservation-of-rights clause.* As used in a book contract, the clause that confirms what rights have been granted to the publisher and what rights have been held back, or "reserved," by the author.

*Reserves.* A portion of the royalties or other money owed to author under a book contract which is held back by the publisher against various contingencies, including the likelihood that some books reported as sold in one accounting period may be returned to the publisher in the future. See *Returns.*

*Reserve against returns.* See *Reserves, Returns.*

*Retail price.* See *Cover price.*

*Returns.* Books that have been ordered from the publisher by a bookstore or other retail outlet and then returned to the publisher for a refund or a credit, usually because the book was not purchased by a retail customer. In the case of mass-market paperbacks, only the covers are returned and the rest of the book is destroyed by the retailer.

*Reversion of rights.* As used in book contracts, "reversion" is the legal mechanism by which rights in a work of authorship are restored to the party that originally granted them, and a "reversionary clause" is the clause in a book contract where reversion of rights is described. For example, the rights granted by an author to a publisher generally "revert" to the author when the book goes out of print, and so the out-of-print clause in a book contract often functions as a reversionary clause.

*Reversionary clause.* See *Reversion of rights.*

*Rider.* See *Exhibit.*

*Right of publicity.* The body of law that protects the right of an individual to control how his or her "name, image, and likeness" or other personal attributes are used for advertising and merchandising purposes.

*Royalties.* A payment of money by the publisher to the author based on the sales of the author's book or the exploitation of other rights in the author's work, usually expressed as a percentage of either the suggested retail price of the book or the publisher's net income.

*Royalty statement.* See *Statement.*

*Secondary* or *subsidiary rights.* The rights in a work of authorship that the publisher owns or controls but intends to exploit through third parties. For example, in a contract between an author and a book publisher, the right to exploit the author's work in another medium—a movie, an audiocassette recording, an electronic book, etc.—are generally regarded as secondary or subsidiary rights. See *Primary rights.*

*Selection rights.* See *Permissions.*

*Sell-off period.* The period of time following the expiration or termination of a contract, usually a licensing agreement, during which the publisher may continue to sell existing inventory but may not manufacture new product.

*Sequel* and *prequel.* A "sequel" is a work that adds to, continues, or completes the story line of another work that is set earlier in time. A "prequel" is a work that introduces or leads up to the story line of another work that is set later in time.

*Series.* Two or more related works published under the same title, logo, or format.

*Short form.* An informal term used to identify a legal document that is intended to confirm some but not all of the rights and duties of the parties to an agreement or other transaction. See *Instrument of Recordation, Deal memo, Long form.*

*Side letter agreement.* An agreement, usually in letter or memo form, between an author and a publisher on some specific or limited matter related to the author's work but not covered in the book contract itself. See *Exhibit.*

*Softcover rights.* See *Paperback rights.*

*Special sales.* The sale of a book by its publisher on terms other than a conventional wholesale transaction in ordinary channels of trade in the book industry, i.e., sales in bulk quantities to a single purchaser ("bulk" sales); sales at a wholesale discount greater than the publisher's customary discount schedule ("deep discount"); sales of books to a corporation for in-house or other corporate uses ("corporate" sales); sales to a college, hospital, or other institution for in-house promotional use ("institutional" sales); and sales of books for use as a premium to promote the sale of other goods and services ("premium" or "promotional" sales). Such sales are usually at made at a reduced wholesale price and on a nonreturnable basis. See *Bulk sales, Returns.*

*Statement.* A formal statement of account by which the publisher reports to the author on the royalties and other revenues, if any, generated by the exploitation of the author's work, and the charges, if any, owed by the author to the publisher. Often called a "royalty statement" even though a typical statement reports *all* credits and debits and not merely royalties.

*Subvention.* See *Grant.*

*Successors, assigns, and licensees.* A "successor" is a general term that refers to a person who succeeds to the rights and assumes the burdens of another person, whether by voluntary action or by operation of law, and is often used to describe a corporation that has merged with another corporation. An "assign" is one to whom ownership of rights have been voluntarily conveyed. A "licensee" is one to whom permission has been given for limited *use* of rights.

*Suggested retail price.* See *Cover price, Invoice price.*

*Television rights.* The right to use the contents of an author's work in the preparation and exploitation of a television program such as a movie-of-the-week, a special, a mini-series, or a series. See *Video rights.*

*Trade.* As used in the publishing context, the book trade; and more particularly, the conventional channels of distribution and sale of books through bookstores and other retail outlets where books are customarily sold.

*Trade dress.* A form of trademark consisting of the design, configuration, and physical appearance of a product, including, for example, the cover design and overall appearance of a book or other print product. See *Trademark and unfair competition.*

*Trademark and unfair competition.* The body of law that defines and protects the rights in a word, image, or other symbol that identifies the source of goods and services, including, for example, the name or logo of a publishing house, a series of related titles, etc. See *Trade dress.*

*Trade* or *quality paperback.* A paperback or softcover book, usually printed on high-quality paper with a page (or "trim") size comparable to a hardcover book and distributed primarily through bookstores and other retail outlets in the book trade. See *Mass market or "Rack" paperback.*

*Transcription rights.* A phrase used in older contracts to apply generally to the use of the contents of an author's work in various other media, often limited to microfilm, microfiche, transparencies, film strips, and other photography-based media, but sometimes more broadly defined as photographic, phonographic, tape, wire, magnetic, electronic, and so on. Although "transcription rights" are still mentioned in contracts now in general use, many of the subsidiary rights once encompassed under a transcription rights clause are better defined and allocated under other headings. See *Audio rights, Electronic rights, Microfilm or microfiche rights.*

*Translation rights.* The right to prepare and publish a translation of a work of authorship into one or more specified foreign languages. See *Foreign rights.*

*Unfair competition*. See *Trademark and unfair competition*.

*Vetting*. The process of reviewing a manuscript, usually conducted by an attorney, to determine if the author's work poses any risks of liability such as copyright or trademark infringement, defamation, invasion of privacy, or other legal defects.

*Video rights*. The right to use the contents of an author's work in the preparation and exploitation of a home video product such as a videocassette or laser disc. Video rights are sometimes considered "allied and ancillary" to motion picture rights and/or television rights, and some contracts specifically define motion picture rights and/or television rights to include video rights. See *Motion picture rights, Television rights*.

*Warranties, representations, and indemnities*. As used in the typical book contract, a series of guarantees that the author's work is free from legal defects, and a promise by the author to protect the publisher if a legal claim on the basis of the author's work or the book contract itself arises.

*Wholesale discount*. The amount subtracted from the suggested retail price or invoice price of a book to determine the wholesale price, usually expressed as a percentage, i.e., "40 percent off the retail price." See *Cover price, Invoice price*.

*Work-for-Hire*. A "legal fiction" under the copyright law of the United States by which the party who employed or commissioned an author to create a work of authorship is deemed to be the author of the work as well as the owner of all rights in the work.

# INDEX

Page numbers in **boldface type** refer to the Model Contract. Page numbers in Roman type refer to the main text. Page numbers in *italics* refer to the Glossary.

# ACKNOWLEDGMENTS

Foremost among those who supported and sustained the writing of this book is my superbly accomplished wife, Ann B. Kirsch, whose beauty, wisdom, and love have always made all good things happen in my life.

My children, Jennifer and Adam, each one a writer like their mother and father, have always encouraged my work with high spirits and good humor and rewarded Ann and me with the deepest joy and delight, pride and pleasure.

The idea for *Kirsch's Guide* originated with Tony Cohan, publisher of Acrobat Books, and I happily express my appreciation to him for befriending me, setting me on the author's path after a long hiatus, and making the whole enterprise of writing books about publishing law such a pleasure. Tony is a Renaissance man in the best sense—author, publisher, musician, a man of many gifts and much wisdom.

Crucial to the successful completion of the book were my editor, Victoria Gold; the cover designer, Clive Piercy; the graphic designer, Bill Morosi; and Eric Carter, the anchorman at Acrobat Books. Knowing Tony Cohan as I do, I am not at all surprised to find such warm, gifted, and engaged people at work on the books from Acrobat.

This book is dedicated to my law partner and cherished friend, Dennis Mitchell, and the sentiments expressed in the dedication are heartfelt and accurate. Truly, none of my books would have been written without his support and encouragement.

Another colleague of mine, Larry Zerner, has always been generous with his acuity, vivacity, and wit. Larry brought his own publishing law expertise to bear on the page proofs of *Kirsch's Guide*, and he is always quick to report a promising literary sighting on the Internet.

With a full heart, I thank Judy Woo and Angie Yoon, who are

essential figures in the day-to-day operation of our law practice, not only because they make our work lives so rewarding but because each is so lovely, gracious, patient, kind, and caring.

Among my colleagues in the legal profession, I owe a special debt of gratitude to Scott Baker, Ed Komen, Lon Sobel, Les Klinger, David Nimmer, Paul Goldstein, and Gregg Homer, each of whom has been willing to share his expertise and good judgment whenever asked.

I am proud and gratified to express my heartfelt appreciation to Jan Nathan, director of the Publishers Marketing Association, one of the truly great people in American publishing. Jan is deeply experienced, superbly well-informed, energetic, witty, and the best friend an independent publisher ever had.

For sharing their friendship, vision, energy, and enterprise with me over many years, I thank Linda Pfeffer, Jina Elgin, Kathryn Leigh Scott, Geoff Miller, Laurie Fox, Linda Chester, Vikas Bhushan, Tao Le, and Chirag Amin.

Even if I cannot mention each of their names, every client who has entrusted a publishing matter to the care of Kirsch & Mitchell has contributed in a crucial way to this book, and I am deeply grateful to all of them.

## ABOUT THE AUTHOR

Jonathan Kirsch is an attorney specializing in copyright, trademark, and publishing law. He is a partner in the firm of Kirsch & Mitchell, 2029 Century Park East, Suite 2750, Los Angeles, CA 90067. Telephone: (310) 785-1200. Fax: (310) 286-9573. E-Mail: ursus@aol.com

Kirsch is also a contributing writer for the *Los Angeles Times Book Review*, author of *The Harlot by the Side of the Road: Forbidden Tales of the Bible* and *Moses: A Life*, and literary correspondent for National Public Radio affiliate KPCC-FM in Southern California.